MEN OF GRANITE

TRUE STORIES OF NEW HAMPSHIRE'S FIGHTING MEN

BY WILLIAM E. MCGEE

PETER E. RANDALL PUBLISHER LLC
Portsmouth, New Hampshire
2007

ISBN10: 1-931807-65-5
ISBN13: 978-1-931807-65-4

Library of Congress Control Number: 2007908777

Peter E. Randall Publisher LLC
P.O. Box 4726
Portsmouth NH 03802

www.perpublisher.com

Book design: Grace Peirce

Cover photo credit: Old Man of the Mountain, Franconia Notch.
NHDTTD/Dick Hamilton photo.

Book Web site: www.menofgranite.com

Dedication

To Dr. Robert G. LeBlanc, PhD, Professor Emeritus, University of New Hampshire whose knowledge, vitality and humanity touched so many lives. Whose own life was tragically cut short on 9-11-2001.

Good friends are never forgotten.

All profits from the sale of this book go to the Robert G. LeBlanc Memorial Scholarship Fund administered by the University of New Hampshire Foundation, Durham, NH.

Contents

Acknowledgments

Larry Berkson, Historical Society, Pittsfield, New Hampshire

John Clayton, *New Hampshire Union-Leader*, Manchester

Ms. Sally Fellows, Archivist, City Hall, Manchester

Mr. John Fortier, son of Lt. Col. Normal Fortier

Mr. Thomas E. Graham, Historian, New Hampshire National Guard, Boscowen

Dr. Stephen Grove, Historian, U.S. Military Academy, West Point, New York

Ms. Rosanne Neri, ROTC Aerospace Studies, University of New Hampshire, Durham

Bonnie Oropallo, Bon-Lin Secretarial Service, Syracuse, New York

Col. William Saavedra, USAF History Support Unit, Bolling Air Force Base, Washington, D.C.

John Slonaker, Historian, Army War College, Carlisle Barracks, Pennsylvania

The family of Lt. Leon Jacques; Mrs. Marion Jacques Dube and son Steven Jacques

The family of General Frank Merrill; son Thomas Merrill and niece Mrs. Anne Merrill Bassette

The family of General Melvin Zais; Mrs. Patricia Light Zais and son Col. Barrie Zais

Foreword

IN 1963 I WAS A PRIVATE IN THE U.S. ARMY HERE IN THE states and Bill McGee was flying helicopters in Viet Nam. He sent me letters telling me about putting iron stove lids under his seat to protect from small arms fire. He also wrote me about shooting water buffalo to keep the Viet Cong hungry, and provide steaks for his unit's mess hall.

This was before anyone I knew was aware of Viet Nam. I had to go to the post library at Fort Belvoir to find the place on the globe. Couple years later Bill and I were no longer on active duty and every one knew where Viet Nam was.

Bill is my oldest and dearest friend. We go way back. In 1948 Bill and I were Boy Scouts together in Troop Four, Milford, New Hampshire. Bill's uniform was always neat and squared away. He kept his bedroom neat. He had a mint collection of the very first Walt Disney comic books. He was on the Milford High varsity basketball team and got good grades in school. He was an altar boy at St. Patrick's Church. Bill was the only one of our bunch who became an Eagle Scout.

I was always a little amazed that he continued to be my friend. He succeeded in all the things that I wanted to succeed in but could not. Also he was taller and better looking than I and had a lot more success with girls. Many of us, back then, joined Explorer Scouts. We Explorers held dances in the Boy Scout rooms in the town hall. "Explorers" was a perfect name for us. We'd get into uniform for the dances. We looked good in uniform. Also we felt more confident around the girls.

Our Scoutmaster was John LaTourette. Mr. LaTourette had come home from World War II to teach school and live the

American life. We adored him. He was patient and practical and knew all about Boy Scout stuff like building campfires and sleeping in the woods.

At the University of New Hampshire, Bill joined the Reserve Officers Training Corps. He loved the uniform and he loved the Army. For his entire life Bill McGee has had two great passions: the Boy Scouts and the military. I have never had a conversation with him that did not include both subjects. So it was inevitable, Bill would someday write a history of the Scouts . . . or he would write a military history.

When he told me he was researching a history of New Hampshire military heroes I knew it would be done with love and it would be thorough. The fact that it is a delight to read is frosting on the cake. This book will be a resource to students and historians for years to come. Researchers and teachers will thank Bill McGee for this work.

As I thank him.

Bill McGee amazes me.

Fritz Wetherbee

Acworth, New Hampshire

October 2007

Introduction

HIGH ABOVE FRANCONIA NOTCH, THE GATEWAY TO northern New Hampshire, was the profile of the Old Man of the Mountain.

Daniel Webster once said, "Men hang out their signs indicative of their respective trades; shoe makers hang out a gigantic shoe; jewelers a monster watch, and the dentist hangs out a gold tooth, but up in the mountains of New Hampshire, God Almighty has hung out a sign to show that he makes men."

These are the true stories of New Hampshire's fighting men—soldiers, sailors, marines, and airmen who made significant contributions in their service to their country from the French and Indian War to Iraq.

Eleven Medal of Honor recipients.

Men who were the namesakes of three Army forts, an Air Force base, two Army airfields, and four Navy destroyers.

Admirals, generals, privates and corporals—submariners, parachutists, and fighter pilots from New Hampshire . . .

Granite Staters . . .

Men of Granite.

FRENCH & INDIAN WAR

1755–1763

BRITAIN AND FRANCE FOUGHT FOUR WARS IN AMERICA between 1689 and 1763. The first, King William's War, which lasted from 1689 to 1697, was indecisive. The two major engagements involved were Sir William Phips' expedition of New Englanders occupying Port Royal in Acadia (Nova Scotia) and the French and Indians burning the English town of Schenectady, New York.

The second was Queen Anne's War, 1702-1713. The French, with their Indian allies, massacred the inhabitants of Deerfield, Massachusetts. Spain, now allied with France, attacked South Carolina from its stronghold, St. Augustine, Florida. A new British interest in Canada inspired a joint expedition of British troops and New Englanders against Quebec. The Quebec attack was repulsed by the French, but Acadia was conquered again. This resulted in Britain's acquisition of Nova Scotia, Newfoundland, and the Hudson Bay region.

King George's War, 1739-1748, was notable mainly for the success of Sir William Pepperrell whose force seized French Louisburg on Cape Breton Island (1745). A peace treaty mandated the return of the captured territory.

The fourth conflict known in America as the French and Indian War, focused on the western territories on the upper Ohio River and Lake Champlain region in upper New York. Both Britain and France wanted to build a fort at the fork of the Ohio River. The French erected Fort Duquesne (later Pittsburgh) after maneuvers in which young George Washington played a part. The French wiped

1

out the British under General Edward Braddock (July 9, 1755). For the next two years, the war went against Britain. Fort Oswego (New York), on Lake Ontario, was destroyed in 1756 as was Fort William Henry on Lake George in 1757.

Britain then turned to its great war minister, William Pitt, who inspired the nation with a passion for victory. In 1758, British forces conquered Forts Louisburg, Duquesne, and Frontenac. These successes opened the way to acquire Canada. Quebec fell in 1759 and Montreal in 1760. By the Treaty of Paris, in 1763, Britain acquired Canada and in America the land west of the Mississippi River.

The four British-French wars contributed materially to the growth of self-government in the thirteen American colonies. In the thirty-eight years of war, Britain could send only a small fraction of its army. The colonies were repeatedly required to provide both soldiers and money to support the wars. The colonial assemblies used their aid as a bargaining chip to gain privileges extending and intensifying their spirit of freedom. The battlefields developed such military leaders as George Washington, John Stark and Robert Rogers and his Rangers.

Robert Rogers

Major, Rogers' Rangers
French and Indian War

Born:	Nov. 18, 1731, Methuen, Massachusetts
Died:	May 18, 1795, London, England
Buried:	London, England
Battles:	Louisburg, Cape Breton, 1757
	Fort Carillon, Ticonderoga, 1758
	St. Francis, Canada, 1759
	Montreal, Canada, 1760

Wrote the first manual of warfare in the Americas

ROBERT ROGERS CONCEIVED THE IDEA OF A SMALL UNIT OF skilled woodsmen, well-trained, highly disciplined, and equipped to fight using hit and run tactics. These tough patriots would march all night in all weather to be ready for a surprise attack at dawn. These men were rangers, Rogers' Rangers. His Rules for Rangers (see page 11) are still used by Rangers today.

Robert Rogers was born to James and Mary Rogers on November 18, 1731, in Methuen, a small Massachusetts town north of the Merrimack River near the New Hampshire border. James and Mary were of Scottish descent who emigrated from Ireland. Robert was the fourth of their five sons, the youngest was a daughter, Mary.

Because James held no legal title to his land in the Massachusetts Bay Colony, he and some neighbors moved thirty-five miles north to the "great meadow" of New Hampshire in 1738. James purchased 21,090 acres at Mountalona (now Dunbarton) some ten miles south of Rumford (now Concord).

Young Robert received no formal education, but paternal guidance and the family Bible provided the basics of reading and writing. In his published journals, Rogers refers to his early education as woods lore and woodcraft he learned from local Indians.

The Rogers boys helped clear their family land for planting. Trees were felled, stumps and rocks had to be removed before plowing. It was a hard life, made more difficult by the threat of frontier raids by French-led Indians. In 1745, Robert, now fourteen, joined Capt. Daniel Ladd's company of militia to hunt down the marauders. He was probably happy to leave the toil and tedium of farming for the freedom of the forests and the thrill of the hunt. By the following spring, Robert was back helping till the family fields. That fall, he was among the first to enlist in Capt. Ebenezer Eastman's company of militia.

James Rogers' original land claims were reduced to two hundred acres following a dispute between Massachusetts Bay and the original land grantee, Capt. John Mason. The area of Mountalona became a new town—Starktown, later called Dunbarton. In 1752, Robert left farming for the lure of the frontier forest.

In March 1753, he and twenty men trudged north on snowshoes to survey the fertile Coos Meadows as authorized by the New Hampshire Assembly. Their guide was John Stark, who had seen the meadows a year before when he had been captured by Indians.

In September 1753, Robert Rogers purchased land in the town of Merrimack, and from that time he was usually identified in deeds as a member of that community.

Robert, although a keen observer and interpreter of woods and Indian lore, was not so astute in his financial dealings. He was duped into receiving and then passing some counterfeit money. A trial was held in Portsmouth on February 7, 1755. Robert and others were released on bond while the real counterfeiter escaped.

The drums of war were beating. The French in Canada encircled the English colonies along the Atlantic seacoast. The French invaded Nova Scotia, erecting forts and inciting the Acadians to revolt. On February 12, 1755, Gov. William Shirley, of Massachusetts, issued a call for volunteers for a regiment to drive the French out of Nova Scotia. Robert Rogers seized this opportunity to change his image from that of counterfeiter. He offered to recruit twenty men for the Massachusetts Regiment.

Meanwhile, the theater of war had enlarged. The New Hampshire Assembly voted in March to raise a regiment of five hundred men to force the French out of Crown Point, whose fort was located at a strategic narrows of Lake Champlain on the New York side. The New Hampshire Grants, now Vermont, was on the eastern side of the lake.

Rogers was ordered by Governor Benning Wentworth to come to Portsmouth to recruit men for the New Hampshire regiment. By April 24, Robert had brought in fifty men. His unit became Company One. He was its captain and John Stark was his lieutenant. Rogers' company of men were sworn in as private soldiers in a company of foot in a regiment, under command of Joseph Blanchard.

Rogers' company marched to Albany, New York, then northward to join Sir William Johnson's New York force of farmers, tradesmen, mechanics, and laborers at Lake George. Johnson sent Rogers and two others to reconnoiter the French fort at Crown Point. They returned with accurate information. Other scouting parties were reluctant to venture too far from the safety of their encampment at the log fort that later would become Fort William Henry. Rogers and only a few others remained at the fort over the winter of 1755-56.

During the winter, Rogers led a series of scouts and raids on the French that laid out the basis of his "ranging tactics." These revealed two of Rogers' characteristics—his aggressiveness and his uncanny woodsmanship. He would conduct his forays during the extremes of winter and into the heart of the enemy-held territory, and still return with few, if any, casualties.

News of Rogers' expeditions spread throughout the English colonies. Newspapers were filled with details and even his military colleagues were impressed with his feats. Robert Rogers was summoned to Boston, where he met with William Shirley, Governor of the Massachusetts Bay Colony and commander-in-chief of the British Army in North America. Governor Shirley appointed Rogers captain of an independent company of rangers on May 23. The new unit of sixty privates, two sergeants, and four officers would receive the same pay as British regular soldiers, twice as much as what provincial troops earned.

An excited and enthused Robert Rogers returned to Portsmouth and Rumford to recruit New Hampshire woodsmen for his company of Rangers. Robert's brother, Richard, became his first lieutenant. His trusted friend, John Stark, became a lieutenant second in rank to Richard. By mid-April, thirty-seven new recruits were on the march west to Fort Number Four on the Connecticut River. The company split into two units and made their ways separately to Fort William Henry on May 11.

For the remainder of 1756, scouting parties were sent to observe the French army strengthening their Fort Carillon (Ticonderoga) and up into Lake Champlain to take a few prisoners. A second ranger company was formed with Richard Rogers as its commander. Thirty Stockbridge Indians were incorporated into the two ranger companies.

In January 1757, Rogers led a raid against Crown Point. His men were each issued two weeks food rations, sixty rounds of powder and ball. Each man had snowshoes slung over his back, over the other shoulder hung his food knapsack, below it a canteen with diluted rum, under the right arm hung a powder horn. A blanket went over the head like a monk's hood and fastened in their waist-belts. Mittens were tied to the neck by cords to prevent loss. Muskets were carried like clubs over their shoulders. Reaching the frozen lake, the men donned skates and proceeded swiftly northward.

Halfway between Carillon and Crown Point, they were detected and became engaged in an all-day skirmish against a larger force of French and Indians.

The rangers withdrew during darkness and dragged themselves back to Fort Henry. Although they killed many more of the enemy, it was Rogers' worst loss of men. Of the seventy-four engaged, thirteen were killed, nine wounded, and seven taken prisoner.

Gov. William Shirley's military successor, John Campbell, Earl of Loudoun, could see that the success of Rogers' scouting and skirmishes was not by luck or chance. Rogers trained and directed his rangers by carefully thought-out tactics. Loudoun wanted to know these rules and requested that Rogers tell him. The result was the first written manual of warfare in the New World.

In response to Rogers' request, Loudoun commissioned him on April 6, 1758, to major of the Rangers in his majesty's service.

The rangers also received deserved official recognition by the issue of uniforms replacing their homespun clothes and leather hunting shirts. The new uniform was green, signifying woodsman. The outer coat was a short jacket similar to grenadiers and drummers. Underneath was a waistcoat lined with green serge. Linen or canvas drawers extended down to the knees and brown leggings up the rangers' thighs. The footwear was moccasins. Officers on parade wore tricorns piped with silver edging. Men wore plain tricorns with a sprig of evergreen stuck on the side. When on scouting missions, they preferred to wear the flat Scotch bonnets.

Their tools of the trade remained the same brown bess muskets as the regular British soldiers. The standard issue cartouche (cartridge box) replaced the leather pouch. A leather sling over the right shoulder held bayonet and tomahawk. Another sling carried a metal canteen and at the waist, a sheathed knife. Haversacks carried rations, and blankets were rolled and slung over the left shoulder.

The 1760 assault on Montreal was planned to have three forces converge on the city simultaneously. Lord Jeffrey Amherst's force would come down the Saint Lawrence River. General Murray would advance from Quebec, and General Haviland, with Rogers' six Ranger Companies and two Indian units, would smash through from the south. Three British armies, of thirty-two thousand men, converged on Montreal and on September 7, 1760, the French capitulated. Montreal and the entire country of Canada became subject to the British king.

The French also ceded their holdings in the American western frontier. Robert Rogers was sent to carry the Union Jack to the French forts west of Fort Pitt. This assignment offered Rogers a new lease on life. Five years of war had given him only the temporary rank of major, his service had involved him in debt, and creditors were pressing him for payment.

With written orders from Lord Amherst, Rogers set off for forts at Detroit and Michilimackinac, on September 13, 1760. With two ranger companies and a guide, the group in fifteen whaleboats began their trek upriver against the Saint Lawrence current, into Lake Ontario. They had to portage around Niagara Falls to reach the river to Lake Erie and westward to Detroit.

On November 23, they camped at the mouth of the Huron River and met with the Ottawa and Huron war chiefs, most likely including Pontiac. A pipe of peace was smoked and gifts were exchanged. The new Indian allies accompanied Rogers' party to Fort Detroit, where Captain Bellestre read the terms of the French surrender at Montreal. The French rule in the west ended with the surrender of Fort Detroit.

Rogers returned to New York and at age twenty-nine, made his decision to remain in the army. Amherst offered him a captain's commission in the regular British Army and the chance to fight the Cherokees in South Carolina. Rogers gladly accepted, but the problems of his indebtedness persisted. He had accumulated bills of more than six-thousand pounds to pay for his men and their equipment. Both the colonies of New Hampshire and Massachusetts refused to make good on their share, then the Crown refused its liability, leaving Rogers up to his neck in debt.

Although his financial affairs were not going well, there was a happy side to his life. He returned to Portsmouth, and married twenty year old Elizabeth Browne, his beloved Betsey. They were married June 30, 1761, in Queen's Chapel by her father, Rev. Arthur Browne.

In South Carolina, Rogers petitioned the governor to appoint him Superintendent of Southern Indians. He did not receive the appointment. By the summer of 1762, Rogers was suffering from malaria and returned to Betsey in New Hampshire. His creditors were still dogging him.

In 1763, Rogers was sent west again to aid the British at Fort Detroit, now fighting the massed Indians in what was called "Pontiac's War." Rogers' heroic stand covering the retreat of the British soldiers prevented the annihilation of the entire force. In October, Pontiac ceased the fighting. Rogers returned to New York, where he was jailed by his creditors. He was "broken out" of jail by soldiers of the Royal Americans Battalion who sympathized with Rogers' plight. He returned to New Hampshire only to learn that General Gage refused to honor the instructions of General Amherst stating that Rogers should receive full pay for his service. Gage in fact refused him any pay.

Rogers, in desperation, fled to England leaving his Betsey behind. He hoped that he could petition the government directly for his back pay and allowances. He published two books at his own expense to bolster his financial claims. His descriptions of the native copper and the possibility of a northwest passage through the American West to the Pacific Ocean drew much interest.

The British government must have been intrigued by the territory and the possibility of a northwest passage. Rogers was appointed commander of Fort Michilimackinac and superintendent of the Indians there and west of that post.

Rogers returned to America in January 1766, hoping to receive back pay for his military service and begin his new career as governor of the western wilderness. General Gage again denied his financial requests and told Sir William Johnson to spy on Rogers at his new post. Johnson was all too eager to undermine Rogers to maintain his own supreme position as the Crown's liaison with the Indians.

Rogers returned to New Hampshire to pick up his wife, and the couple began their long journey to Michilimackinac. They stopped at Sir William Johnson's home, west of Albany just north of the Mohawk River. They proceeded via Lake Ontario and Lake Erie to the fort located on the peninsula separating Lake Huron and Lake Michigan. Rogers did an excellent job managing the fort and dealing with both traders and Indians.

In September 1767, Gage and Johnson, armed with letters from Joseph Hopkins and Benjamin Roberts, falsely accused Rogers of treason. Rogers was arrested and clamped in irons. He and Betsey were taken to Detroit and later to Montreal for trial by court martial. Betsey, now carrying their child, went on to Boston to enlist support for her husband. In February 1769, their son Arthur was born. He was christened by his grandfather in Portsmouth.

Finally, in March, Rogers was acquitted by the court martial, but General Gage persisted in slandering him. During his tenure at Michilimackinac, Rogers had not been paid by Gage. Again Rogers sailed for England. Eventually he was allowed to receive his back pay, but Gage again blocked the payment of his military expenses. In October 1772, Rogers was put into Fleet Prison, London, at the suit of his creditors. Filing under a new bankruptcy law, Rogers was released from Fleet Prison after twenty-two months, in August 1774. Finally, in the spring of 1775, he received his retirement pay, enough for passage to America. After six years of disappointment and failure, he sailed back to his native land, a broken man of forty-three bearing the marks of debtor's prison. He hoped to return to a quiet future with his wife and son.

Landing in America in September 1775, Robert Rogers knew little about the struggle for liberty. He was arrested in Philadelphia on suspicion of being a British spy, as he was a retired major in the British army on half pay. Because that was his only offense, he was released when he promised not to take up arms against America.

He visited his brother James en route to Portsmouth to be reunited with his wife and son. He left New Hampshire to pursue land grants. Rogers secretly applied for a commission from Congress, but members were suspicious of his motives. He was arrested again and General Washington examined him in person. Washington also suspected that Rogers was a British spy. There was no place for Robert Rogers in the American army. He escaped prison in July and ten days later offered his services to General Howe. Howe empowered Rogers to raise a battalion of rangers. Recruiting numbers of loyalists, he quickly filled the battalion ranks. The problem was that these recruits were farmers or merchants and scarcely knew one end of a gun from the other. British regulars looked down on the new "Rangers" with deserved contempt.

Rogers, now a lieutenant colonel, commanded and led the Queen's American Rangers until January 1777, when he was asked to retire. Rogers quietly stepped aside instead of complaining. He probably had little heart for combat against his American countrymen.

In January 1778, Elizabeth Rogers filed a petition for divorce, which was granted. In November that same year, the New Hampshire Legislature passed an act naming individuals, including Rogers, who were not to return to its soil. These two actions devastated him.

In April 1779, Sir Henry Clinton still had a desperate faith in Rogers and asked him to raise two battalions of King's Rangers.

His brother James was to be second in command. The recruits they expected to come pouring in from New England and Canada never came. Troubles with his officers in Quebec in December took Rogers away from the field. By now, Rogers was drinking, which only made matters worse.

Rogers probably left America in 1782 with the defeated British Army and returned to London a lonely, broken exile. He was in and out of debtor's prison. His last sad days were passed in Southwark, where his heavy drinking continued. Robert Rogers died May 18, 1795. He was buried in a churchyard next to the Elephant & Castle Inn, London, far away from his beloved Betsey and the green hills and fields of New Hampshire.

His legacy lives on in the spirit of the U.S. Army Rangers.

Standing Orders, Rogers' Rangers

1. Don't forget nothing.
2. Have your musket clean as a whistle, hatchet scoured, sixty rounds powder and ball, and be ready to march at a minute's warning.
3. When you're on the march, act the way you would if you was sneaking up on a deer. See the enemy first.
4. Tell the truth about what you see and what you do. There is an army depending on us for correct information. You can lie all you please when you tell other folks about the Rangers, but don't ever lie to a Ranger or officer.
5. Don't never take a chance you don't have to.
6. When we're on the march we march single file, far enough apart so one shot can't go through two men.
7. If we strike swamps, or soft ground, we spread out abreast, so it's hard to track us.
8. When we march, we keep moving till dark, so as to give the enemy the least possible chance at us.
9. When we camp, half the party stays awake while the other half sleeps.
10. If we take prisoners, we keep 'em separate till we have had time to examine them, so they can't cook up a story between 'em.
11. Don't ever march home the same way. Take a different route so you won't be ambushed.
12. No matter whether we travel in big parties or little ones, each party has to keep a scout 20 yards ahead, 20 yards on each flank, and 20 yards in the rear so the main body can't be surprised and wiped out.

13. Every night you'll be told where to meet if surrounded by a superior force.
14. Don't sit down to eat without posting sentries.
15. Don't sleep beyond dawn. Dawn's when the French and Indians attack.
16. Don't cross a river by a regular ford.
17. If somebody's trailing you, make a circle, come back into your own tracks, and ambush the folks that aim to ambush you.
18. Don't stand up when the enemy's coming against you. Kneel down, lie down, hide behind a tree.
19. Let the enemy come till he's almost close enough to touch. Then let him have it and jump out and finish him up with your hatchet.

—MAJ Robert Rogers

THE AMERICAN REVOLUTIONARY WAR

1775–1781

SHORTLY AFTER THE END OF THE FRENCH AND INDIAN WAR, British statesmen of Britain found themselves with the problem of paying for that war which had left a national debt of 130 million pounds sterling. Another question was, who would pay for the ten-thousand British regulars garrisoned in North America? George Grenville's ministry reasoned that because the colonists would benefit most from the victory in Canada and on their frontiers, won for them by British arms, the colonists should pay. These ministers failed to recognize that in the course of these wars, some colonies had financed part of the campaigns as well as having furnished troops.

Soon the colonial merchants began to feel the pinch of the efforts of the English ministry to make up its financial deficit by the strict enforcement of the old Trade and Navigation Acts. Among these indignant colonial merchants were those of Portsmouth. Exasperated by the duties imposed upon them, the colonists resolved to renounce the use of every article of English manufacture or production. The *New Hampshire Gazette* urged the people "to dispense with superfluities, and practice economy for the sake of liberty and their country."

The Stamp Act and the Townshend Acts were as ill received in New Hampshire as they were in the rest of the colonies. Had England let the sleeping dog lie, the course of history might have been significantly different.

The Tea Act of 1773 was next in a sequence of many acts. It had been passed primarily to help the East India Company through its financial straits. Its provisions gave to the East India Company a monopoly on tea brought into the colonies. This tea was not subject to as high a tax or duty as were other teas, therefore it could easily undersell any competitors. These competitors were the colonial merchants. Although the colonists could buy tea at a cheaper price, they sympathized with the merchant class in this gross injustice. The merchants of Boston retaliated with their famed Tea Party.

The men of Portsmouth handled a similar situation with much more savoir faire. On June 25, 1774, a ship anchored in Portsmouth Harbor and prepared to land twenty-seven chests of tea. An orderly gathering of citizens and merchants took place and voted, that the tea should go out of this port and harbor immediately, and not be landed in this province.

Whether or not the British had the right to tax, there was no popular backing for taxation here. The colonists objected because of the restrictions and the high prices of goods, such as English gloves and clothes. The merchants protested because their profits were being cut. The merchants carried considerable influence in the colonies and did much to arouse the feelings of animosity of the people toward the Crown. One of the common arguments was if the British could seize John Rowe's wharf or John Hancock's ships, they could just as easily move in on barns, fields, livestock. Many a New Hampshire settler from Ireland could see the similarity of events here and in Ireland, which was eventually drained by British taxation.

The British regular soldiers garrisoned in Boston were a common sight. They acted only in compliance with the orders of their superiors, as did their officers. In carrying out their orders they were scorned and became the object of ridicule and hatred. On the night of March 5, 1770, occurred the unfortunate Boston Massacre. The whole affair was local and might have been buried except for one man, Samuel Adams, the intense, master propagandist.

These incidents seem to be pertinent only to Massachusetts, but they affected New Hampshire too. It is reasonably true that New Hampshire sympathized with Massachusetts due to their common bond. That is, both colonies had the same royal governors from 1699 to 1741 and the inhabitants of both colonies came from common stock. New Hampshire's religious outlook was also characteristically Puritan. Its local government conformed to that of Massachusetts Bay, to which colony it looked for political leadership.

The overt actions of the New Hampshire colonists against British rule took many forms. First was the formation of the Committee of Correspondence by the Provincial Assembly. Governor Wentworth tried in vain to restore order to the unruly New Hampshire assembly. He finally resorted to ordering the assembly to disband; "I require and hereby command you in his Majesty's name, forthwith to disperse." This was in vain. They rose when he entered to declare their proceedings void, but as soon as he left, they resumed their seats and went on with their business.

The Assembly appointed Major John Sullivan and Colonel Nathaniel Folsom to be delegates on the part of the Province, to attend and assist in the General Congress of Delegates from the other Colonies. To Sullivan went the honor of speaking first at the convention in Philadelphia. He reported that his assembly had instructed him to devise, consult, and adopt measures to secure and perpetuate their rights, and to restore that peace, harmony, and mutual confidence which once subsisted between the parent country and her colonies.

The most brazen action of New Hampshire's citizens was the raid on Fort William and Mary in New Castle. On December 15, 1774, Major John Sullivan led a group of patriots on the second raid of the fort. Included among the spoils taken in the two raids of December 14 and 15 were sixty muskets, sixteen light cannons, and one hundred barrels of powder. These bold attacks were precipitated by the fact that the king had forbidden the export of gunpowder to America, and also be the news that a "ship of war was daily expected from Boston to take possession of Fort William and Mary." Had any blood been spilled in this endeavor, the American Revolution might have started in New Hampshire, preceding the "shot heard round the world" by four months.

The province now had guns and powder with which to fight, if the need arose. New Hampshire also had men experienced in warfare. During the French and Indian War the militaristic spirit had been aroused. No colony furnished as many men in proportion to its population as did New Hampshire. A large portion of the men and officers who comprised the famous battalion of rangers under Major Robert Rogers were from this province. During the later part of the war, New Hampshire had furnished about five thousand men. The militia was thoroughly organized with large percentages of men and officers having seen active duty.

The battles at Concord and Lexington incited the colonists, and they realized that their position was a dangerous one. The New Hampshire Committee of Safety, organized in May 1775, sent out messages to several towns to send delegates to a convention to be held at Exeter on April 21, to consult for the general safety. At this convention Colonel Nathaniel Folsom was appointed Brigadier General to command the New Hampshire troops that had gone or might go to the aid of Massachusetts. It was also recommended that several towns in the province provide money and food in case of an emergency, and properly equip as many men as possible to march at a minute's notice.

Meanwhile, formal notices had been sent to towns to elect and send delegates to an assembly in Exeter to be held on May 17. At the convention, the members voted for raising companies and set the terms of enlistment. The convention also provided for the raising and commissioning of three continental regiments of light infantry. In December 1775, the convention at Exeter divided the militia into twelve regiments. Four regiments were minute men, constantly trained and at the ready. When in active service, they received the same pay as the continental soldiers, six shillings per day.

After New Hampshire ratified the Declaration of Independence, the two houses of its legislature decided to change the militia system. In September 1776, an act was passed providing for two classes of soldiers within the militia, a training band and an alarm list. Both classes included all males between the ages of sixteen and fifty years of age. Each officer and soldier had to furnish himself with a firearm, clothes, ammunition, and other necessary equipment. Whenever the militia was on active duty, the men became subject to the fifty-nine Articles of War. These articles set forth the rules and regulations of soldierly conduct. The rules were very strict and any infringement or violation of any article resulted in a trial by court martial. In 1776, New Hampshire had a battalion of three hundred men posted at fortifications and nine regiments in the field—three regiments of regulars in the Continental Army and six regiments of militia as reinforcements.

Upon hearing the reports of the actions that took place at Concord and Lexington, John Stark, like many other patriots of his state, took his musket and rode to Medford, Massachusetts.

As Stark rode, he passed other volunteers from New Hampshire and urged them to rendezvous at Medford. On April 22, 1775, Stark was elected, by its members, colonel to command this regiment of New Hampshire volunteers. Stark assured the committee at Cambridge that his regiment would be under Massachusetts control until the Exeter convention acted to finance it. There were so many volunteers to join Stark's regiment that he had to make up fifteen companies of seventy men each. Within five days after Concord and Lexington, the men began drawing pay.

On May 20, the convention at Exeter voted to raise a force of two thousand men and to assume control of those from New Hampshire already in the field. On May 23, delegates organized the troops into a brigade of three regiments to be commanded by General Folsom. James Reed and Enoch Poor were appointed colonels of two of the regiments, leaving the other colonelcy open for John Stark when he would resign his commission under the Massachusetts government. Stark went to Exeter and received his commission on June 3, 1775. On that same day it was voted that Stark would command the First New Hampshire Regiment of light infantry. The ten companies of the regiment of sixty-two men each, at Medford would be the first or oldest regiment.

Previous to this, Stark informed the New Hampshire Congress of an alarming situation. Many of the enlistees expected to draw arms from the provincial stocks and they had no arms of their own. "As no arms are to be procured here at present, (they) must inevitably return from whence they come. . . I humbly pray that you . . . adopt some measure or measures whereby they may be equipped." This same need was felt throughout the colonies and continued until Silas Deane and Benjamin Franklin secured aid from France in the form of thirty-thousand Model 1763 Charville muskets. In March 1777, a ship bearing twelve-thousand muskets arrived at Portsmouth. This windfall put the American army back in business, ending its dire shortage of shoulder arms.

Uniforms were another aspect of regimental organization. In the early part of the Revolution, the volunteers wore the clothes they enlisted in. Some of the troops assumed the dress recommended by Washington, "a hunting shirt and long gaiter breeches made of tow cloth, steeped in a tan vat until it reached the color of a dry leaf." This was called the shirt uniform, or rifle dress. On March 23, 1779, Congress authorized Washington "to fix and prescribe the uniform as well as with regard to color and facings . . . of the clothes to be worn by the troops of the respective states and regiments." In accordance with this resolution, General Washington issued the following order: "The following are the uniforms that have been determined for the troops of these States respectively; New Hampshire, Massachusetts, Rhode Island, and Connecticut—blue faced with white, buttons and linings white."

Between the time when the volunteers arrived at Medford and the Battle of Bunker Hill, the troops were drilled. Although there were some veterans of the French and Indian War, most of the volunteers were raw recruits. Stark had a sufficient knowledge of army organization and routine to see that the manual of arms was taught properly. It was Stark's nature to sanction just enough discipline to inculcate order and cooperation. He had little taste for dress parading.

On June 16, 1775, the night before the battle, under General Prescott's orders, the troops on Bunker Hill began digging and building redoubts. The following morning, Stark, his executive officer, and three hundred men arrived at the hill to make a ground reconnaissance. As they arrived, the British began cannonading the hill. Stark, seeing that his whole regiment would be needed soon, returned to Medford with this detachment. When the orders came to march, the First Regiment was ready. Stark's response was immediate and his regiment was the first present, although he received orders an hour later than the other troops and had two miles farther to go.

Arriving at Bunker Hill, Stark directed his men to take up positions along a rail fence about nine hundred feet long. He also ordered that a stone wall be erected from the end of the rail fence across the beach of the Mystic River. This anchored one end of the Americans' line of defense. The line of New Hampshire men behind the rail fence was two deep with enough room between men to permit ease in reloading.

After these hasty fortifications were established, the British troops began their advance. Colonel Stark stepped in front of the line, thrust a stick into the ground about eighty yards away and remarked to his soldiers, "There, don't a man fire till the red-coats come up to that stick, if he does I'll knock him down." The British lines advanced, possibly puzzled by the lack of resistance. When they reached Stark's stick the First Regiment opened fire, delivering with such accuracy that the British line wavered and broke. A second frontal attack on the rail fence netted the British the same results, withdrawal.

On the third attack, General Howe directed cannon fire on the middle of the patriots' line and onto the redoubt. This barrage was followed by a charge with fixed bayonets, which overwhelmed the defenders. The middle of the line broke, then the entire line gave way and the Americans retreated. Stark's men were the last to leave the field and retreated with the order of veteran troops.

Stark, in his report of the battle to the congress in Exeter said, ". . . but we remain in good spirits, being well satisfied that where we have lost one, the enemy have lost three." The actual count of casualties of the First Regiment was twelve men and three officers killed, forty-five wounded.

In September 1775, General Washington was burdened with maintaining an army through the winter months, a policy not used in the French and Indian campaigns. At this time Stark's regiment was cut down to ten companies totaling only 229 men who were willing to continue in the service of the United Colonies during the winter.

It was not until March 1776 that the regiment broke camp in Medford. On March 16, Stark received orders to proceed to Norwich, Connecticut. At Norwich, Stark's regiment was placed under the command of General Heath. Under Heath, the colonial regiments marched to New York in anticipation of invading Canada. While they were quartered in New York, an epidemic of smallpox decimated the troops, Stark himself being a temporary casualty.

June 5, 1776, the First Regiment arrived at the mouth of the Sorel River near Three Rivers. Stark, having recovered from his illness, joined his regiment there. Upon the death of General Thomas and the withdrawal of Wooster, General John Sullivan was put in command of the expedition. Sullivan immediately took the initiative when there was no call to. This was based on his thirst for glory, and not on sound logic. In his council of war, all of Sullivan's officers, including Stark, opposed Sullivan's plan.

The campaign at Three Rivers was a fiasco. The troops completed crossing the Sorel River too late for the proposed night attack. The guide of one wing led them through a swamp, betraying their intended surprise, and the guide of the other wing led his charges to a frontal attack of the enemy's fortified position. With surprise out of the question and a British fleet in the Saint Lawrence in position to fire upon them, retreat was inevitable. Even the retreat was accomplished with the greatest of disorder. Sullivan in his report to General Washington said that the reason for this failure was the sickness of the troops.

With the defeat of Arnold at Montreal, the position of Sullivan's brigade at Three Rivers was precarious. Although Sullivan was unwilling to withdraw, he was unanimously opposed by his council of war. Some luck was with Sullivan, for as his brigade was retreating, the British ships in the St. Lawrence were becalmed and could not harass the Americans in their retreat. Stark and his First Regiment served Sullivan well in this action by acting as the rear guard until the brigade safely reached Crown Point. Not a boat or a piece of artillery was lost. Colonel Stark and his staff were in the last boat that left shore. They were in sight when the advanced guard of the enemy arrived amid the smoking ruins of St. John's.

In the summer and fall of 1776, the First Regiment was garrisoned at Fort Ticonderoga and did little more than become bored with garrison duty there. General Gates proposed a furlough to the New Hampshire men. "It would most certainly be for the immediate benefit of the service that … the three regiments commanded by Stark, Poor, and Reed, march to Portsmouth where they can not only be recruited but recovered and refreshed." The request was denied by General Schuyler because these troops would soon be marching south to New Jersey to aid General Washington.

Washington's troops were quartered on the right bank of the Delaware River in a position to protect Philadelphia. The British commanders were unwary and lax in discipline, it being the middle of winter. General Howe suspected little trouble from Washington's depleted and ill-equipped forces. However, General Howe did have reason to worry. For the previous month, Washington had been collecting boats and scows for thirty miles up and down the river, and the depleted ranks were swelled by the arrival of the New Hampshire brigade.

On Christmas Day 1776, a council of war was called at which Washington is reported as saying to Colonel Stark, "We are to march tomorrow on Trenton, you are to command the right wing of the advanced guard and General Greene the left." It is interesting to note that Stark, a mere colonel among so many general officers, was designated to play such an important role in this battle. Some historians have conjectured that Washington, after his recent defeat at Long Island, was in a position that would allow no failure. Comparatively few of the officers present had been battle-tested, and indecisiveness could prove fatal. Stark was an experienced commander and his regiment was composed of seasoned and hardened veterans.

Washington divided his command into three divisions to be led by Irwine, Cadwalder, and himself. The plan was to ferry the three divisions across the Delaware at night and attack Trenton from three directions, while the enemy was recuperating from its holiday celebrations. The ferrying of the troops across the ice-filled Delaware was delayed and it was not until four in the morning that Washington's division was ready to march. (Both Irwine and

Cadwalder failed in their attempts to cross the river.) Washington divided his force. He took the Pennington Road and Sullivan's brigade of New Hampshire troops moved down the road nearer the river. The orders were to commence the attack as soon as either group reached Trenton.

The right wing, under Stark, arrived at about eight o'clock. The company under Captain Frye was the first to alarm the Hessians by surrounding one of their outposts. Stark's First Regiment leapt to the attack and dealt death wherever they found resistance and broke down all opposition before them.

A group of Hessians took refuge in a house and their firing slowed the Americans' advance. Captain Frye ordered a Sergeant Stevens to take a squad and dislodge the Hessians. The squad fired upon the house, broke down the door, and, using bayonets, silenced the enemy.

Colonel Ralle, the Hessian commander, attempted to organize a counter-attack, but he was fatally wounded and the German mercenaries fled in confusion toward Princeton. Washington, seeing this retreat, ordered a detachment to stop it. Captain Frye's company was again foremost in action. Frye, a heavy man, was not able to keep up with the rapid advance of his troops, ordered them to continue under Sergeant Stevens. These few men reached a patch of woods before the Hessians appeared on their retreat down the road. The squad jumped out at the Hessians yelling fiercely. The astonished Hessians immediately surrendered to the New Hampshire men although they outnumbered them by four to one.

With the route of retreat cut off, the remaining Hessians surrendered. About nine hundred men and officers of Von Ralle's Hesse Cassel Regiment were taken prisoner. The American troops withdrew from Trenton with their prisoners and that same night recrossed the Delaware.

That Christmas night when Washington crossed the Delaware was the most critical movement of his career. The terms of service of the greater part of his little army expired on New Year's Day, and but for the success of Trenton, they would have almost certainly disbanded. Colonel Stark, aware that the fate of the nation depended on the reenlistment of the New Hampshire regiments, told the men of his First Regiment that if they left the army, all would be lost. He reminded them of their deeds at Bunker Hill and at other battles in the Canadian campaign. He assured them that if Congress did not pay their wages, he would make it up to them. Hearing Stark's proposal for a six week extension of their enlistment, the men of the First Regiment were with him to a man.

The British, smarting from the defeat at Trenton, began massing troops at Princeton in hopes of effecting a decisive victory to destroy the rising American morale. The British located Washington's camp near Trenton and briefly cannonaded it, confident of their success in the following morning's battle. Washington realized that he was outnumbered and implemented a ruse. By leaving behind a minimum number of troops to pose as guards and keep the camp fires going, Washington was able to withdraw his entire force without being detected by the British.

With this force, on December 28, 1776, the Americans marched to Princeton, which was now garrisoned by only three regiments. Washington would have achieved complete surprise in this maneuver had he not met by chance a British Regiment on its way to Trenton. The Pennsylvania militia, at the head of the column, broke and retreated. Washington charged to the front with the New England troops, who fought until the British ranks retreated. These troops were followed into Princeton, where they put up only slight resistance. The town was surrendered with three hundred British. Meanwhile, the British at Trenton, perplexed at attacking a deserted camp, fled in panic to Brunswick. Details as to the American divisions and their precise actions in the Battle of Princeton are sketchy, therefore, the parts played by Stark and the First Regiment of New Hampshire are obscure.

Colonel Stark was a patriot-soldier and was rank conscious for neither prestige nor money, but he rightly felt that his seniority and ability should have been recognized. The first occasion when Stark was passed over for advancement was when the New Hampshire Congress promoted Colonel Folsom to brigade commander in May 1775. This marked the beginning of Stark's growing resentment toward politically appointed officers. The breaking point for Stark occurred in February 1777 when he learned that Colonel

Enoch Poor had been commissioned brigadier general by the Continental Congress on the recommendation of the New Hampshire Congress. Because the quota allow for only one brigadier for New Hampshire, Stark was passed over again.

As soon as Colonel Stark heard this, he went to Exeter and resigned his commission. The Congress voted Stark a vote of thanks for his meritorious contributions to the American cause.

Stark's exact date of resignation is not known, but Joseph Cilley was promoted to colonel commanding the First New Hampshire Regiment on February 23, 1777. Cilley, acting on Washington's orders, which reached him by way of Exeter, led his regiment to Fort Ticonderoga. All of the First Regiment did not arrive until May. The First, with her sister regiments, now under Colonels Scammell and Dearborn, drilled in preparation for the expected meeting with General Burgoyne.

On August 22, 1777, two regiments from New York joined General Poor's brigade. A week later Morgan's regiment of riflemen also joined. On September 9 the brigade marched to Stillwater, near Saratoga, New York, and camped there. Three days later the forces advanced to Bemis Heights and fortified their positions. On September 19, at about noon, the Americans engaged the enemy.

Morgan's regiment charged first, followed by the New Hampshire regiments, which charged the British line with such ferocity that it broke and retreated in disorder, leaving its cannons on the battlefield. Colonel Cilley ordered his regiment to hold one of the cannons at all costs, which his men did. The troops of the First Regiment repulsed repeated attacks from the British to regain their lost artillery piece. Finally the New Hampshire men turned the cannon and fired it upon the British. Two sources agree that Colonel Cilley himself aided in the defense, loading, and firing of this piece.

The immediate results of the Battle of Bemis Heights was the loss to General Burgoyne of the eighty cannon and about four hundred officers and men, either killed or captured. The long term result of this battle was the demoralization of Burgoyne and his troops. Although Cilley's regiment was in the thick of the battle, it did not sustain a single fatality. Forty-six men were wounded and twelve were missing.

After the action at Stillwater, the enemy fortified a position about a mile from the Americans at Bemis Heights. The number of the American forces swelled as two thousand militiamen joined the camp. On October 7, the British attacked the left wing of the Americans' position. This attack was turned into a rout by the Americans. The failure of the British precipitated their hasty withdrawal from their position. When the American commanders heard of the British action, they ordered a pursuit.

On October 9, the pursuing Americans caught the British at Saratoga. The British, realizing that they were surrounded, called for a cease-fire to draw up terms for a surrender. On October 17, 1777, the British Army of the North, under Burgoyne, surrendered. Prior to this battle, Burgoyne had written to Lord Germain that "the Hampshire Grants country unpeopled and almost unknown in the last war, now abounds in the most active and rebellious race on the continent and hangs like a gathering storm upon my left."

The victory of the Americans at Saratoga was made possible by the gallant and timely actions of two militia forces far from the Saratoga battlefields. The Mohawk Valley militia under General Herkimer defeated Barry St. Leger's troops at Oriskany (New York), preventing them from joining Burgoyne. The New Hampshire militia, under John Stark, marched to Bennington (Vermont) and defeated a British supply column, preventing the sorely needed supplies and reinforcements from reaching Burgoyne's army.

The American victory at Saratoga marked the turning point of the Revolution. The surrender of an entire British army had a great psychological effect on the American cause, raising the morale and giving our envoys to France something concrete to bargain with. The British evacuated Fort Ticonderoga and Crown Point, as agreed in the terms of the surrender. By the end of 1777, the British held only the cities of New York, Philadelphia, and Newport. Six months later, the center of the war shifted to the south.

After successive marches, the First Regiment joined the army under Washington, near Philadelphia, on November 21, 1777. On December 16, the army marched to Valley Forge to set up winter quarters. Just the mention of Valley Forge brings to mind the sickness, starvation and the ragged clothing of the men. This was the perpetual state of the continental soldiers for the duration of the war.

The morale of those men who were not sick, was lifted by the instruction of Baron Von Stueben, who drilled the men in the manual of arms and thereby kept their minds temporarily off their hardships. At times, when Von Stueben became exasperated with drilling Americans, he would swear in German, then in French, and then in both languages together, finally pleading for someone to "swear for me in English." This only endeared him more to the Americans.

May 16, 1778, was a day of great celebration for the men of the continental army, as it marked the arrival of the news of the alliance of France with the United Colonies and a relief from carrying the full burden against the British.

General Charles Lee's division was drawn up in a field near the courthouse in Monmouth, New Jersey, on June 28th. The regiments were not in battle formations, as Lee had neglected to tell his subordinates of the impending British attack. When the two elements came in contact with each other, there followed a number of skirmishes, in which American orders seem to have been countermanded as soon as they were given. Lee had no plan and no grasp of the situation. He then gave the order to retreat. Washington, who was attacking the British rear guard, could not believe that the division under Lee was retreating, and rode forward himself to learn the truth. Washington severely reprimanded Lee on the spot. Washington then turned the retreating Americans about to meet the enemy. After the battle, Alexander Scammell, acting under Washington's orders, placed Lee under arrest.

The First Regiment attacked the rear guard of the British as part of Washington's division. The First Regiment was then brought up to relieve an attack on Stirling's flank. In that encounter, a part of the New Hampshire troops, under Colonel Cilley, behaved with such distinguished bravery as to receive the notice of General Washington. Washington inquired, "What troops are these?" Cilley replied, "True-blooded Yankees, sir!" "I see," said General Washington, "They are my brave New Hampshire boys."

After the battle dead had been buried, Poor's New Hampshire brigade marched north. At Wardsession they met the other wing of the American army. The troops marched through southern New York and finally set up their winter quarters near Redding, Connecticut, and spent the winter of 1778–1779 there.

In the spring of 1779, after a series of raids and massacres of settlers in New York's Cherry Valley and Pennsylvania's Wyoming Valley, by British-led Iroquois Indians, General Washington ordered a punitive campaign. General John Sullivan was chosen to lead an American army of forty-five hundred men against the Indians of western New York.

Sullivan's army consisted of three New Hampshire regiments under General Henry Dearborn; a New York brigade under General James Clinton; General William Maxwell's New Jersey brigade; a Massachusetts regiment; some artillery; and a company of Virginia riflemen.

Washington's orders were explicit for Sullivan's force to burn the villages of the Seneca, Cayuga and Onondagas and to destroy all crops and orchards. They were told not to negotiate with the Indians, to simply destroy everything so the British would have to supply and maintain their Indian allies through the coming winter.

Sullivan's army defeated the Tories and Indians, led by General Butler and Chief Joseph Brant on August 29, 1779, at Newtown (Elmira, New York). The American force marched up the shores of Seneca and Canandaigua Lakes and destroyed more than forty villages, hundreds of acres of corn, and peach and apple orchards. They drove back the Iroquois to Fort Niagara for the coming winter.

After this successful campaign, General Sullivan resigned due to deteriorating health. The New Hampshire regiments spent the winter of 1779–80 near Danbury, Connecticut.

In April 1780, the First Regiment marched to West Point, where the men were garrisoned until August. They then marched into lower New York and back to West Point to spend the winter of 1780-81 garrisoned on Constitution Island. At the close of 1780, the three New Hampshire regiments of continentals were reduced to two, Colonel Reed commanding the Second Regiment and Colonel Cilley the First Regiment. In July 1781, after Colonel Cilley resigned from the service, the New Hampshire government appointed Colonel Alexander Scammell as commander of the First Regiment.

That same month, Scammell marched at the head of his troops to New York City, where the regiment joined the French army. The French were in better uniforms and perhaps in a better state of discipline than the Americans, but no corps exceeded the light infantry commanded by Scammell. The column marched from New York to the south in order to engage General Cornwallis. The forces met at Yorktown, Virginia, where the British, with only six thousand men, were in a defensive position. Washington, at that time, had under his command eight-eight hundred American troops and seventy-eight hundred French troops.

During the siege of Yorktown, Colonel Scammell was mortally wounded. One day, presuming that a battle would ensue, Scammell considered it his duty to place himself at the head of a reconnaissance patrol. Another colonel on this same patrol was Light-horse Harry Lee, who gave the following account: "Advancing close to the enemy's position, Scammell fell in with a detachment of the British legion dragoons, who instantly charged our party. In the fight, Scammell was mortally wounded and taken prisoner." Henry Dearborn, who had been a captain under Stark when the First Regiment was founded at Medford, was appointed to replace Colonel Scammell as commander of the First New Hampshire Regiment.

On the night of October 14, 1781, the First Regiment attacked the right redoubt as part of the action of the New England light infantry in combination with the French. This mission was successful, as was the entire siege of Yorktown, which resulted in Cornwallis's surrender of the British forces in America.

In the fall of 1781, the First Regiment, under Dearborn, marched back to New York State. In 1782, the men were stationed at Saratoga with no duties other than to act as the relief for Colonel Willet's troops, whose service terms had expired. In November 1782, Dearborn's First Regiment joined the main army at Newburgh (near West Point), and remained there until the peace of 1783.

The First Regiment received notice to disband on April 4, 1783. The First New Hampshire Regiment, the sole representative of the New Hampshire line, was the last, or at least among the very last, to lay down arms. The payrolls show that the men camped on the Hudson River during the month of December 1783, and there is little doubt that they were disbanded before January 1, 1784. This would give the regiment a length of continuous service of eight years and eight months—nearly nine years in the service of their country as an unequalled record among the continental regiments and a proud heritage for the state of New Hampshire.

John Stark

Brigadier General
New Hampshire Volunteer Regiment
American Revolutionary War, 1775-1781
Captain of Rogers' Rangers
French and Indian War, 1755-1763

Born:	August 28, 1728, Nutfield, New Hampshire (now Londonderry)
Died:	May 8, 1822, Manchester, New Hampshire
Buried:	River Road Cemetery, Manchester
Battles:	Ft. Carillon, 1757, Ticonderoga, New York
	Louisburg, 1758, Nova Scotia
	Bunker Hill, 1775
	Trenton, 1776
	Princeton, 1776
	Bennington, 1777

OF THE MANY TITLES USED TO DESCRIBE JOHN STARK—
hunter, trapper, farmer, sawmill operator, husband, father, military
leader—the one to best characterize him is patriot.

John Stark was born in 1728 in Nutfield (now Londonderry,
New Hampshire). When he was eight years old his family moved
to Derryfield (now Manchester). His father built a small house by
Amoskeag Falls on the Merrimack River.

In the spring of 1752, Stark went trapping with some compan-
ions up Baker's River near the present town of Rumney. Although
it was a time of peace, Stark and a friend named Eastman were
taken prisoners by the Abenaki Indians near Stinson Lake. The two
hostages were taken to the Indian village near St. Francis, where
they were forced to run the gauntlet. Each had to repeat a sentence
in Algonquin as he ran between the lines of Indians. Neither understood the meaning of the words. Eastman was nearly killed by the
blows but made it through. Stark expected the same, but as he ran
the Indians laughed at him. He was yelling, "I will kiss all your
young maidens."

While held prisoner, Stark learned the customs and language of his captors. When commanded to hoe corn, he threw down the hoe and said it was women's work and not fit for warriors. Instead of beating him they adopted him into the tribe. Stark was eventually ransomed for about a hundred dollars, a sum he quickly paid through trapping.

His travels had taken him and Eastman through the Coos Meadows, probably the first white men to see that country. Their glowing accounts of this area led to its settlement after the French and Indian raids were over.

When his friend Robert Rogers raised his famous company of rangers, John Stark volunteered. He was commissioned a second Lieutenant in the first company of rangers, attached to Colonel Blanchard's regiment. The rangers fought against the invading French army which enlisted the help of Indian tribes. The British were at war with the French and called upon the American colonists to aid them. Most of Rogers' Rangers' raids were in the Lake Champlain area of New York. In 1757, John Stark was promoted to captain and commanded the second ranger company.

In 1758, hearing of his father's death, John took a leave of absence to settle his estate. At this time he was a frequent visitor to the Page homestead in Dumbarton, where he met Elizabeth Page—his beloved Molly. They were married on August 20, 1758, and settled in the Page home.

After many weeks of inactivity, Stark was all too eager to accept General Jeffery Amherst's request to build a road from Crown Point, New York, to Fort Number Four in Charlestown, New Hampshire, across what is now the state of Vermont. This was no easy undertaking. Stark and his rangers were a rough and independent bunch and were made to feel inferior to the British army. Discipline was severe and difficult for the American rangers to understand or endure. The French capitulated in 1760, and Stark, after a dispute with his superiors, was glad to go home to build up his family property. He bought the land his brothers and sisters had inherited and became the sole owner of a large estate. He and Molly were now living with his mother in Derryfield (Manchester).

Resentment of British rule and of the presence of British soldiers in the American colonies came to the surface as more and more taxes were imposed. The Stamp Act of 1765, the Boston Massacre in 1770, and the tea tax were bitter pills for colonists to swallow. When the shots were fired at Concord and Lexington, they echoed around the world.

John Stark was working at his sawmill on the Stark farm in Manchester when he heard the news of those shots. It was said that he grabbed his musket, jumped on his horse without putting on his coat, and headed for Medford, Massachusetts. As he rode, he passed other volunteers from New Hampshire. He urged them to rendezvous at Medford. On April 22, 1775, Stark was elected by the New Hampshire volunteers to serve as colonel of the New Hampshire regiment of volunteers.

For the next three weeks the troops were drilled. Some, like Stark, were veterans of the French and Indian War, but most were raw recruits. Although Stark was not a technician, he did have knowledge of army routine and organization and taught the men the manual of arms. He also understood that just enough discipline was required to achieve order and cooperation, while too much only bred resentment.

On the morning of June 17, 1775, Stark and three hundred of his men arrived at Bunker Hill to "get the lay of the land." When the British ship HMS *Lively* began cannonading the hill, Stark returned to Medford to get his entire regiment. Capt. Henry Dearborn's company was first in the order of march. He was walking beside Stark and suggested they quicken the pace. Stark fixed him with a steely gaze and replied, "Dearborn, one fresh man in action is worth ten fatigued ones," and continued his deliberate pace. Arriving at Bunker (Breed's) Hill, Stark directed his men to take up positions along a rail fence about nine hundred feet long. He also ordered that a stone wall be erected from the end of the rail fence to the beach of the Mystic River. This would anchor the colonists' line of defense.

The line of New Hampshire men behind the rail fence was two deep, with enough room between men to permit ease in reloading their muskets. As the British troops began their advance, Colonel

Stark stepped in front of the line and thrust a stick into the ground about eighty yards distant. He said to his men "Don't a man fire till the red-coats come up to that stick, if he does, I'll knock him down."

On the British side of the river, the decision was made to mount a full frontal assault. This was the standard procedure on European battlefields—the British assuming the rebels would break and run. The British lines of redcoats advanced up the hill, possibly puzzled by the lack of resistance. When they reached Colonel Stark's stick, the First New Hampshire Regiment opened fire with such accuracy that the British line wavered and broke. A second frontal attack on the rail fence netted the same result—withdrawal.

On the third attack, General Howe aimed cannon fire on the middle of the line. This barrage was followed by a British charge with fixed bayonets, which overwhelmed the defenders. The Americans retreated. Stark's men were the last to leave the field and retreated with the order of veteran troops.

Stark's regiment of 679 lost twelve men and three officers killed and forty-five wounded. The British sustained 1,054 casualties of their twenty-three hundred troops. Washington's estimate of American casualties in all regiments at Bunker Hill was 450 killed, wounded, or missing.

The New Hampshire regiment wintered at Medford and broke camp on March 17, 1776. They joined General Heath in Connecticut, then marched to New York in anticipation of invading Canada. The campaign, under General John Sullivan at Three Rivers, failed and the Americans had to retreat. Stark's First New Hampshire Regiment served General Sullivan well, acting as the rear guard until the brigade safely reached Crown Point. The summer and fall of 1776 were spent garrisoned at Fort Ticonderoga.

General Schuyler ordered the New Hampshire Brigade south to assist General Washington, whose troops were quartered on the right bank of the Delaware River in position to protect Philadelphia. Being mid-winter, the British commanders were unwary and lax in discipline. General Howe did have reason to be concerned. Washington had been collecting boats and scows up and down the river for the previous month and his depleted ranks were now augmented by the arrival of the New Hampshire Brigade.

General Washington called a council of war on Christmas Day 1776 and said to Colonel Stark, "We are to march tomorrow on Trenton, you are to command the right wing of the advanced guard and General Greene the left."

It is interesting to note that Stark, a mere colonel among so many generals, was designated to play such an important role in this battle. After Washington's recent defeat at Long Island, he was in a situation that would allow no failure. Of the officers present, few had been battle-tested. Stark was an experienced commander and his regiment was composed of "seasoned and hardened veterans."

The plan was for three divisions of Washington's command to cross the Delaware at night and attack Trenton from three directions. Two divisions failed to cross the ice-filled river, but Washington's force including the First New Hampshire, made it across. Washington divided his force; he took the Pennington Road and Sullivan's New Hampshire troops (moved) down the road nearer the river.

The right wing under Colonel Stark, arrived about eight o'clock. The Company, under Captain Frye, surrounded a Hessian guard post. The rest of the First New Hampshire leapt to the attack and killed many Hessian mercenaries with musket fire and bayonets. Colonel Von Ralle, the Hessian commander, attempted to form a counterattack, but was fatally wounded. Some Hessian soldiers fled in confusion toward Princeton, but Captain Frye's men captured them. About nine hundred men and officers of Von Ralle's German Hesse Cassel regiment were taken prisoner.

That Christmas night was critical in Washington's career, for the terms of enlistment for the volunteers would expire on New Year's Day. If not for the success at Trenton, the little army might have disbanded. Colonel Stark, aware that the fate of the new nation depended on the reenlistment of the New Hampshire regiments, told them, "If Congress does not pay your arrears, my own private property should make it up to them."

The British, smarting from their defeat at Trenton, began massing troops at Princeton in hopes of a decisive victory to destroy the rising American morale. The British located Washington's camp near Trenton and briefly cannonaded it, confident of their success the following morning. Washington effected a ruse. Leaving only a few men to keep camp fires going, he withdrew his main force undetected and attacked Princeton. On December 28, 1776, the town was surrendered with three hundred British troops.

John Stark was a patriot-soldier who felt that his seniority and military ability should be recognized. He had been passed over in 1775, when the New Hampshire Congress promoted Colonel Folsom to brigade commander. The breaking point for Stark came in February 1777 when the Continental Congress appointed Enoch Poor brigadier general. The quota allowed for only one brigadier from New Hampshire.

When Stark heard this, he returned to Exeter and resigned his commission, receiving their vote of thanks for his services. Stark pledged his immediate assistance to New Hampshire should it be needed.

After four months as a private citizen, Stark accepted a commission as brigadier general of the New Hampshire Militia, with the proviso that he be answerable only to New Hampshire. This was a wise decision, for when ordered to join General Schuyler at Saratoga, Stark refused and instead marched his contingent of fifteen hundred to Bennington.

Just before the August 16th battle, Stark stood on a rail fence and told his men, "Over there are the Hessians. They were bought for seven pounds and 10 pence a man. Tonight the American flag floats over yonder hill or Molly Stark sleeps a widow." Stark's New Hampshire men won the battle, which prevented British reserves and supplies from augmenting Burgoyne at Saratoga. More than two hundred British and Hessians were killed and seven hundred captured. The eventual American victory at Saratoga was the turning point in the Revolutionary War. In 1805 Thomas Jefferson wrote, "The victories of Bennington, the first link in the chain of successes which issued in the surrender of Saratoga are still fresh in the memory of every American...I salute you, venerable patriot and general, with affection and reverence."

The war dragged on for four more years. General Stark, now in his fifties, would go home during the colder months to recuperate from the rheumatism, which would bother him the rest of his life.

When the Revolutionary War ended, Stark settled down to farm life again. He and Molly had ten children, five boys and five girls. In 1783, John Stark was ordered by General Washington to report to headquarters where he received the personal thanks of the Commander-in-Chief and the rank of major general by brevet.

In 1809, Stark was invited to attend a banquet of Bennington veterans. At age eight-one he was too infirm to attend, but sent a letter reminding the men of the time they "taught the enemies of liberty that undisciplined freemen are superior to veteran slaves." Stark closed with his now famous phrase, "Live free or die. Death is not the worst of evils."

Molly stark died of typhus in 1814 at age seventy-eight. John lived to his ninety-fourth year and died May 8, 1822, reportedly the last surviving continental general of the American Revolution. In 1945, the New Hampshire Legislature adopted "Live Free or Die" as the state motto. John Stark's love for the cause lives on.

References:
E. Everett, *John Stark*, New York, 1902
H.P. Moore, *A Life of General John Stark*, Boston, 1949
C. Stark, *Memoir & Official Correspondence of Gen. John Stark*, 1877

JOHN SULLIVAN

Major General, Continental Army
American Revolutionary War

Born: February 17, 1740, Somersworth, New Hampshire
Died: January 23, 1795, Durham, New Hampshire
Buried: Durham, New Hampshire
Battles: Siege of Boston, 1775-1776
            Three Rivers, Canada, 1776
            Long Island, 1776
            Trenton, 1776
            Princeton, 1777
            Brandywine, 1777
            Germantown, 1777
            Newport, 1778
            Newtown, 1779

JOHN SULLIVAN'S PARENTS EMIGRATED FROM IRELAND to Maine in 1723. He was born in Somersworth on the banks of Salmon Falls, and studied law in the office of Samuel Livermore, in Portsmouth, New Hampshire. In 1760, at age twenty, he married Lydia Worcester. Sullivan practiced law in Berwick, Maine, until 1763, when the couple moved to Durham, New Hampshire, where he set up his own law office. The couple's children, three sons and a daughter, grew up in Durham. Two other children died as infants.

In 1772, Sullivan was appointed major of the New Hampshire militia and in 1774 and served as a delegate to the First Continental Congress in Philadelphia, taking his seat on September 5. He returned home and in December received Paul Revere's warning of a threatened attack by the British. Sullivan and John Langdon organized a group of patriots who captured Fort William and Mary located at the entrance to Portsmouth Harbor. They seized sixteen cannons, sixty muskets, and one hundred barrels of gunpowder, which were hidden on farms and forests for later use.

Sullivan was a delegate to the Second Continental Congress in May 1775, and there he was appointed a brigadier general in the Continental Army. In July, he joined Washington's troops near Boston, garrisoned at Winter Hill, and served there until March 17, 1776, when the city was evacuated. Sullivan then received orders to join the northern army in the campaign at Three Rivers, Canada. When General John Thomas, the expedition's overall commander, was killed, Sullivan succeeded him. His plan of attack at Three Rivers failed and the colonial army was forced to retreat. Sullivan was replaced by General Horatio Gates. Sullivan returned to Philadelphia intending to resign, but was persuaded by Continental Congress President John Hancock to remain in the army.

On August 9, 1776, Sullivan was promoted to major general and was sent with his men to Long Island. He was captured by the British during the Battle of Long Island on August 27. He was later exchanged for British General Richard Prescott and sent to Philadelphia, carrying overtures of peace from Lord Howe.

Sullivan rejoined Washington's army, and in December 1776 crossed the Delaware River to surprise the Hessian mercenaries at Trenton. During that winter of 1777, Sullivan's units fought the British at Princeton, Germantown, and Brandywine. In March 1777, he returned to New Hampshire to expedite preparation for military operations that summer. In July, Sullivan joined generals Nathaniel Green and Henry Knox in protesting the rapid promotion of DuCoudray, a newly arrived French Officer. All three threatened to resign, but the situation was resolved when DuCoudray drowned. It made some enemies for Sullivan in Congress however. To make matters worse, Sullivan led an expedition August 21, 1777 to retake Staten Island which failed. Sullivan regained some favor when his troops arrived in Philadelphia in time to defend against General Howe's attack on the city.

In 1777, Congress proposed to remove Sullivan from his command while the Staten Island matter was investigated. His enemies added charges of cowardice at Brandywine. General Washington refused to recall Sullivan and the charges proved to be false.

During winter 1777-78, Sullivan and his troops were with Washington at Valley Forge. In August 1778, he conducted the siege of Newport, Rhode Island. The operation depended on the French fleet defeating the British fleet. This key maneuver failed when the French fleet and army withdrew to Boston thus leaving Sullivan without support. Although he met and repulsed the British attack, he was forced to withdraw his command to the mainland. He remained in Providence until March 1779, when he was sent to command a small army consisting of General James Clinton's New York brigade, Dearborn's brigade, and Maxwell's New Jersey brigade in an expedition to destroy the Iroquois and their British loyalist allies in and along the western frontier of New York State. Washington's orders were that he wanted "total destruction and devastation of their settlements...essential to ruin their crops now in the ground and prevent planting more. Our future security will be in their inability to injure us, and the distance to which they are driven."

The Sullivan-Clinton campaign against the Cayuga and loyalists was most effective. The forty-five hundred colonial soldiers burned forty Indian towns or villages, torched 160,000 acres of corn, and girdled the bark of thousands of fruit trees. The Sullivan-Clinton force defeated a strong combined force of British loyalists and Iroquois warriors under the command of Joseph Brant and Sir William Johnson at Newton (Elmira), New York on August 29, 1779. This sent three-thousand refugees out of central New York to British Fort Niagara 120 miles away. The land surveyed on the Sullivan campaign eventually became the military tract that New York used to pay its veterans after the Revolution.

Sullivan's health was shattered by five years of continuous service, and he resigned his commission on November 30, 1779. He returned to Congress in Philadelphia in 1780-1781.

John Sullivan became attorney general of New Hampshire in 1782-86 and served as speaker of the State Assembly, 1785. He was governor (then called president) of the state three times: in 1786, 1787, and in 1789. In 1788 he was chairman of the state convention, which ratified the federal constitution (the ninth state to do so, making it the law of the land).

He was appointed U.S. district judge of New Hampshire in 1789, holding that office until his death in 1795.

JOSEPH CILLEY

Sergeant, Rogers' Rangers
French and Indian War
Colonel, First New Hampshire Regiment
American Revolutionary War

Born:	1734, Nottingham, New Hampshire
Died:	August 25, 1799, Nottingham, New Hampshire
Buried:	Nottingham, New Hampshire
Battles:	Indian Wars, 1760
	Boston, 1775
	Three Rivers, 1776
	Long Island, 1776
	Trenton, 1777
	Princeton, 1777
	Saratoga, 1777
	Bemis Heights, 1777
	Monmouth, 1778
	Newtown, 1779

JOSEPH CILLEY WAS A SELF-TAUGHT LAWYER AND A SOLDIER, judge, and politician. His parents, Captain Joseph Cilley and Alice (Else) Rawlins (Rollins) Cilley, moved from Newbury, Massachusetts, in 1727 to Nottingham, New Hampshire. They built a log cabin and raised young Joseph there.

Cilley was of medium height and weight, stood erect, was quick in his perceptions and actions, and dauntless in the face of danger. In 1758, he enlisted as a private in Major Rogers' battalion of rangers. He served with the rangers in New York and raids in French Canada. He was promoted to sergeant. Cilley took part in John Sullivan and Langdon's raid on Fort William and Mary, near Portsmouth, New Hampshire, in capturing British weapons and barrels of powder.

Upon hearing the news of the battle at Lexington, Massachusetts, Cilley recruited one hundred volunteers from the Nottingham area and led them to Boston. He was appointed a major in Colonel

Enoch Poor's second New Hampshire regiment and in 1776 became a lieutenant colonel. On April 2, 1777, he was appointed colonel, commanding the First New Hampshire Regiment, replacing John Stark, who had resigned.

During the winter of 1776, Cilley's and Stark's New Hampshire regiments tasted the first victories of the long war at Princeton, New Jersey, crossing the Delaware River on Christmas Eve to catch the Hessian troops napping. Then it was on to Trenton. These two successful attacks on British forces were crucial in raising American morale and encouraging Congress to lengthen enlistments to three years.

Possession of the Hudson-Champlain Valley was essential to keep New England from being cut off from the rest of the country. Cilley's regiment was ordered to Fort Ticonderoga in May 1777 to strengthen that fortress. In July, Cilley's unit became part of the summer retreat across the Hudson River and eventually to Bemis Heights. There, on September 19, the two armies engaged in a devastating battle that ended in a draw.

By October 7, the British, under General Burgoyne, decided to make a stand at Freeman's farm near Saratoga. The First New Hampshire Regiment entered the battle facing the elite grenadier regiment and British light infantry. The firing was so intense that Cilley's men had to move forward, out of the smoke of their own muskets, to fire again. The grenadiers stood firm and were cut to pieces.

During the advance, British twelve-pound cannons were captured. Amid the cheers of his men, Colonel Cilley straddled one cannon, waved his sword, and yelled that he was dedicating the cannon to the patriot cause. The New Hampshire men turned the cannon on the retreating enemy. With the British surrender at Saratoga, the northern campaign was over. The regiment marched south.

For Colonel Cilley's valiant actions at the battle of Monmouth in July 1778, the New Hampshire Legislature presented him with a pair of pistols in March 1779. He proudly carried them during the Sullivan-Clinton expedition against the Torys and Indians in upper New York at the Battle of Newtown (Elmira).

He was distinguished by his courage and patriotism; beloved by his soldiers for his humanity; and trusted by officers for his integrity, character, and prompt decisions. He later served as General of the New Hampshire Militia.

After the Revolutionary War, he became justice of the peace for Rockingham County and held that position for life. In politics he was a Jeffersonian Republican. He served in New Hampshire State Senate 1790-1791, in the House, 1792 and was councilor 1797-1798. He died at his homestead in Nottingham at age sixty-five. His grandson, Joseph, fought in the War of 1812.

ALEXANDER SCAMMELL

Colonel, First and Third New Hampshire Regiments
Adjutant General, Continental Army
American Revolutionary War

Born:	March 27, 1747, Mendon (Milford), Massachusetts
Died:	October 6, 1781, Yorktown, Virginia
Buried:	Unknown
Battles:	Long Island, 1776
	Trenton, 1777
	Princeton, 1777
	Saratoga, 1777
	Yorktown, 1781

SCAMMELL'S PARENTS EMIGRATED FROM ENGLAND IN 1738. His father, a prominent physician, died when Alexander was only six years old. A minister friend of his father saw that young Alexander was raised properly. Alexander worked his way through Harvard, graduating in 1769. His first job was as a schoolteacher in Plymouth, Massachusetts. He studied law in the office of John Sullivan in Durham, New Hampshire.

When the Revolutionary War broke out, he became a major in Sullivan's brigade of militia. In October 1776, Scammell served as a brigade major in Charles Lee's division. In November 1776, he was promoted to colonel, commanding the third New Hampshire Regiment.

Colonel Scammell was present at the evacuation of Fort Ticonderoga and led his regiment at the two battles of Saratoga (Freeman's farm and Bemis Heights), where General John Burgoyne's troops were soundly defeated.

Scammell became General Washington's aide-de-camp. He later served as the Continental Army's Adjutant General, from January 5, 1778, through January 1, 1781.

During the Benedict Arnold/Major André affair, General Washington was so grieved by Arnold's treachery that he could not bear to watch the hanging of the British major. André, when captured, was wearing civilian clothes and was tried and convicted as a spy, not as a military combatant. Washington directed Scammell to supervise the hanging.

Scammell resigned his continental commission to take command of the First New Hampshire Regiment in 1781. During the Yorktown campaign, Scammell led four hundred light infantrymen on a reconnaissance mission behind British lines. In the darkness, he fell in with ranks of Tarleton's Legion. Scammell was shot in the back and taken prisoner.

Seeing that their captive had been fatally wounded, the British released Scammell to the Americans. He died shortly thereafter. His body was buried in the vicinity of the Yorktown battlefield but is unmarked and forgotten.

Scammell was not forgotten, however, by his friend and comrade-in-arms General Henry Dearborn, who succeeded him as commanding officer of the First New Hampshire Regiment. Dearborn named a son, Henry Alexander Scammell Dearborn. Although Alexander Scammell's burial place is unknown, there is a monument to him in Bellingham, Massachusetts, near the place where he grew up.

Lafayette, on his last visit to America, 1824–1825, proposed a toast to a gathering of Revolutionary War veterans, "To the memory of Yorktown Scammell."

Enoch Poor

Brigadier General
American Revolutionary War

Born:	June 21, 1736, Andover, Massachusetts
Died:	September 8, 1780, Hackensack, New Jersey
Buried:	Hackensack, New Jersey
Battles:	Louisburg, 1755
	Stillwater, 1777
	Freeman's Farm, 1777
	Bemis Heights, 1777
	Monmouth, 1778
	Newtown, 1779

ENOCH POOR WAS BORN, RAISED AND EDUCATED IN Andover, Massachusetts. He was a descendent of Daniel Poore. In 1755, Enoch enlisted as a Private in a militia company as part of General Jeffery Amherst's expedition against the French held town of Louisburg, Nova Scotia. In 1745, Poor's father had been a soldier during King George's War, when Louisburg was captured by the British. This military action expelled the Acadians from Canada, some of whom fled to Louisiana, speaking a dialect called Cajun.

After returning home from the war, Enoch eloped with Martha Osgood. The newlyweds made their home in Exeter, New Hampshire. Poor became a shipbuilder and within a few years, became a prominent citizen. He served on various town committees. In 1775, he was elected to the Provincial Assembly.

Upon hearing of the Battle of Lexington, the Assembly raised three regiments of militia. Enoch Poor was selected to become the Colonel commanding the Second New Hampshire Regiment. John Stark would command the First and James Reed would lead the Third Regiment. While Stark's and Reed's units went to Boston and fought at Bunker Hill, Poor's Second Regiment remained in Exeter and Portsmouth. After the battle, the Second Regiment went to Boston and Poor led his unit in the siege when the British evacuated Boston on March 17, 1776.

After that, Poor's regiment joined General John Sullivan's third brigade, which linked up with General Montgomery's northern army. Montgomery's expedition was to capture the city of Montreal. The Canadian campaign was a disaster with General Montgomery being killed on December 31, 1776. Poor led the survivors of his regiment back to Fort Ticonderoga. After recruiting and rearming, the regiment was renamed as the eighth Continental Regiment. Poor's unit joined Washington's main army in December at the winter quarters in Morristown, New Jersey.

On February 21, 1777, Congress commissioned Enoch Poor as a Brigadier General. That spring, his brigade of three New Hampshire and two New York regiments was sent back to Fort Ticonderoga. Poor's brigade was now part of the northern army under command of General Benedict Arnold. The American military units were at the right place at the right time to thwart British General Burgoyne's advance from Canada toward New York City.

The first engagement of Saratoga was at Freeman's Farm. Poor's brigade held the American's left flank (to the west) aiding Colonel Daniel Morgan's attack. The brigade kept General Fraser's redcoats engaged while Benedict Arnold led attacks to the center of resistance.

At the second Saratoga battle, Bemis Heights, Poor's brigade was again on the American's left flank, closest to the center of the advancing British. Poor's men faced Major John Acland's grenadier battalion, whose musket fire proved ineffective. Acland ordered a bayonet charge. Poor held his unit's fire until the charging British grenadiers were almost upon them. When the brigade opened up with the massed fire of fourteen hundred muskets, the charge was broken. Major Acland was wounded and captured along with the British artillery. Burgoyne surrendered giving the American Army its first decisive victory—the turning point of the revolution!

After the British surrender at Saratoga, Poor's brigade joined Washington in Pennsylvania and shared the hardships of the long, cold winter at Valley Forge. General Poor did his best to overcome the privations and suffering of his men. Poor wrote to the New

Hampshire legislature about the deplorable conditions and low morale, "I am every day…awakened by the lamentable tale of their distresses. If they desert, how can I punish them when they plead in justification that the contract on your part is broken?"

In the summer of 1778, Poor led his brigade across New Jersey pursuing the British. At the Battle of Monmouth, the brigade fought gallantly under Lafayette.

The following year, General Poor commanded the Second or New Hampshire Brigade in General John Sullivan's expedition against the British-led Indians of western New York. Following the orders of Washington, Sullivan's army laid waste to many Indian villages, burning crops and orchards. Along the way the Americans defeated the Tories and Indians at Newtown.

In May 1780, the Continental Congress gave Lafayette command of a division. Lafayette selected Enoch Poor to train a brigade of light infantry. Poor was honored to do so, but the unit saw no action being assigned to garrison duty in New Jersey.

Some sources suggest that Enoch Poor was shot in a duel near Hackensack, New Jersey, and died as a result of the wound. The army surgeon attending him reported that Poor died of typhus. General Poor was buried with full military honors in a churchyard in Hackensack. Both Washington and Lafayette attended the funeral. In Washington's report to congress he noted, "He was an officer of distinguished merit, one who as a citizen and soldier had every claim to the esteem and regard of his country."

In 1824, Lafayette visited veterans in New Hampshire. At a banquet in his honor, Lafayette gave this toast, "To light infantry Poor and Yorktown Scammell."

GEORGE REID

Colonel, Second New Hampshire Regiment
American Revolutionary War

Born:	1733, Londonderry, New Hampshire
Died:	1815, Londonderry, New Hampshire
Buried:	Unknown
Battles:	Bunker Hill
	Brandywine
	Long Island
	Germantown
	White Plains
	Trenton
	Saratoga
	Newtown

REID'S PARENTS WERE AMONG THE FIRST SETTLERS OF Londonderry. George grew up as a farmer and married Mary Washburn in 1765 and they lived in Londonderry.

When war with England broke out in April 1775, Reid organized a company of militia. As captain, Reid led his sixty-man company to Medford, Massachusetts, near Boston, and joined up with John Stark and his companies of New Hampshire volunteers. Both units fought at the Battle of Bunker Hill on June 17, 1775.

On January 1, 1776, John Hancock, president of delegates of the United Colonies, appointed Reid to be a captain in the First New Hampshire Regiment commanded by John Stark.

In February of 1777, Stark resigned and Joseph Cilley was made colonel, commanding the First New Hampshire. George Reid became a lieutenant colonel of the Second New Hampshire Regiment commanded by Colonel Nathan Hale. When Hale was captured in the summer of 1778, Reid was made colonel in command of the Second New Hampshire Regiment.

Reid held a commission throughout the Revolutionary War. He spent the winter of 1777–78 at Valley Forge and served with

General John Sullivan in the campaign against the British-sympa-thizing Cayuga Indians in New York's western territory.

In 1783, Reid was breveted (temporary grade) colonel in the Army of the United States by an act of Congress. In 1785, John Langdon, president (governor) of New Hampshire, appointed Reid to the post of brigadier general of the state militia.

A year later, in 1786, General Reid put down a minor rebellion against the New Hampshire Legislature at the request of his wartime commander, John Sullivan, who was then president of New Hampshire. Reid was despised for this action and received numerous death threats. In 1791, George Reid was appointed sheriff of Rockingham County. The Reid family moved from their farm to a house in Londonderry. He died there in 1815 at age eighty-three.

LEWIS & CLARK EXPEDITION

1804–1806

Ordway Statue at Fort Lewis,
Washington. US Army photo.

John Ordway

Sergeant, U.S. Army
Lewis and Clark Expedition
May 14, 1804–September 23, 1806

Born: 1775, Bow (Dunbarton), New Hampshire
Died: circa 1817, probably Missouri
Buried: Unknown

JOHN ORDWAY WAS HAND-PICKED FOR THE EXPEDITION by Captain Meriwether Lewis. Ordway was a regular army sergeant in the First Infantry Regiment, stationed at Fort Kaskaskia in the Illinois territory. Lewis knew him from previous service at Pittsburgh. Ordway was the only one of the three original sergeants to come directly from regular military service.

Sergeant Ordway was from the Northeast, born in Bow, New Hampshire, while nearly everyone else in the expedition crew was from Virginia, Kentucky, or the frontier. Ordway was well-educated. He could read, write, and keep account records as well as command men. Other than Captains Lewis and Clark, only three or four of the other men could read and write.

John Ordway kept a detailed journal of the two-year expedition. It was purchased for three hundred dollars by Lewis and Clark who planned to incorporate it into their book. Ordway's journal was lost or misplaced after Lewis' death in 1809 however, and not found until a century later. It was published in 1913 and was notable for its details in naming the hunters, salt makers, and scouts at the various places where they stopped during the expedition. That human element was missing from earlier journals. Ordway's descriptions of the Indian tribes they encountered also provided valuable historical data.

At the end of the expedition, Sergeant Ordway accompanied Captain Lewis, Chief She-He-Ke, and a band of Osage Indians to Washington, D.C. He was then discharged, and returned to New Hampshire to marry Gracey. He bought several land warrants issued to other men, and returned to the Cape Girardeau district of Missouri and settled there in 1809. He became quite prosperous from his land holdings. By 1817, both he and Gracey had passed away.

Any discussion of the Lewis and Clark expedition should begin with mention of how this vast unexplored region, the Louisiana Purchase, came to be an American territory. The most important act of President Thomas Jefferson's administration was the acquisition of Louisiana, then consisting of the northwestern half of the United States from the Mississippi to the present state of Montana.

The French had settled the southern region while the English established their thirteen colonies along the Atlantic seaboard. After the French and Indian War, France ceded Louisiana to Spain. In 1800, Spain secretly agreed to return the territory to France. Spain at the time was weak and no menace to the U.S. France was a mighty power ruled by the ambitious Napoleon.

Disturbed by this, Jefferson sent James Monroe and Robert Livingston on a special trip to Europe. Their mission was to buy New Orleans from France. Much to the surprise of the Americans, Napoleon decided to sell, not only New Orleans, but also the whole of Louisiana from the mouth of the Mississippi to Montana. Because Napoleon was planning to resume war against Britain, there was a chance the British would seize New Orleans. It seemed better to sell the province to the Americans and have the money for other projects.

Napoleon offered to sell Louisiana for fifteen million dollars. Livingston and Monroe immediately accepted and signed a treaty, which was accepted by President Jefferson and the Senate in 1803. The U.S. had acquired more than eight hundred thousand square miles of territory, nearly doubling the size of the nation.

Even before the land purchase, Jefferson had proposed an exploration of that area. In a confidential message to Congress, he asked for an appropriation of twenty-five hundred dollars, which was granted. To lead this party Jefferson selected his private secretary, Meriwether Lewis, age twenty-nine, a regular army captain. Lewis requested that he share the command with his good friend William Clark, thirty-three, who had seen considerable Indian fighting as a militia officer.

Both men had much experience of command and life on the frontier. This may account for the remarkably few emergencies that arose during the two years, four months, and two days of the expedition. As it happened, these wilderness soldiers were masters of every situation. Although Clark received a regular army commission as a Lieutenant, Lewis stated that during the expedition they would be referred to as "Captain" Lewis and "Captain" Clark. To cover this official disparity of military grades when documents were signed, Lewis signed as "Captain, First Infantry," and Clark signed as "Captain of a Corps of Discovery."

Selection of their personnel was critical. During the winter of 1803-04, Captain Lewis visited Kaskaskia and recruited two of his best men from Captain Russell Bissell's company of the First Infantry. One of these was Sergeant John Ordway, a New Hampshire Yankee, who Lewis knew in 1800-01 when they were both constantly in and out of the quartermaster's office in Pittsburgh. Sergeant Ordway was one of the very few enlisted men who could read and write and the journal he kept proved invaluable. Pvt. Patrick Gass was the other.

Captain Bissell flatly refused to let two of his best men go. Patrick Gass was "an old regular" who had fought Indians, but was also an experienced carpenter, sure to be useful when the expedition needed to build canoes, forts, and cabins. Lewis, armed with presidential authority, overruled Captain Bissell and obtained both men. Two other sergeants, Charles Floyd and Nathanial Pryor completed the NCO (non-commissioned officer) slots. Thirty-six privates filled the ranks and were later joined by guides and interpreters as well as York, Clark's Negro servant, and Scannon, Lewis' Newfoundland dog.

On Sunday morning, May 13, 1804, everything was ready at last. Three boats were loaded with provisions, ammunition, and twenty-one bales of Indian trade-goods. Provisions included fourteen barrels of parch meal, twenty barrels of flour, seven barrels of salt, fifty kegs of pork, fifty bushels of cornmeal, tools of every description and abundant drug and medical instruments.

All of this was packed into three vessels—a twenty-two-oar keelboat or bateau manned by soldiers of the permanent party, and two large pirogues of six oars each. One pirogue, rowed by soldiers not in the crew of the Corps of Discovery, returned back down the river in the spring.

The keelboat was the type of craft the men were familiar with, fifty-five feet long and drawing only three feet of water. It was decked over for ten feet in the bow with a cabin astern. Along the sides were lockers, whose lids could be raised for protection in case of an attack. At first, the boats were badly loaded, and at St. Charles they stopped to redistribute the load aft so the bows would ride over underwater obstacles.

Discipline, at first, was poor among the crew. When the two commanding officers were away from camp, they left Sergeant Ordway in charge. Privates Fields and Shields refused to report for guard duty. Ordway reprimanded the two at parade in front of the entire company. The two offenders squirmed, but went on to distinguish themselves during the expedition. The commanding officers highly approved of the conduct of Sergeant Ordway.

In April, those men who were still technically civilians were formally enlisted into the Army. The detachment was organized into three squads with a sergeant in command of each. John Ordway became the acting first sergeant, third in command under Captains Lewis and Clark.

On May 21, after the reloading of the boats at St. Charles and the arrival of Lewis, the expedition got under way. On the twenty-sixth, the captains assigned special duties to the three sergeants. One took the helm of the keelboat, a second commanded the guard amidships, managed the sail, supervised the oarsmen, watched the shore enroute, and posted the guard at night on shore. The third sergeant, in the bow, kept a sharp lookout for snags in the river and for possible enemies on shore. The expedition's constant alertness was instrumental for its success. A surprise inspection found some of the arms in bad order. An inspection a week later found all the rifles clean.

The first months up the Missouri passed without many incidents of note until the death of Sergeant Floyd who died July 31 of "the camp colic"—probably appendicitis. He was buried with military honors on a bluff overlooking the Missouri River near what is now Sioux City, Iowa. The men, allowed to elect a successor to Sergeant Floyd, chose Patrick Gass, who already held a sergeant's warrant in the First Infantry.

The severity of previous court martial punishments of Willard, Hall, and Reed had not quite ended the bad discipline. On October 13, Private John Newman spoke mutinously to Captain Lewis. He was arrested and that same night went before a court martial of enlisted men. The court sentenced Newman to seventy-five lashes and to be eliminated from the permanent party engaged for North Western discovery. Both Hall and Newman remained with the group, but were reduced to simple laboring hands.

Newman's was the last court-martial of the expedition and had produced the desired effect. Disgrace and dismissal were penalties more severe than the lash. Having eliminated troublemakers, the captains found their men loyal and diligent through all the perilous miles they traveled together.

The expedition continued up the Missouri, encountering curious Indians on the shores. The group would put in to meet with the chiefs of the Sioux, Arikara, and Mandan. Lewis would repeat his now familiar standard speech of how the great white father in Washington would send them trade goods and all necessities. All the chiefs received medals and clothing. The parleys suffered for lack of good interpreters.

With winter approaching, quarters had to be built. The site selected for Fort Mandan was on the left bank of the Missouri about fifty miles upstream from the present city of Bismarck, North Dakota. Hunters began to lay in a meat supply and others felled trees and cut them to length. Sergeant Gass, originally a house-builder, directed the construction of the storehouse and sleeping huts. Captain Clark designed the fort in a triangle shape. The stout long cabins formed two sides, opening inward. The base of the triangle was closed by a semicircular stockade of large posts. Fort Mandan was not only strong, but it was also warm. Gaps between the log walls were chinked with mud. By mid-November the party moved into their quarters.

On November 11, 1804, a young, pregnant squaw walked into the white man's camp. This was Sacagawea, a Shoshone woman who had been captured by the Minnetaree tribe and sold to Toussaint Charbonneau, a rough and tumble river trader and woodsman. As the captains came to know Charbonneau, they realized that whatever his shortcomings, he and Sacagawea would be a valuable team. Charbonneau could interpret among the river Indians and Sacagawea's knowledge of Shoshone offered their only chance of conversing with the Rocky Mountain Indians. Sacagawea's baby, a boy, Jean Baptiste Charbonneau, was born on February 11, 1805, after a prolonged labor.

During the cold of January and February, the boats, which they left in the river, became iced in. The men decided to heat water inside the boats by dropping in hot stones. Evidently they tried heating sandstone, which bursts as it is heated. Sergeant Ordway remarked, "come to heat the stone, they flew in pieces as soon as they got hot."

Winter near the Arikara village brought other problems. The squaws here were more brazen than the Sioux women and placed a value on their favors of twenty strands of blue beads. It is perhaps no accident that the Lewis and Clark expedition used up its supply of blue beads far too soon.

Sergeant John Ordway was a model soldier and a pillar of strength, but he had his weaknesses and prominent among them was women. While his thoughts may have been on two young ladies, Betsey and Gracey, both of whom lived near his father's home near Concord, New Hampshire, he was married to neither at the time. Ordway was in a receptive mood toward the Mandan squaws. Accepting the offer of a broad-minded Mandan husband, he took the warrior's squaw as a wife-for-the-night. Infatuated with the white sergeant, the Indian woman attempted to run away. Her husband followed and the explosive matter was defused by Captain Clark and the tribe's Chief. Ordway probably breathed a sigh of relief when he returned from the expedition.

When spring came, the party readied the newly made canoes and repaired the old bateau and pirogues. Nine boxes of plant and animal specimens and curios were packed with live animals in cages. Most important was Clark's map which he had made during the long winter, and a long letter to President Jefferson. The consignment safely reached St. Louis in July. Corporal Richard Warf-ington, whose enlistment expired, was in charge of the precious cargo. He was joined by a small group of men whom the captains considered least valuable.

The commanders felt they could rely completely on the thirty-two men who finally set forth for the long journey to the Pacific Coast. On June 13, 1805, they came to the Great Falls of the Mis-souri, in present Montana. The portage around the falls took nearly a month of back-breaking work. On August 12 they reached the head of navigation near the Continental Divide, some seventy-three hundred feet above sea level.

The expedition took the Nez Percé trail to the Bitterroot Range, then west through Lolo Pass to the Clearwater River, which led to the Snake River and finally to the Columbia River. On October 16, 1805, the men encountered Indians astonished to see their first white men. The only hint that the Pacific Ocean was not far away was by noticing woolen trade blankets that could have come only from ships plying pacific coastal trade routes. On November 7, the party camped on some heights from which they could see the Pacific Ocean at last.

They established their winter camp, Fort Clatsop, near the present Astoria, Oregon. Their diet of elk meat was broken by three hundred pounds of blubber from a whale washed up on the nearby beach. During the winter, the two captains diligently copied their route maps, sketched geographical features, and recorded plant and animal observations.

In late March 1806, Lewis and Clark gave "certificates of kind-ness" to the natives and started their return journey. The party divided briefly to explore parts of Montana. They joined up just below the mouth of the Yellowstone River and rapidly descended the Missouri to arrive at St. Louis on September 23, 1806. Here most of the men were eager to turn their land claims into cash, even though Congress had not yet formally authorized the claims.

Sergeant Ordway, thrifty Yankee that he was, bought the claims of Baptiste LePage, William Warner, and Silas Goodrich, paying two hundred dollars for the first two and two hundred fifty dollars for the third, thereby acquiring 960 acres in addition to his own 320. Ordway accompanied Captain Lewis and a party of Indians to Washington to meet with President Jefferson.

The expedition's importance to U.S. history is still in the process of interpretation and assessment two centuries later. It was key in the acquisition of the Oregon country.

Lewis was made governor of the Louisiana Territory. Clark was appointed brigadier general of the Louisiana militia. William Clark married Judy Hancock and went on to fight in the War of 1812. Merriwether Lewis dallied through several trivial affairs and never married. He became involved in various unprofitable ventures and his financial situation was in a quagmire. As Lewis was returning to Washington, traveling the Natchez Trace, a trail through Tennessee, he was either murdered or committed suicide.

Sergeant Ordway's journal was purchased by Lewis and Clark for three hundred dollars. Ordway left the Army and returned to New Hampshire to marry Gracey. They traveled to the Cape Giradeau district in Missouri and settled near New Madrid in 1809. Ordway purchased a large amount of land and began farming it.

In December 1811, three major earthquakes struck the area. Between five hundred and one thousand people perished. By the time a fifth earthquake hit, on February 7, 1812, scarcely a house remained standing. These quakes changed the course of the Mississippi River and destroyed entire towns and their records.

Little is known of Ordway after that. Scholars speculate that his farmland was rendered useless from the earthquakes and that he and Gracey died in poverty before 1817.

Although traces of Sergeant John Ordway's life end abruptly, his service to his country is memorialized by a larger-than-life statue at Fort Lewis, Washington. Erected in 2006, Sergeant Ordway's memorial is the only statue of an American enlisted man. Its plaque honors him and all first sergeants who have served in the U.S. Army.

References:
Lewis and Clark—Partners in Discovery, John Bakeless, Dover, 1975
Undaunted Courage, Stephen E. Ambrose, 1996

WAR OF 1812

1812–1815

BRITAIN DID NOT WANT WAR WITH THE UNITED STATES; she had enough to do in Europe fighting Napoleon. Nor did most Americans want war. War would mean the end of a profitable neutral commerce and probably the destruction of the American merchant marine by the vastly superior British navy.

Americans who lived far from the sea opposed Britain. Those living along the Canadian border wanted control of Canada for its fur trade, its farmland, or its Saint Lawrence River outlet. American frontiersman favored taking Canada to eliminate the menacing Indians who had the support of Britain. Notable here was Tecumseh, who had formed an Indian confederacy in the Great Lakes area around the present state of Indiana. Tecumseh's cause suffered a set-back in 1811 at the Battle of Tippecanoe against the troops of William Henry Harrison, territorial governor of Indiana.

Some antagonism toward the British came from traders living in Florida, which was controlled by Spain. Spain was now allied with Britain and the two were viewed as twin enemies. The desire to take both Canada and Florida accentuated the war feelings in the United States.

Yielding to pressures, President James Madison reluctantly asked Congress for a declaration of war, which was approved on June 18, 1812. Opposition came mainly from maritime interests and New York and New England seacoast towns, the most likely targets for British attacks. This division of opinion made fighting the

War of 1812 difficult. Congress adjourned that year without voting war taxes!

Little was expected of the American navy, it having only a score of fighting vessels against Britain's six hundred. American merchant ships converted into privateers did well, taking three hundred British merchant vessels the first year of war. "Old Ironsides," the U.S.S. *Constitution,* defeated the *Guerrier* in a dramatic sea battle. Eventually, strength won out. By 1814, the British navy controlled all the waters off the American coast.

The first American land campaigns also failed. British General Brock and his Indian ally, Tecumseh, captured Detroit August 1812 without firing a shot. The Americans suffered another defeat at Queenston Heights, near Niagara Falls, in October 1812, because some American militiamen refused to cross into Canada. However at this battle, General Brock was killed.

Shifts in command brought some victories in 1813. With a quickly built flotilla, Oliver Hazard Perry defeated a British squadron of ships in the Battle of Lake Erie on September 10. This victory enabled General William Henry Harrison on October 5 to move into upper Canada, where his troops defeated the British and Indians in the Battle of the Thames where Tecumseh was killed.

As encouraging as these small victories were, they did not turn the tide of the war. By 1814, more capable field commanders were taking charge, such as young Winfield Scott. Scott, General Brown's second in command, was an imposing presence, standing six foot five and broad shouldered. Scott was also a professional soldier.

Most of the training of the Left Division, U.S. Army, was in General Scott's hands. Through April, May, and June he drilled the troops endlessly, imposing firm but fair discipline. Some men lacked a uniform and those of the majority of the division were worn and ragged. Realizing the importance of the uniform on his unit's morale, Scott requisitioned fresh supplies. Instead of blue uniform coats, he received a consignment of gray woolen fatigue jackets, with which he had to make do. Shortage of blue cloth also meant that the West Point cadets began wearing gray uniforms in 1814, and they have continued to do so ever since, thereby perpetuating the memory of Scott's Left Division.

Congress, too, was realizing the extent of war needs and funding. At the same time, the enemy was becoming stronger. As the war in Europe began to favor Britain, she could send more veteran troops to fight the Americans. Although the Americans won the battles at Chippewa (July 14, 1814) and at the Battle of Lundy's Lane, near Niagara Falls (July 25, 1814), they could not take Canada.

In the meantime, there was also action in the South. In 1813, American troops took Mobile, the last Spanish-occupied fort in west Florida. But Spain, backed by Britain, held east Florida. Creek Indians on August 30, 1813, nearly wiped out a large number of Americans at Fort Mims in Alabama country. General Andrew Jackson, of Tennessee, organized a force of frontiersmen and inflicted a severe defeat of the Creeks and their Cherokee allies at the Battle of Horseshoe Bend on March 27, 1814. Although this battle is not well remembered, it was one of the most significant engagements of the War of 1812.

Britain's strategy was to invade America at three points. In August 1814, British troops captured Washington, D.C. They burned the White House and the Capitol in retaliation for the Americans burning York (Toronto) in 1813. The force then moved northward toward Baltimore, but were stopped at Fort McHenry on September 13, 1814. The nighttime cannonading of the fort was observed by Francis Scott Key who penned the words to the poem that became our National Anthem.

Two days earlier, in the Battle of Lake Champlain, Commodore Thomas Macdonough had defeated a large British force, under Sir George Prevost, pressing south from Canada into New York State. In December 1814, the third invasion force landed in Louisiana. General Andrew Jackson arrived in time to muster a defensive force of citizens, including some of Jean Lafitte's pirates, to augment his troops. On January 8, 1815, Jackson's men, hiding behind cotton bales and fences repulsed the British attack inflicting heavy losses on veteran units such as the Forty-Second Highland Regiment—The Black Watch.

Just as the United States failed in its attempt to invade Canada, so had Britain failed in its invasion of the United States.

The Treaty of Ghent was signed declaring the war a draw. Still, the war was anything but indecisive. During hostilities, the Americans had eliminated the Creek Indians' power in the South and broken Tecumseh's confederacy in the Northwest. These victories cleared the way for frontier settlers.

The war also showed Spain's weakness. Without British aid, they would have lost east Florida. When British aid was withdrawn in 1819, Spain ceded east Florida to the United States. As a result of the peace treaty of 1814, the Rush-Bagot agreement of 1817, which limited fortifications on the Great Lakes, was signed. This became a permanent peace between the United States and Canada.

Many of the officers who served with the Left Division achieved high rank and profoundly influenced the Army's development during the next half century. General Brown became General-in-Chief in 1821. He died in 1828 at age fifty-two. Winfield Scott ended the war as a brevet major general. For the next thirty years, he concentrated on introducing sound training methods. In 1846, Scott commanded the American army during its successful campaign in Mexico. He, too, became General-in-Chief and was still serving as such when the Civil War broke out.

The lessons of the Revolutionary War having been forgotten by 1812, it can be said that the modern U.S. Army had its origin in the Niagara campaign of 1814, especially in the Battles of Chippewa and Lundy's Lane. The War of 1812 made many reputations and two presidents—Andrew Jackson and William Henry Harrison. It also enhanced national pride, contributing to the building of a new nation.

HENRY DEARBORN

Major General, U.S. Army
American Revolutionary War
War of 1812

Born: February 23, 1751, Hampton, New Hampshire
Died: June 6, 1829, Roxbury, Massachusetts
Secretary of War, 1800-1808
Minister to Portugal, 1822-1824
Battles: Bunker Hill
            Quebec, Canada
            Ticonderoga
            Freeman's Farm
            Valley Forge
            Monmouth
            Newtown
            Yorktown
            York (Toronto), Canada

HENRY DEARBORN ATTENDED THE DISTRICT SCHOOL in Hampton, New Hampshire, then studied medicine under Dr. Hall Jackson, of Portsmouth. He began his medical practice in Nottingham Square, New Hampshire. As trouble with England neared, Dearborn organized a company of militia and was elected Captain. When the news of the fight at Concord and Lexington reached them, Henry led his company of sixty men to Cambridge. There, his unit became part of Colonel John Stark's First New Hampshire Regiment and took part in the Battle of Bunker Hill, June 17, 1775.

In September, Dearborn volunteered to join General Benedict Arnold's expedition to Quebec. During that difficult and hazardous trek through the Maine wilderness, Dearborn commanded one of the companies of musketmen. He kept a journal, which became an important source of information about that campaign. Near the end of the march, he fell ill and was left to recuperate at a cottage on the Chaudiére River.

He recovered and was able to rejoin the force in time to take part in that disastrous assault on Quebec City by the units of General Arnold and Gen. Richard Montgomery on December 31, 1775. In that battle, Montgomery was killed, Arnold was seriously wounded, and Dearborn was taken prisoner. He was confined for a time at Quebec, paroled in May 1776, and repatriated the following March.

Soon after his release, he was appointed a major in the Third New Hampshire Regiment, commanded by Colonel Alexander Scammell. In September 1777, he was transferred back into the First New Hampshire Regiment, now under the command of Colonel Joseph Cilley. Dearborn took part in the New York campaign against Burgoyne, fighting at Fort Ticonderoga and Freeman's Farm (Saratoga). He spent the winter of 1777–78 at Valley Forge, Pennsylvania.

Dearborn took command of the First New Hampshire at the Battle of Monmouth, New Jersey, in June 1778. The regiment won special commendation from General Washington. In the summer of 1779, Dearborn's regiment and Colonel Clinton's New York Regiment formed General John Sullivan's army in a campaign against tribes of the Iroquois Confederacy that aligned themselves with the British. Only the Oneida tribe sided with the Americans. That force laid waste to the villages, gardens, and orchards of the Seneca, Cayuga, and Onondaga of Central New York. This destruction of summer crops would deprive the British and Indians of sustenance during the coming winter.

Dearborn left the New Hampshire line regiment to join General Washington's staff where he served during the siege and the final British surrender at Yorktown, Virginia, in October 1781. In June 1783, Henry Dearborn received his discharge from the army and settled in Kennebec County, Maine, then a district of Massachusetts. He became a brigadier general and later a major general of militia. In 1790, he was appointed U.S. Marshal for the District of Maine. He represented this district of Massachusetts as a Republican in the Third and Fourth U.S. Congresses (1793–97) but did not play a prominent role there.

When Thomas Jefferson was elected president, he appointed Dearborn his Secretary of War. He served in this post throughout Jefferson's eight years in office (1800-1808). As Secretary of War, he helped plan for the removal of the Indians beyond the Mississippi River. In 1803, Fort Dearborn was built, and named in Henry Dearborn's honor. Fort Dearborn was located near the mouth of the Chicago River along Lake Michigan. It was the major fort in the western frontier and established the authority of the U.S. government in that region. From it grew the city of Chicago. In March 1809, Dearborn resigned his cabinet position to become collector for the Port of Boston.

In January 1812, it looked like the United States might go to war with British Canada. President Madison appointed Dearborn senior major general of the U.S. Army and placed him in command of what was expected to be the most important theater of war. That was the northeast sector from the Niagara River to the New England coast. Dearborn, like General William Hull, had exhibited exemplary military qualities as a young officer in the Revolutionary War, but those qualities appear to have withered with age and a long period of disuse.

Dearborn prepared plans for a four-pronged attack on British positions in Montreal, Kingston, Niagara, and Detroit, but showed no enthusiasm for the execution. After setting up headquarters in Albany, Dearborn went to Boston to supervise recruiting and coast defenses. His stay in Boston was prolonged for weeks past the declaration of war. As a result, no actual preparations were made for attacking any position east of Detroit. This enabled British General Brock to mass his entire force against Hull at Detroit, compelling Hull's surrender, with two thousand American Soldiers.

The year ended with another American defeat, at Queenston on the Niagara River, and Dearborn's futile march from Plattsburgh toward Montreal. Upon reaching the border, the American troops refused to cross into Canada and returned to their garrison.

The campaign in the spring of 1813 against Kingston on the northeastern end of Lake Ontario was another fiasco. Secretary of War John Armstrong ordered an attack on Kingston. Dearborn overestimated the British strength there and received permission to attack York (Toronto) instead. Dearborn captured York on April 27, 1813, incurring heavy losses and to no military advantage. The British were so enraged with the sacking of York that when they overran Washington, they burned the White House.

Dearborn took Fort George at the mouth of the Niagara River on May 27, but the British army escaped and inflicted severe losses on the two pursuing U.S. detachments. Dearborn became ill and active command was passed to General Morgan Lewis. Meanwhile, Sackett's Harbor, the American base at the east end of Lake Ontario, had been left exposed to the British fleet and army at Kingston. A surprise attack on May 28 inflicted heavy damage and nearly captured the fort. The northern campaign had been so badly led that Secretary of War Armstrong relieved Dearborn of his command on the frontier. He was, however, given command of New York City.

Dearborn was honorably discharged from the Army on June 15, 1815. President Madison nominated him for secretary of war, but Congress protested and Madison withdrew the nomination. In 1822, President James Monroe sent him to Portugal as U.S. minister, a post he held for two years. He returned at his own request and retired to Roxbury, Massachusetts, where he died five years later.

References:
Revolutionary War Journals of Henry Dearborn, 1775–1783

John McNeil Jr.

Brigadier General
War of 1812

Born: 1784, Hillsborough, New Hampshire
Died: 1850, Washington, D.C.
Buried: Unknown
Battles: Chippewa
            Niagara Campaign
            Lundy's Lane

DURING THE WAR OF 1812, JOHN MCNEIL WAS COMMISSIONED a captain in the Eleventh U.S. Infantry Regiment on March 12, 1812. He was promoted to major on August 15, 1813, within the same regiment. The Eleventh Infantry played a major part in the Niagara Campaign.

McNeil fought at Chippewa, a landmark battle because it was the first time the U.S. Army defeated veteran British regulars in open combat. He was breveted a lieutenant colonel and later colonel for his bravery at the Battle of Lundy's Lane.

McNeil married Elizabeth A. Pierce, the eldest daughter of General Benjamin Pierce. Pierce was a well respected leader during the Revolutionary War and a future governor of the State of New Hampshire (1827-28 and 1829-30).

General Pierce was a strong backer of Andrew Jackson. When Jackson became President of the United States (1829-1837) he appointed Pierce's son-in-law, McNeil, to be supervisor of the Port of Boston. This was an important and prestigious position, which McNeil held for twenty years until his death in 1850.

JAMES MILLER

Brigadier General
War of 1812

Born: April 25, 1776, Peterborough, New Hampshire
Died: July 7, 1851, Temple, New Hampshire
Buried: Harmony Grove Cemetery, Salem, Massachusetts
Colonel Twenty-First U.S. Infantry Regiment
First Governor of Arkansas Territory
Battles: Chippewa
           Lundy's Lane
           Fort Erie

JAMES MILLER WAS BORN IN PETERBOROUGH, NEW HAMPSHIRE in 1776. He set up his law practice in nearby Greenfield. In 1803, he joined the state militia there and rose to command one of its artillery units. Miller was an efficient and disciplined drill master. He was noticed by General Benjamin Pierce, a Revolutionary War hero with a strong interest in the militia.

General Pierce recommended that Miller be commissioned a major with the Fourth U.S. Infantry Regiment, which was stationed at Fort Independence in Boston Harbor. Miller's commission was dated March 3, 1809.

In 1811, Miller's unit was ordered to Vincennes (Indiana territory) to fight Indians there. He was promoted to colonel for his actions during the unit's move west. The Fourth Regiment was ordered to Detroit in 1812 to join General Hull's army. War with Britain was declared in June 1812. Hull was determined to attack Canada, but was defeated and surrendered to the British. Two thousand Americans were taken prisoner at Fort Detroit.

Colonel Miller was part of the prisoner exchange in 1813. In 1814, he became part of the real action of the war. As colonel, commanding the Twenty-First Infantry Regiment, Miller led his men at the Battles of Chippewa, Lundy's Lane, and Fort Erie. When ordered to capture an enemy artillery battery on the high ground at Lundy's Lane, he replied to General Jacob Brown, "I will try, sir."

On their third attempt, Miller's men accomplished their mission. This action earned for him the nick-name, "hero of Lundy's Lane."

On the night of that battle, Miller secretly led his regiment of three hundred men up the hill. Shrubbery and a rail fence gave them some cover while Miller waited to attack. The men jumped the fence, firing as they charged the surprised British. Hand-to-hand fighting ensued, and the Americans captured the battery of artillery—cannons, ammunition, wagons, and all.

In September 1814, Miller's regiment helped protect Fort Erie from British invasion. For his bravery in that battle, he received a Gold Medal from the U.S. Congress. The award was presented by fellow New Hampshireman Daniel Webster, Secretary of State, at a park in New York City. Miller was made a brigadier general by Congress and was honored with the gift of a dress sword presented by the State of New York.

Miller left active military service in 1819 to become the first governor of the Arkansas Territory. (Miller County, Arkansas, is named in his honor). He became ill and refused a seat in Congress.

In 1823, poor health caused him to return to his farm in Temple, New Hampshire. When his health was restored, he accepted the appointment as customs collector for Salem and Beverly, Massachusetts. He held that position from 1824 through 1848. He then returned to his farm in Temple, where he died of a stroke in 1851.

JOSEPH P. CILLEY

Captain Twenty-First Infantry
War of 1812

Born: Jan. 4, 1791, Nottingham, New Hampshire
Died: Sept. 16, 1887, Nottingham, New Hampshire
Buried: Nottingham, New Hampshire
Educated: Atkinson Academy
Battles: Niagara Campaign
           Lundy's Lane

JOSEPH P. CILLEY WAS THE NAMESAKE AND GRANDSON of Revolutionary War General Joseph Cilley. He was born and raised in Nottingham, New Hampshire, and grew up hearing the deeds of his famous grandfather.

As the drums of war began to beat in 1812, twenty-one-year-old Joseph volunteered to serve in the New Hampshire Regiment. He first served as an ensign and later joined the Twenty-First Regiment United States Infantry. He was breveted a captain, commanding a company in the Twenty-First, which fought in the Niagara Campaign.

At the Battle of Lundy's Lane, his company was ordered to take a hill. As Captain Cilley led his company up the hill, he was wounded in the leg. The musket ball caused a compound fracture. His wound never healed properly and he was in pain for the rest of his life. Captain Cilley was wounded a second time, blinding him in one eye.

After the war, Joseph Cilley returned home to resume agricultural pursuits, but he still wanted to serve his state and country. In 1817, he was appointed quartermaster of the New Hampshire Militia. In 1827, Cilley became the aide-de-camp to Governor Benjamin Pierce.

He was a member of the Liberty Party and from June 13, 1846, through March 3, 1847, filled the U.S. Senate seat vacated by Levi Woodbury. Woodbury's resignation was to prepare a campaign to run for president, challenging President Martin Van Buren. After his service in Washington, Cilley returned to farming in Nottingham, where he died on September 16, 1887, at age ninety-six.

FATHER OF WEST POINT

1817–1833

SYLVANUS THAYER

Brigadier General, U.S. Army
War of 1812
Superintendent of West Point

Born:	June 9, 1785, Braintree, Massachusetts
Died:	September 7, 1872, Braintree
Buried:	West Point Cemetery
Education:	Dartmouth College, 1807
	U.S. Military Academy, 1808

BRIGADIER GENERAL SYLVANUS THAYER IS REVERED BY the cadets of the U.S. Military Academy as "the Father of West Point." He was one of the early superintendents of the academy, located in New York. He was also an early proponent of engineering education in America.

Thayer was born in Braintree, Massachusetts on June 9, 1785, the fifth of seven children of farmer, Nathaniel Thayer, and his wife, Dorcas. In 1799, at the age of fourteen, he was sent to live with his uncle Azariah Faxon and attended school in Washington, New Hampshire. At his uncle's home, he met General Benjamin Pierce, a Revolutionary War veteran like his uncle Azariah.

In 1803, Thayer entered Dartmouth College, graduating in 1807 at the head of his class. At the request of General Pierce, Thayer received an appointment to West Point from President James Madison. Thayer graduated from the military academy in one year and was commissioned a second lieutenant in the Corps of Engineers in 1808.

For four years he was concerned with the construction of coastal defenses around Boston and New York. During the War of 1812, he served as chief engineer of the northern army on the Niagara frontier and Lake Champlain. He also served as chief engineer and brigade major directing the fortification and defense of Norfolk, Virginia.

In 1815, he was breveted a major and was given five thousand dollars to travel to Europe with Colonel William McRee to study methods of educating military engineers so that he could rescue West Point from incipient decay. The academy had a reputation for laxity of discipline and academic standards. There was also an uncertainty about whether to emphasize civilian or military studies.

Thayer studied for two years at the French École Polytechnique. While traveling in Europe, he amassed a collection of science and mathematics textbooks that now form a valuable archive for historians of mathematics.

In 1817, President James Monroe ordered Thayer to West Point as its superintendent. Under his guidance, the academy became the nation's first college of engineering. He accomplished sweeping reforms by setting new standards for admission, establishing minimum levels of academic proficiency, and creating a system to measure cadet progress. A commandant of cadets was appointed to regulate discipline and the military curriculum. Thayer formed a board of visitors to inspect the academy annually to recommend adjustments to the curriculum. He also established an academic board of faculty to develop academic policy.

Thayer believed that the arts and sciences are important. He wanted graduates to act with distinction in the conduct of civilian offices they might enter. Courses in English and French, natural sciences, social sciences, and ethics were staples. The cadets also studied civilian applications of West Point's curriculum. By 1831, the military engineering course was redesignated civil engineering and had lost most of its military overtones now leaning toward construction of buildings, arches, canals, bridges, and other public works.

Suspicion that the academy was an incubator of a military aristocracy led to tensions between Thayer and President Andrew Jackson's administration. Thayer resigned in 1833 as a colonel to supervise the construction of fortifications and harbor improvements in Massachusetts and Maine. He became commander of the Corps of Engineers in 1857, but took sick leave the following year. Thayer retired in 1863 as a brigadier general.

In 1867, he endowed Dartmouth College with thirty-thousand dollars to create the Thayer School of Engineering. Thayer located and personally recommended Lieutenant Robert Fletcher to Dartmouth President Asa Dodge Smith. Fletcher became the school's first professor and dean. The Thayer School admitted its first three students to a graduate program in 1871. Thayer spent his last three years arranging the school's curriculum. He also donated funds for a public library in his hometown of Braintree.

Sylvanus Thayer died on September 7, 1872, at his home in Braintree, where he was buried. He was reinterred at West Point Cemetery in 1877. A statue was erected there in his honor bearing the inscription in which he is called the Father of the United States Military Academy.

References:

West Point, A History Of The U.S. Military Academy, by Sidney Forman, 1950.
Duty, Honor, Country; by Stephen Ambrose, 1999.

THE MEXICAN WAR

1846–1848

THE MEXICAN WAR BEGAN AS A BRAZEN BIT OF SABER rattling by President Polk. After the annexation of Texas in 1846, Polk sent ten U.S. Army regiments to the Rio Grande in an attempt to force Mexico to sell California and the Southwest to the United States. Because the Rio Grande was in disputed territory, Mexico regarded the act as an invasion and war quickly broke out.

In the first battle in May 1846, General Zachary Taylor's two-thousand regular army troops, although outnumbered, routed the overconfident Mexicans by superior marksmanship and expert use of artillery.

Facing a force of more than thirty-thousand troops, Taylor could not advance into Mexico without reinforcements. Volunteers proved easy to come by and within a few months fifty-thousand U.S. recruits had enlisted for glory and adventure in the Halls of Montezuma. The "wild volunteers," as General Taylor called them, massed in Texas, where they soon became impatient with drilling in the blazing summer sun. These raw recruits spent much of their time drinking, brawling, and earning the contempt of the regular soldiers.

But when Taylor finally thrust into Mexico, the new soldiers fought ferociously. The fortified city of Monterey fell on September 25 at a cost of nearly five hundred casualties. Taylor ended his campaign with a narrow victory at Buena Vista, which was won only when a cavalry charge broke the surrounding Mexican lines. The charge was led by Colonel Jefferson Davis, whose comrades in arms included young West Point graduates such as Robert E. Lee, Ulysses S. Grant, and George McClellan.

While Taylor slogged his way southward, General Stephen Kearny's Army of the West marched from the Missouri to California. They did not encounter significant resistance until they approached San Diego. Within a month, the province of California was secured. In the main theater of the war, the crushing blow was delivered by General Winfield Scott, who attacked inland from Vera Cruz and on September 14, 1847, captured Mexico City.

The swift victory over Mexico heaped glory on the army and two of its generals—Zachary Taylor and Franklin Pierce, who served under Scott, would become U.S. presidents in the next decade and Ulysses Grant who was elected twenty years later. But the Mexican War cost thirteen-thousand American lives, the great majority to diseases such as dysentery and smallpox.

After the war, the army had the additional burden of protecting the half-million square miles of territory it had won. The Indian tribes of the southwest—Navajo, Apache, and Ute—would keep the U.S. soldiers busy there for the next forty years.

FRANKLIN PIERCE

Brigadier General—Mexican War
Fourteenth President of the United States

Born: November 23, 1804, Hillsborough,
             New Hampshire
Died: October 8, 1869, Concord, New Hampshire
Buried: Old North Cemetery, Concord
Education: Bowdoin College, Maine, 1824

FRANKLIN'S FATHER, BENJAMIN PIERCE (1757-1839) WAS A general in the Revolutionary War and served as governor of New Hampshire from 1827 to 1829. Two of his older brothers fought in the War of 1812. Young Franklin was brought up in an atmosphere of public service. He attended schools in Hancock and Francestown and Phillips Exeter Academy. In 1824 he graduated third in his class from Bowdoin College. His classmates there included Henry Wadsworth Longfellow and Nathaniel Hawthorne.

Pierce studied law for three years in Portsmouth, New Hampshire, and Northampton, Massachusetts, and finally with Judge Edmund Parker in Amherst, New Hampshire. He was admitted to the New Hampshire bar in 1827. Pierce married Jane Means Appleton on November 10, 1834. They had three children, two of whom died due to childhood diseases.

In 1829, he was elected to the New Hampshire Legislature and in 1832 was made Speaker of the House. He entered the U.S. Congress in 1833 and developed a close friendship with Andrew Jackson, supporting him on important issues. His four years in the House of Representatives were uneventful. In 1837, Pierce was elected to the U.S. Senate, but was overshadowed by political greats such as Henry Clay, John C. Calhoun, and Daniel Webster. Pierce was the youngest senator and seldom spoke. He resigned in 1842 to become the district attorney of New Hampshire.

When the Mexican War broke out, in 1846, he enlisted as a private in a company of volunteers at Concord. Soon after, he was commissioned a colonel of the Ninth Infantry Regiment. On March

3, 1847, Pierce was commissioned brigadier general of volunteers even though he had no military experience.

He accompanied General Winfield Scott on his march on Mexico City. Pierce served in several hostile engagements, was under fire, and conducted himself well. He was severely injured at Contreras when he was thrown from his horse. He returned to New Hampshire to practice law.

The Democratic National Convention met in Baltimore in June 1852 with Lewis Cass, James Buchanan, and Stephen A. Douglas as the leading presidential candidates. After thirty-five ballots, the Virginia delegation voted for Pierce. On the forty-ninth ballot, he received 282 votes to six for all other candidates. The "dark horse" candidate from New Hampshire narrowly defeated General Winfield Scott, the Whig candidate, and became the fourteenth President of the United States.

Two months before taking office, he and his wife saw their eleven-year-old son killed when their train was wrecked. Still grieving, he entered the White House in a state of nervous exhaustion.

During his administration, Pierce favored the purchase or annexation of Cuba. He also wanted to expand America's commerce, first with federal subsidies for shipping and second by opening new areas for trade. Pierce sent Commodore Perry to Japan to "induce" them to open their ports to trade with America in the first act of "gunboat diplomacy." Perry successfully negotiated the trade agreement.

President Pierce also supported the plan for linking California with the rest of the country by means of a transcontinental railroad. The best route was via the Southwest through Mexican-held territory. James Gadsen was sent to purchase land on the southern border of New Mexico. The tract of fifty-thousand square miles was purchased for ten million dollars and was known thereafter as the Gadsen Purchase. Pierce included in his cabinet a Mexican War compatriot, Jefferson Davis, of Mississippi, as Secretary of War. When Congress voted to fund the railroad survey, Jefferson Davis was the overseer.

In his inaugural address, Pierce advised against reopening the slavery question. Nevertheless, the conflict over the extension of slavery into the territories was the great event of his administration. Senator Stephen A. Douglas' plan to settle the Northwest by removing the Indians, connecting Chicago to the Pacific Northwest by railroad, and opening the territory to slavery would be his ticket to the next presidency. This was a plan to thwart the southern interests for a southern Pacific railroad. Douglas won the support of the middle west and western Missouri and some powerful interests in the South. His plan was supported by the Kansas-Nebraska bill, which contained a clause giving settlers the right to decide whether or not they would have slaves. Thus, the Missouri Compromise of 1820, prohibiting slavery in the Louisiana territory, except Missouri, was repealed.

President Pierce signed the bill, thereby aiding the South in its desire to extend slavery into the western territories. This virtually ruined his administration. He also organized Kansas and Nebraska as territories and supported the pro-slavery party in Kansas in an effort to prevent Kansas's admission to the Union as a free state. He believed that this would satisfy the South and a civil war would be avoided. Pierce was under the influence of Jefferson Davis (who later became President of the Confederate States of America) and this may account for his stance on several important public questions. Pierce felt that the U.S. Constitution guaranteed slavery as an institution and that the only way to avoid civil war was to support the southern point of view.

After retiring from the presidency, he traveled in Europe for three years. Pierce was opposed to the methods of the abolitionists, but supported the North when the Civil War did break out. He spent his last years at his home in Concord, New Hampshire, beloved by his personal friends but nearly forgotten by his countrymen.

JOHN G. FOSTER

General, U.S. Volunteers
Mexican War
American Civil War

Born: 1823, Whitefield, New Hampshire
Died: 1874, Nashua, New Hampshire
Buried: Nashua
Education: USMA, West Point, 1847
Battles: Vera Cruz, Mexico
             Molino del Rey, Mexico
             Fort Sumter, South Carolina
             Fort Macon, Georgia

JOHN FOSTER GREW UP IN NASHUA AND PREPPED FOR
West Point at Crosby's Nashua Literary Institute. After graduating
from West Point, in 1847, he was assigned to Washington, D.C.
as a second lieutenant of engineers. When the war with Mexico
broke out, Foster was assigned to a company of sappers, miners,
and pontoon builders in Mexico. He participated in the siege of
Vera Cruz and in September 1947 at Molino del Rey. He, like many
others, contracted malaria and was sent home to recuperate. When
he returned to Mexico, he was breveted a first lieutenant then promoted to captain and cited for his brave and meritorious conduct.

After the Mexican War, Foster was assigned as an engineer
to work on coastal fortifications and in the coastal survey office in
Washington. From 1855 to 1857, he was an assistant professor of
engineering at West Point.

In 1858, Foster worked on building Fort Sumter, in the
Charleston, South Carolina, harbor. He was commissioned a full
captain July 1, 1860, after fourteen years service. During 1861, he
was in charge of strengthening the fortifications of Charleston
Harbor in the anticipation of war. Foster was in command when
the garrison at Fort Moultrie was transferred to Fort Sumter, and
was second in command when Fort Sumter was attacked—the act

signaling the start of the Civil War. Foster was present when the fort surrendered and was evacuated April 12-14, 1861. He was breveted a major for his gallantry during the bombardment of the fort.

After the surrender of Fort Sumter, Foster worked on northern coastal fortifications. He was appointed brigadier general of volunteers in October 1861. General Foster led his regiment in two actions in North Carolina; the capture of Roanoke Island and that of New Bern. He also participated in the taking of Fort Macon, Georgia. Foster was in command of the Department of North Carolina July 1862 through July 1863 and had several regiments of New Hampshire volunteers under his command. He was breveted a major general of U.S. volunteers in July 1863.

Foster's next command was the Department of Ohio, from December 1863 to July 1864. He suffered serious injuries after a fall from his horse and asked to be relieved. After the Civil War, he served in the Department of Florida, but the climate and atmosphere brought on another attack of malaria. In 1869 he was assigned to Boston to make improvements in Boston harbor.

When he died, General Foster's funeral in Nashua was a huge event. All businesses were closed and many buildings were draped in mourning black. Eight Civil War generals guarded the hearse and Col. George Bowers, a compatriot from the Mexican War, led the funeral escort of U.S. Army troops.

Jesse A. Gove

Colonel, 22nd Massachusetts Volunteer Regiment
Mexican War
American Civil War

Born:	1824, Weare, New Hampshire
Died:	1862, Gaines Mill, Virginia
Buried:	Unknown
Education:	Norwich University, Northfield, Vermont
Battle:	Gaines Mill, Virginia

AFTER GRADUATION FROM NORWICH UNIVERSITY, JESSE Gove served as a lieutenant during the Mexican War, 1846–1848. He then returned to New Hampshire and read law at the Concord law offices of Pierce & Minot (Franklin Pierce had also served in the Mexican War).

Gove was admitted to the New Hampshire bar and served as Deputy Secretary of State from 1850 to 1855, but he missed the military and secured a commission as captain of dragoons in the Regular Army. Gove was serving in Utah when the Civil War began.

In 1861, Gove was commissioned as colonel of the 22nd Massachusetts Volunteers. The 22nd joined the Army of the Potomac and Gove was killed in action at Gaines Mill, Virginia.

American Civil War

1861–1865

THE AMERICAN WAR OF THE 1860s WAS NOT A CIVIL WAR in the usual sense of the term. The opponents were not fighting for control of the government, but rather over the attempt of one side to become a separate nation. The Confederate States of America (the South) was an organized, responsible government possessing the attributes of sovereignty. *Civil War* is, however, about as accurate as any description and is therefore, the generally accepted term for this bloody conflict.

The industrial age in America caused changes in both the north and south, two quite different societies. The problems arose from the ways in which these societies adjusted to industrial changes. The biggest difficulty was how the North and the South viewed the institution of slavery. Without slavery, the problems could probably have been worked out through ordinary politics.

Eli Whitney's invention of the cotton gin, a device that made it possible for textile mills to use short-staple cotton, which the southern farmers grew in abundance, was a catalyst. In ten short years, the demand for cotton grew from 7 percent of America's exports to 57 percent. The South had become a cotton empire relying solely on the labor of four million slaves.

Slavery was not the only source of discord however. The South was concerned that the North might control the federal government. The South developed the concept of state's rights as a matter of self-protection. Although various compromises were proposed, it was, in the end, slavery that was the main cause of the Civil War.

John Brown's raid on the federal arsenal at Harpers Ferry to seize weapons and arm slaves sent shock waves through the South. After that abortive raid, there was no chance of peacefully ending the bitter sectional arguments or differences.

In 1860, Abraham Lincoln was elected president. Lincoln received less than a majority of popular votes, but a solid majority of the electoral college. On March 4, 1861, he would become President of the United States . . . but not of all the states. South Carolina's legislature remained in session until after the election. Once it saw the results, it held a convention in Charleston and on December 8, 1860, voted for South Carolina to secede from the Union.

This was the catalyst the other southern states needed. By February, South Carolina had been joined by Mississippi, Alabama, Florida, Louisiana, and Texas. On February 8, delegates from the seceding states met in Montgomery, Alabama, to form a new nation—the Confederate States of America. A provisional constitution was adopted, which was replaced by a permanent document very similar to the U.S. Constitution. Jefferson Davis, of Mississippi, was elected president.

As yet, no blood had been shed and Senator John Crittenden, of Kentucky, attempted a final compromise. Lincoln refused to sign it because it included slavery. In his inaugural address, Lincoln had said that he would do all in his power to "hold, occupy and possess" the places and property belonging to the federal government that lay in confederate territory. He referred chiefly to Fort Sumter, near the mouth of Charleston Harbor in South Carolina.

The commanding officer at Sumter was Major Robert Anderson; his second in command was a New Hampshireman, Captain John G. Foster. The garrison of sixty-eight soldiers had enough food for two weeks flew a U.S. flag in defiance of the newly formed confederacy. Attempts were made to induce Washington to evacuate the fort. Lincoln sent word to resupply Fort Sumter, a clear indication that the Union intended to hold it indefinitely.

Jefferson Davis ordered General P.G.T. Beauregard to open fire and bombard the fort into submission. After a thirty-four-hour artillery bombardment, Major Anderson lowered the flag and turned over the fort to the confederacy. The spectacular bombardment of Fort Sumter was the visible symbol that the war had begun.

President Lincoln immediately had the states put seventy-five thousand militia at the service of the federal government. This call to arms brought a rush of enthusiastic recruiting throughout the north. At the same time, it put four more states into the confederacy: Virginia, North Carolina, Tennessee, and Arkansas, which had been waiting and hoping for a peaceful solution, now chose the South.

Although various states' militia had men on hand, they were not trained for combat, nor were they ready to fight as cohesive units. A militia regiment was composed of a company from this town, another company from that town, and so on, with ten companies scattered across a state. In most cases, those individual companies had never been brought together to maneuver as a regiment. Even a first-rate militia company would be of little value in battle if it had never worked as a part of a larger unit.

However, both sides were equally unready. The militia companies were led by officers elected by the rank and file. Some officers were elected because they were "leading citizens" and some just because they were good vote getters. Very few were chosen because they had qualifications for military command. The Fifth New Hampshire Regiment was an exception, choosing the experienced Edward Cross as its leader.

There were regular officers on duty, but the federal government did not know how best to use them. General Winfield Scott was General-in-Chief, but now in senility. Scott had wanted to keep the regular army intact. He did not want his regular officers resigning to take commissions leading amateurs from their home states. Most of the general officers did come from the regulars, but some political leaders were given important commands.

The Confederacy was more systematic. Jefferson Davis was a West Pointer with field experience in the Mexican War, and had served as Secretary of War. About a third of the West Pointers in the regular army had resigned to serve with the South. Robert E. Lee had been offered the command of the principal field federal army.

He rejected the offer to stand with his native state of Virginia. Davis made Lee a full general.

The war aims of the opponents were simple. The Confederacy would fight for independence and the North would fight for reestablishment of the Union.

The Civil War had many distinct features. It was the largest war the world had ever known. The telegraph was used as a military instrument, aerial observation from balloons was developed, and railways proved to be of prime importance. Railroads delivered troops and supplies in a timely way; rail lines were the arteries sustaining both sides and rail centers became major targets. Among the Civil War's firsts were the use of ironclad battleships—the *Monitor* and the *Merrimac*, and the electrically exploded torpedo, and the sinking of a vessel by a submarine.

War aims govern war strategy. The Confederacy realized it was at a disadvantage in the areas of manpower, industrial strength, and riches. President Jefferson Davis, therefore, would take the defensive position and make the powerful North come to fight on the South's home ground. The South encompassed a huge territory and the supply lines of the North would be long, immobilizing many troops just for their protection. The North's navy was large, but the southland's coast was vast and thus nearly impossible to seal off or blockade.

Finally, the southern soldier would have a clearer picture of what he was fighting for: to protect his home from the northern invader. Meanwhile, the northern soldiers were fighting for "the Union," an abstraction, a concept that might wear thin once the real war weariness set in.

Neither side anticipated a prolonged war. The militia had been called to federal service for its limit of ninety days. Many thought the war would be over before their term of service expired. In these early days of patriotism, both sides attracted far more volunteers than they could equip.

The uniform of the U.S. Army (the North) was the standard dark blue wool coat and light blue trousers. However, assorted volunteer units on both sides wore gaudy and impractical uniforms; most with flamboyant names such as the Tigers, the Game Cocks, the Susquehanna Blues, and the Rough and Ready Grays. In the early days, some of the "blues" were southern units and some of the "grays" were northern. After some battlefield confusion, the South adopted a more recognizable national gray uniform.

Two northern regiments were allowed variation from the standard army blue. These were the First and Second Regiments of Volunteer Sharpshooters, conceived and commanded by Colonel Hiram Berdan. The Sharpshooters wore a distinctive green uniform and used Sharps rifles with telescopic sights instead of smoothbore muskets. Berdan, a New Yorker, was a national champion marksman for fifteen years prior to the Civil War. He convinced the U.S. War Department that units of sharpshooters would be of benefit. He was made a colonel and empowered to raise two regiments. Berdan recruited men mainly from the Northeast. Men qualified by shooting ten bulls-eyes "off hand" at one-hundred yards and another ten "at rest" from two-hundred yards.

Companies F and G of the Second Regiment of Sharpshooters were comprised of hardy New Hampshiremen. The green-clad sharpshooters fought at the second battle of Manassas, South Mountain, along Antietam Creek at Sharpsburg, Fredericksburg, Chancellorsville and Gettysburg. Many were killed in action, some were captured and died in prison, but most survived to return to New Hampshire.

Richmond, Virginia, became the capital of the new Confederacy. Richmond and Washington, D.C. were the principal centers of troop concentrations, with Virginia the main battleground. The Confederacy would later regret its emphasis on the East and its neglect of New Orleans and Vicksburg to the west.

The first major battle of the war was the first Manassas (or Bull Run). General McDowell led thirty-five thousand Yankee troops out of Washington to meet southern Generals Beauregard and Joe Johnston at a creek called Bull Run near Manassas, Virginia. The fight was poorly conducted on both sides due to the inexperience of both men and officers. As General Kirby-Smith's brigade turned the tide against the North, the federal troops' retreat broke into a panicked rout sending Yankee soldiers and civilian curiosity seekers scurrying back to Washington. This easy victory for the South merely enhanced its hope for a short war. The Union defeat reconciled the north to the possibility of a long and vigorous conflict.

On July 25, 1861, George McClellan was promoted to General-in-Chief of the northern armies, replacing Winfield Scott. After the Battle of Bull Run, there was little heavy fighting until early 1862. The North succeeded in curtailing southern supplies by blockading ports of North Carolina and capturing the city of New Orleans. The ironclad southern ship *Merrimac* caused some sinkings and damage during March 1862. When the North's iron-clad *Monitor* appeared the following days, the *Merrimac* retired to Norfolk and was blown up when the Confederates evacuated the city in May.

Confederate losses along the coastal areas were accompanied by serious setbacks to the west in Kentucky and Tennessee. The forces of Commodore Andrew Foote and Brigadier General Ulysses S. Grant led to a pivotal victory at Fort Donelson, on the Cumberland River, on February 2, 1862. They captured fifteen thousand men, rifles, guns, and supplies the Confederacy could not spare. Following this success, the North moved on to occupy Memphis and looked toward Vicksburg next. The military success at Fort Donelson was important not only for capturing men and materials, but also for its morale effect. Northerners were inspired to renewed support of the war, while southerners were discouraged with their new government's conduct of the war.

Confederate General Albert Johnston surprised Grant at Pittsburg Landing before Grant could be reinforced. April 6 was the bloodiest day of the war up to that time. In the Battle of Shiloh, Johnston was killed but Beauregard continued the battle. Finally, on April 7, Grant received reinforcements from Major General Lew Wallace and three divisions of Buell's army.

Meanwhile, in the East, General McClellan was ordered by President Lincoln to move the Confederates from the Munson Hill area near Washington. McClellan planned his peninsula campaign attacking and advancing up between the York and James Rivers to Richmond. Confederate General Joseph Johnston evacuated Yorktown and withdrew safely toward Richmond. On March 11, McClellan was relieved of his command to pursue the Confederates up the Virginia peninsula. As the federal army marched up the Chickahominy River toward Richmond, General Johnston was badly wounded and succeeded by Robert E. Lee. The battle was renewed but Lee withdrew to Richmond. General Thomas "Stonewall" Jackson and General Lee did not display any military brilliance in these battles but did manage to save Richmond.

Against McClellan's protest, the Army of the Potomac was withdrawn from the Virginia peninsula back toward Washington. General Pope's federal army of Virginia was to cover McClellan's withdrawal. General Lee split his force, and with one wing commanded by Stonewall Jackson soundly defeated Pope at the second battle of Manassas on the old Bull Run battlefield.

With Pope defeated and Lee threatening, President Lincoln again placed McClellan at the head of forces protecting Washington. Lee sent Stonewall Jackson to capture Harpers Ferry, and moved the Confederate Army north. McClellan moved quickly to counter Lee's advance. The two forces met at Sharpsburg—Antietam Creek on September 17, 1862. This was the bloodiest single day's fight of the entire war, with casualties on both sides exceeding twenty thousand men.

McClellan let opportunity slip through his fingers by not following Lee's retreating army after this battle. His incompetence was finally recognized and he was replaced by General Burnside. McClellan never led troops in the field again.

Five days after Antietam, Lincoln issued his intention to declare all slaves to be free—the Emancipation Proclamation. The ultimate effect of this decree both in America and abroad was an important declaration of the North's war aim.

The last significant battle of 1862 was that of Fredericksburg, Virginia. This was an enormous federal disaster. General Burnside's troops repeatedly attacked over open ground, an entrenched confederate force on the higher ground on Mayre's Heights. Confident Confederate soldiers were impressed by the bravery of the attacking federal troops and began to doubt that the war would go in the South's favor. After Fredericksburg, Burnside was replaced by General Hooker. After these defeats, the morale of the Union army soldiers and civilians at home was at its lowest point.

In April 1863, General Hooker boosted the mood of his troops with better rations, some furloughs, and training. He planned an offensive against Lee near Chancellorsville, Virginia. He had nearly surrounded Lee's forces, when Stonewall Jackson outflanked Hooker. Initially the Union sensed victory as they received favorable battle reports from Thaddeus Lowe's observation balloon. While General Hooker hesitated, Lee quickly sent Jackson with three divisions to the west to crush General Howard's Eleventh Corps. Although the Confederates were victorious at Chancellorsville, Stonewall Jackson was mortally wounded by his own troops while making a night reconnaissance.

Lee, now backed by Jefferson Davis, planned an offense aimed at Washington, Baltimore or Philadelphia. On June 3, Lee headed northward with a force of about seventy-six thousand. On July 1, Lee's army clashed with the Army of the Potomac, now commanded by General George Meade, at Gettysburg, Pennsylvania. After a desperate three-day struggle, culminating in the futile charge by General Pickett against the Union center, Lee retreated. Much to Lincoln's disappointment, Meade failed to pursue Lee. No other significant land actions occurred in the East until the spring of 1864.

Meanwhile, events of great importance were happening in the West. General Grant marched his army down the Mississippi winning a succession of battles and capturing Jackson, the state capital. Grant and his army of forty thousand settled in for a six-week siege of Vicksburg. The siege ended July 4, when General Pemberton surrendered a Confederate force of thirty thousand men. Soon after, on July 8, the Confederate garrison at Port Hudson surrendered. This cut off the South's valuable supply line from Mexico.

In spite of the defeats at Gettysburg and Vicksburg, the Confederates continued to fight. General Morgan led his gray-clad cavalry on raids into Ohio and Indiana. The next big fight in the West was the battle of Chickamauga, Tennessee, September 19-20th, 1863. Union forces under General Rosencrans met Confederate Generals Bragg and Longstreet. This battle, which began with Bragg crossing Chickamauga creek, was the bloodiest two days of the war.

Longstreet flanked Rosencrans's right and sent him and his forces back toward Chattanooga. Only General George Thomas' magnificent stand on the Union left and crucial resistance by Colonel John Wilder's brigade, who had armed themselves at their own expense with repeating rifles, saved the Union army from annihilation. The victory for the Confederates was dearly bought. Their casualties were 2,312 killed and sixteen thousand wounded and missing.

The land campaigns of 1863 were paralleled by important naval actions. The confederate cruiser *Alabama* commanded by Captain Raphael Semmes, sank many tons of federal shipping. CSA ships *Florida* and *Nashville* also played key roles. Confederate raiders destroyed 257 ships during the war and caused the transfer of registry of seven hundred more. The injury to the American merchant marine was so great that it would take half a century to recover.

In 1864, the Union made two important changes. The first was to clarify and simplify the military chain of command, with President Lincoln as the Commander-in-Chief and Grant as the General-in-Chief, and General Halleck in between as the chief-of-staff. The second change was the development of an overall strategy that would eventually bring victory to the Union.

The strategy Lincoln and Grant agreed on, called for major drives on three fronts. The Army of the Potomac, under Meade, would move southward to destroy Lee. In the west, General Sherman would annihilate the Army of Tennessee and lay waste to the economic resources around Atlanta, Georgia. Third, General Banks would move his army from New Orleans to Mobile, Alabama, and head north toward Sherman.

In May 1864, Meade moved south across the Rapidan River. The ensuing Battle of the Wilderness saw three days of intense fighting. After the battle, instead of falling back, Meade aggressively continued southward. Grant tried unsuccessfully to flank Lee at Spottsylvania Court House. The two armies met again at Cold Harbor, Virginia, in June. Grant's attack resulted in seven thousand Union casualties. Lee also suffered losses that the Confederates could not replace.

After the repulse at Cold Harbor, Grant shifted forces to Petersburg, Virginia, a railhead twenty miles south of Richmond. Poor leadership by General Butler resulted in the nine-month siege of Petersburg. At one point, a unit of Pennsylvania coalminers dug a tunnel under the Confederate earthworks, placed eight thousand pounds of powder there, and blew a huge gap in the South's defensive line. Union troops charged through the smoking crater, but were repulsed by the Confederates.

Under Lee's orders, General Jubal Early attacked Washington, D.C., in July 1864. Lincoln watched as the raiders were eventually driven back. After this raid, General Philip Sheridan and his cavalry were placed in charge of the capital's defense. Meanwhile, Sherman was marching through Georgia. His troops burned Atlanta in November and by Christmas Eve had captured Savannah.

In the West, Confederate General Hood clashed with Thomas in Tennessee. The Confederates made a futile attack on General John Schofield's force at Franklin, Tennessee, near Nashville. The South lost fifty-five hundred men and five Confederate generals were killed. After the battle at Franklin, Schofield joined Thomas at Nashville and pushed Hood's army out of Tennessee.

In the South, the Union fleet entered Mobile Bay on August 5, 1864, in a spectacular move planned by Admiral David Farragut. After one of the ironclads had been sunk by a torpedo, Farragut gave his famous order, as he was lashed to the rigging of his flagship *Hartford*, "Damn the torpedoes, full speed ahead!"

In February 1865, at Hampton Roads, Virginia, after an unsuccessful peace conference, the Confederate congress took desperate measures to avoid defeat. They adopted a law authorizing recruitment of slaves to replenish the dwindling Southern army. The effort was too little and too late to match the increasing desertion of soldiers and defection of civilians.

In February, Sherman's army reached Columbia, South Carolina, capturing it. The army marched on into North Carolina, defeating Confederates at Bentonville and Goldsboro.

Grant's troops broke the Confederate lines at the Battle of Five Forks, Virginia, on April 1, 1865, killing General A.P. Hill and forcing the evacuation of Petersburg and Richmond the next day.

Lee withdrew to Appomattox Court House and there surrendered his hungry, ragged, and depleted army to Grant on April 9.

To the credit of both Grant and Lee, the nation could and would come back together. General Lee accepted the terms of an unconditional surrender. The Southern troops would go home and get on with their lives. They would not head for the hills to carry on guerrilla warfare. The Confederates burned their flags rather than surrender them, but they did go home.

General Grant was also eager to end the war with a good peace. Under terms signed by both men, there would be no reprisals, Lee and his generals would not be hanged. Confederate officers could keep their swords, sidearms, and horses: "each officer and man will be allowed to return to his home undisturbed by United States authorities." As Union artillery began to fire salutes, Grant stopped it. "We did not want to exult over their downfall," he wrote.

Five days after Lee's surrender, President Lincoln was shot at Ford's Theater in Washington by John Wilkes Booth. Lincoln died on the morning of April 15 and Vice President Andrew Johnson, of Tennessee, became president.

The importance of the Civil War in the stream of American history is immense. The conflict settled once and for all the momentous questions of secession and slavery. It increased national prestige abroad. It gave impetus to nationalism, industrialism, and urbanization.

The Civil War did not secure full rights for the black slaves, now freed. It left a legacy of hatred between the victors and the vanquished that would endure for generations. In terms of human sacrifice and suffering, it left voids in the thousands of families that had lost fathers, brothers, husbands, and sons. Over twenty-two hundred battles and engagements were fought, not including sixty-eight hundred minor actions and skirmishes. The deaths on the Union side were said to be 360,222, of which 110,070 were battle casualties. Over 275,175 Union soldiers were wounded. The total of Confederate deaths are estimated at 258,000, of which 94,000 were battle casualties.

Many brave soldiers died of exposure or malnutrition at prisons and prison camps such as Andersonville in Georgia and Elmira in New York State.

I hope the reader will pardon the author for ending this discourse on such a sad and sorrowful note, but that is war. That is what the soldier carries in his heart and mind until he too will join his fallen comrades.

EDWARD E. CROSS

Colonel—Fifth Regiment
New Hampshire Volunteers
American Civil War

Born:	April 22, 1832, Lancaster, New Hampshire
Died:	July 2, 1863, Gettysburg, Pennsylvania
Buried:	Lancaster
Battles:	Rappahanock Station
	Fair Oaks
	Seven Days' Battles / Malvern Hill
	Antietam
	Fredericksburg
	Chancellorsville
	Gettysburg

Col. Edward Everett Cross commanded an infantry brigade during the American Civil War. He was wounded twelve times and died during the Battle of Gettysburg.

EDWARD E. CROSS WAS THE FIRST SON OF COLONEL Ephraim Cross and his third wife, Abigail Everett. Ephraim was a hatter by trade, but his leadership of the town militia earned him the title "Colonel."

Edward Cross was educated in Lancaster, New Hampshire, public schools. He began his career at fifteen as a printer for the *Coos County Democrat*, a newspaper still published in Lancaster. Cross moved to Cincinnati, where his brother, Nelson, served as a judge. He accompanied the first printing press to travel across the Rocky Mountains, then settled in Arizona. During his time as the editor of the *Arizonian* in Tubac, Arizona, Cross fought two duels over his opinions. The most memorable of the duels is the one with Sylvester Mowry, a mine owner from Tucson.

Cross wrote a series of virulent attacks against Mowry's exaggerated mining and agriculture possibilities of land he owned.

Mowry challenged Cross to a duel, which was promptly accepted. The weapons were Burnside rifles.

The men stood eighty paces apart. Each man fired twice, each missing. Upon the signal to shoot for the third time, Mowry's rifle failed to fire. According to code, he could try another round of ammunition. As the seconds argued duel procedure, Cross calmly folded his arms and waited. Mowry deliberately aimed in the air and fired. High winds during the duel may account for the misses. Impressed with each other's daring, the duelists put down their rifles and shook hands. Cross later withdrew some of his more intemperate remarks.

Cross left the newspaper business and became an agent for the Arizona Mining Company. He later joined Benito Juarez's Mexican Liberal Army and served from 1860 through 1861 as a lieutenant colonel. When he heard the news about Fort Sumter, he resigned his Mexican army commission and returned home to New Hampshire. There, he was appointed colonel of the Fifth Regiment of New Hampshire Volunteers by Governor Nathaniel Berry. The Fifth New Hampshire was mustered in on October 28, 1861, and left for Washington the following day with more than twelve hundred soldiers.

Cross was a physically imposing man, six feet three inches tall, with a full, reddish brown beard. He rode tall in the saddle, erect, "straight as an arrow" according to Charles Hale, his aide. One of Colonel Cross's first acts as commander of the Fifth New Hampshire was to establish training for his officers and non-commissioned officers, as well as discipline and drilling of the men. These measures ensured that the Fifth and the rest of the brigade would be ready for battle. Cross genuinely cared for his men as his strict training was to preserve their lives in combat, and was shown in his sincere letters of condolence to widows and families of those who died.

He was quick to jump to conclusions and was outspoken on political matters. He was pro-Union but not antislavery. These traits did not sit well with the higher officer ranks and may have delayed his military advancement in spite of his splendid and valorous leadership.

Cross and the Fifth New Hampshire saw their first action at Rappahanock Station, Virginia, on March 13, 1862. Remarkably, the Fifth suffered no combat losses and received the dubious title of the "Bloodless Fifth." The irony of that title was reflected in the after-action report of losses sustained by all Union regiments at the conclusion of the Civil War. The Fifth New Hampshire "sustained the greatest loss in the battle during the American Civil War. It lost 295 men, killed or mortally wounded in action, during its four years of service 1861-1865. The losses of the Fifth New Hampshire occurred entirely in aggressive, hard, stand-up fighting; none of it happened in routs or through blunders. Its loss includes 18 officers killed, a number far in excess of usual proportions and indicates that the men were bravely led."

The first major action seen by the Fifth was at Fair Oaks on June 1, 1862, during General McClellan's Peninsula campaign between Virginia's James and York Rivers. Colonel Cross and 170 men were wounded and thirty men of the Fifth were killed.

The Fifth saw more action during the Seven Days' Battles at Savage Station, White Oak Swamp, and Malvern Hill. The next major battle the Fifth participated in was at Antietam on September 17, 1862, fought near Sharpsburg, Maryland. At Antietam, Colonel Cross urged his men to "stand firm and fire low" and to "put on the war paint." The soldiers of the Fifth rubbed black powder from their cartridges on their faces and gave out Indian "war whoops." The Fifth held fast and prevented the enemy from turning the brigade's left flank. The regiments' losses at Antietam were seven killed and 120 wounded of the 319 present for duty.

General McClellan was replaced by General Ambrose Burnside. On December 13, 1862, Burnside committed his troops against an impregnable position held by General Lee at Fredericksburg, Virginia. Among those in the battle were the 20th Maine and the Fifth New Hampshire Regiments, with Cross in the lead followed, by the 69th NY, the Irish Brigade. The Union troops had to cross an open field facing the Confederates behind a stone wall at Mayre's Heights who were shooting down on the fully exposed Union soldiers. The only cover for the attacking Second Corps was behind the dead bodies of their fallen comrades. Colonel Cross was wounded severely while leading the assault. Major Edward Everett Sturtevant was killed during the fruitless charge against the stone wall on Mayre's Heights that day along with seventy soldiers of the Fifth New Hampshire. Colonel John Brook said, "that the bodies found nearest the Confederates' stone wall were those of the 69th New York, 5th New Hampshire, and 53rd Pennsylvania."

Cross was also engaged in a minor role at the Battle of Chancellorsville, May 1863, where he was in command of a small brigade of infantry.

As the Gettysburg campaign progressed, Cross became moody—he told Lieutenant Hale about premonitions of his death saying, "This will be my last battle." Cross's demeanor changed somewhat just before the battle as he walked among the men giving them encouraging words "Give 'em hell, boys!" Cross spoke with young Colonel McKeen of the 81st Pennsylvania indicating that McKeen would command the 148th Pennsylvania that day and was to command the brigade in the event of Cross's death.

As was his usual custom before a battle, Cross would tie a red bandanna on his head, this day he chose to wear a black silk handkerchief. Upon seeing this, General Hancock, the corps commander said to Cross, "This day will bring you a star." Cross shook his head and said quite simply, "No, General, this is my last battle."

As the battle of Gettysburg progressed, the fighting for the Wheatfield had been intense before the arrival of Caldwell's division, headed by Colonel Cross and his brigade. The Confederates were moving quickly across the Wheatfield, but were suddenly halted by the rapid maneuvering of Cross's brigade. The Fifth New Hampshire rushed in and captured several Confederate soldiers and an officer as the enemy was retreating.

Colonel Cross stood among his men issuing orders concerning the prisoners and as he was about to advance his brigade, Cross was shot dead by a Confederate sniper. Colonel Cross would be one of the twenty-seven men of the Fifth New Hampshire to die that day at Gettysburg.

The monument of the Fifth New Hampshire Regiment at Gettysburg battlefield is placed where Colonel Cross was fatally wounded.

Although deserving the "death-bed star" of a Brigadier General, Colonel Cross never received that honor until the New Hampshire State Legislature and Governor in April 2004, promoted him posthumously Brigadier General Edward E. Cross.

References:

Stand Firm and Fire Low, by Col. Edward Cross, Walter Holden, Editor, University Press of New England, 2003.
My Brave Boys: To War with Colonel Cross and the Fighting Fifth, Mike Pride and Mark Travis, University Press of New England, 2001.

THADDEUS S. C. LOWE

Scientist and Inventor
American Civil War

Born: August 20, 1832, Jefferson, New Hampshire
Died: January 16, 1913, Pasadena, California
Buried: Mount View Cemetery, Altadena, California
U.S. Army's First Chief Aeronaut

A SELF-EDUCATED AND SELF-PROCLAIMED "PROFESSOR," LOWE was a scientist and inventor who constructed balloons in order to study atmospheric phenomena. During the Civil War, his flights aloft made observations of Confederate troops both timely and accurate. Lowe sent the first message transmitted by wire from an air vehicle.

He was born the second of six children on a small farm in rural New Hampshire. As a youngster, he learned simple crafts from the local Indians, such as basketry and moccasin making. His meager schooling was limited to the three winter months. His school had few books, so the teacher would lend young Thad hers.

His mother died when he was only ten and Thaddeus was "bound-out" to a family who treated him like a servant. He ran away on July 4, 1843, headed for Portland, Maine, the closest large city. His trek to Portland took two years, working along his way for food and shelter. During his trip, he heard about the airship *Victoria* crossing the Atlantic Ocean. This inspired him to learn as much as possible about ballooning.

In Portland, he worked for the Nash & French Company making shoes. As he watched the workers laboriously cutting the leather shoe pieces, he recalled how his Indian friends wet their knives before cutting leather to make their moccasins. He passed on this technique to the shoe-makers, who were impressed by such a good idea from such a young man.

Thaddeus returned to his New Hampshire home and while there, attended a "magical show" given by a Professor Dincklehoff. Fascinated, Thad attended many performances and was asked to

Thaddeus S. Lowe observing the battle from his balloon Intrepid.
Credits: Matthew W. Brady—National Archives.

become the professor's assistant. He traveled with the show for
two years and became adept at showmanship.

He moved to New York, where he studied science and medicine, but his real interest was aeronautics. He began his own series
of scientific lectures and shows. At one of these performances, he
met his future wife, Leontine Gachon.

He continued his lectures in New York City, but rented a parcel
of land in Hoboken, New Jersey. It was there that Lowe made his
first balloon and his first tethered flight, April 1851. He did quite
well selling rides in his balloon—a dollar for a tethered ride and
five for a free-flight.

In 1858, Thad and Leontine constructed a larger balloon, the *Enterprise* made of the finest Indian silk. The balloon's surface was covered with varnish to prevent the hydrogen from escaping. He made many flights in the *Enterprise*, including a flight from Ogdensburg, New York to Ottawa, Canada. He designed and built a device to aid him in his journeys—the altimeter. Lowe also proposed the idea of a weather bureau to assist his flying great distances. He was an early proponent of trans-oceanic flights.

Although other balloonists had approached the Union army with the idea of military aerial observation, it was Lowe, who in June 1861 was able to demonstrate the technique consistently and successfully. He sent the first telegraph message from a balloon (any aircraft) on June 18, 1861, and was first to successfully direct artillery fire from the air, on September 24, 1861, from Fort Cochran to a target three miles away.

Professor Lowe brought his balloon to Washington, D.C., and on June 11, 1861, he was invited to the White House to discuss his plans with President Lincoln. The president was receptive and promised to give serious consideration to balloon use by the army. One week later, Lowe ascended to an altitude of five hundred feet. Aboard was a telegraph key attached to a line that ran to the White House and the War Department.

Balloon Enterprise,
June 18, 1861

TO THE PRESIDENT OF THE UNITED STATES

Sir:

> *This point of observation commands an area nearly 50 miles in diameter. The city, with its girdle of encampments, presents a superb scene. I have pleasure in sending you this first dispatch ever telegraphed from an aerial station, and am acknowledging indebtedness for your encouragement for the opportunity of demonstrating the availability of the science of aeronautics in the military service of the country.*
> T.S.C. Lowe

The demonstration was impressive and the next day Lowe repeated the performance on the White House lawn for Lincoln and his cabinet. Meanwhile, Confederate troops were in the northern Virginia area and a threat to the security of the District of Columbia. There were reports of large numbers of enemy troops massing nearby at Manassas and Fairfax Court House. Because their exact positions were not known, the Union army asked Lowe to take the *Enterprise* to Falls Church and find the location of the Confederate troops.

On June 22, Lowe ascended near Manassas and Fairfax, but reported nothing of importance. In July, as the *Enterprise* was being towed to Falls Church, his party was overrun by fleeing federal troops and terrified civilian spectators who had been routed at Bull Run (Manassas). As this panicked group reached Washington, they spread rumors of the Confederate army on its way to attack the capital city. Lowe made several balloon ascents and soon relieved their anxiety. Lowe's reports also spared the unnecessary deployment of troops to defend the capital.

On August 2, 1861, Lowe's observation program received a boost with delivery of a new twenty-five thousand cubic foot capacity balloon the *Union*. It was from the *Union* that observers discovered that the Confederates were building earthworks around Washington.

The Balloon Corps was added to the Army of the Potomac in September 1861 when the Secretary of War directed Lowe to construct four more balloons. Thaddeus Lowe was designated Chief Aeronaut and placed in charge of the new service. The corps was under jurisdiction of the Signal Corps.

By January 1862, Lowe's operation consisted of seven balloons and four aeronauts. As the Confederate Army withdrew from the Washington area, the Balloon Corps advanced in various campaigns to the Mississippi River and south to Mobile, Alabama. In June 1863, the Balloon Corps was disbanded.

Recognizing the significance of Lowe's contribution to the evolution of the army aviation concept, in 1960 the U.S. Army named its primary fixed-wing training facility, Lowe Army Airfield at Fort Rucker, Alabama, in his honor.

Thaddeus Lowe also invented a compression ice machine and in 1865 made the first artificial ice in the United States. His other inventions include metallurgical furnaces for gas and oil fuel (1869-1872) and the Lowe coke-oven system in 1897.

Lowe's inventions were widely used making him a wealthy man. In 1888, he moved his wife and ten children to Pasadena, California, where he purchased Oak Mount. A friend, Andrew McNally (of Rand McNally) renamed it Mount Lowe.

Thaddeus Lowe built his mansion and a hotel on his scenic mount. He also had built a three-mile narrow-gauge railway to get tourists to the top. He established the Lowe Observatory with a sixteen-inch telescope. When Lowe died, at age 81, he was working on a giant telescope to further explore the universe and answer questions in his ever-inquisitive mind.

WILLIAM H. APPLETON

First Lieutenant, U.S. Army
Company "H," Fourth U.S. Colored Infantry
American Civil War

Born: March 24, 1843, Chichester, New Hampshire
Died: Unknown
Entered Service: Portsmouth, New Hampshire
Medal of Honor—Date of Issue: 18 February 1891
Battles: Siege of Petersburg, Virginia
               Newmarket, Virginia

CITATION
"The first man of the 18th Corps to enter the enemy's works at Petersburg, Virginia, 15 June 1864. Valiant service in a desperate assault at Newmarket Heights, Virginia, inspiring the Union troops by his example of steady courage."

ALTHOUGH LIEUTENANT APPLETON WAS CITED FOR HIS valor and exemplary leadership at two battles, he and his regiment most probably saw many other engagements and action.

The Fourth U.S. Colored Regiment was part of the Union's Army of the Shenandoah commanded by General Franz Sigel. In the spring of 1864, Sigel was to maneuver up the Shenandoah Valley to Staunton and cut east over the Blue Ridge Mountains toward Richmond in a pincer movement to join Grant's Army of the Potomac.

As Sigel's army advanced up the Shenandoah Valley, it was met by a crack Confederate force at Newmarket and routed. In this battle, the corps of cadets from Virginia Military Institute greatly distinguished itself.

General Grant maneuvered his troops toward Richmond but his assault on June 3 failed and he moved on to the town of Petersburg. Most of the railroads that tied Richmond to the South came through Petersburg. If the Union Army arrived before the Confederates got there, Richmond would have to be abandoned. Lee managed to slip into Petersburg first and man the city's defenses. The Union attacks failed and Grant had to settle for a siege.

This turned into trench warfare strongly resembling that of World War I. Frontal attacks on properly held entrenchments were doomed to failure. It was during this attack that Lieutenant Appleton led the way on an assault that was eventually pushed back.

But Grant saw a new opportunity at Petersburg. A regiment of Pennsylvania coal miners dug a five hundred-foot tunnel under the Confederate lines. Several tons of black powder were placed there and detonated on July 30. It blew an enormous gap in the defensive entrenchments and for an hour or more the way was open for the Union troops to take Petersburg. Somehow the assault failed and Grant's great chance to end the war in one day had vanished.

Of the fifteen Medals of Honor awarded to black soldiers in the Civil War, 14 were awarded for exemplary actions during the siege of Petersburg.

George Eugene Belknap

Rear Admiral, U.S. Navy
American Civil War

Born: January 22, 1832, Newport, New Hampshire
Died: April 7, 1903, Key West, Florida
Buried: Arlington National Cemetery
Commander of Civil War Ironclad Steam Frigate *New Ironsides*

GEORGE BELKNAP WAS APPOINTED A MIDSHIPMAN IN October 1847. He became a passed midshipman on June 1853 and a master in 1855. He was commissioned a lieutenant on September 16, 1855. In this position, he commanded a launch at the capture of the Barrier forts at the mouth of the Canton River, China, in November 1856. He also assisted in undermining and blowing up the forts.

Lieutenant Belknap married Ellen Reed in December 1861. During the Civil War, he commanded attack boats of the *St. Louis* at the reinforcement of Fort Pickens in 1861. Belknap became executive officer and later commanded the ironclad steam frigate, *New Ironsides* in her various engagements at Charleston Harbor from 1862-1864. He was highly praised by Admirals DuPont and Dahlgren for his ability to make attacks and manage his vessel while under enemy fire.

In 1864, Belknap commanded the gun-boat *Seneca* of the North Atlantic blocking squadron. He later commanded the *Canonicus* in two actions against Howlett House Battery and Fort Fisher. After the capture of Fort Fisher, he went to Charleston and was present at the city's evacuation.

Belknap also commanded the same vessel in Admiral Gordon's expedition to Havana in search of the Confederate ironclad, the *Stonewall*. He received further commendations for his efficient handling of this new type of vessel.

In 1866, he married Frances Prescott. In 1867–68, Commander Belknap commanded the flagship *Hartford* of the Asiatic Squadron. From 1869 through 1873, he was on duty at the Boston Navy Yard.

In 1874, Belknap was given command of the steamer *Tuscarora* in taking deep-sea soundings in the North Pacific Ocean. The object of the research to find a route for a submarine cable between the United States and Japan. Belknap discovered a wide, deep underwater trench, which he named *Tuscarora* for his ship. His discovery and notations of the topography of the ocean bed were praised by scientists around the world.

In March 1885, he was promoted to commodore (one star) and appointed superintendent of the Naval Observatory in Washington. Later in his career, he was the senior officer in Honolulu at the time of disturbances during the election of King Kalukaua. At various times he was in command of U.S. Navy yards at Norfolk, Virginia, Pensacola, Florida, and Mare Island, California. Admiral Belknap also commanded the USS *Alaska* in South American waters during the hostilities between Peru and Chile.

He was promoted to rear admiral in 1889. He was forced to retire in 1892 at age sixty after forty five years of active duty. He died in 1903 in Key West.

George Belknap's son, Reginald Rowan Belknap (1871–1959) was also a rear admiral in the U.S. Navy. In 1919, on January fourteenth, the destroyer USS *Belknap* DD-251 was launched.

Father and son are buried at Arlington National Cemetery.

John Adams Dix

Major General
War of 1812
American Civil War

Born: July 24, 1798, Boscowan, New Hampshire
Died: April 21, 1879, New York, New York
Buried: Trinity Church Cemetery, New York City
Education: Phillips Exeter Academy, Exeter, New Hampshire
            College of Montreal
Honors: U.S. Senator, New York, 1845-1849
            U.S. Secretary of the Treasury, 1861
            Governor, State of New York, 1872
            Fort Dix, New Jersey (named in his honor), 1917

IN 1812, AFTER HIS EDUCATION AT PHILLIPS EXETER AND
the College of Montreal, Dix became a cadet in the U.S. Army and
saw service on the Canadian frontier. He resigned from the Army
in 1826 and two years later began to practice law in Cooperstown,
New York. Dix was appointed adjutant general of New York State
in 1830 and was secretary of state from1833 to1839.

He served as a U.S. Senator from 1845 to1849 filling out the
unexpired term of Senator Silas Wright and aligned himself with
the anti-slavery democrats. He retired from politics and for the next
decade was active in railroad promotion and practiced law in New
York City. In January 1861, he was appointed U.S. Postmaster and
afterward, Secretary of the Treasury by President James Buchanan.
While in this post, Dix coined the memorable line, "If anyone
attempts to haul down the American flag, shoot him on the spot,"
part of a message sent to treasury agents in New Orleans ordering
the arrest of the captain of a revenue cutter for his refusal to sail his
ship to New York.

At the outbreak of the Civil War, Dix, as head of the Union
Defense Committee, organized seventeen regiments and was
commissioned a major general of volunteers. Though he saw no
fighting, he helped save Maryland for the Union cause by his active

defense measures. In May 1862, he was sent to Fort Monroe, Virginia, and after the New York draft riots of July 1863, was appointed commander of the Department of the East in New York City. He remained in that position until July 1865, when he returned to civilian life.

Dix was minister to France 1866-1869 and although a Democrat, he was elected governor of New York State on the Republican ticket in 1872.

In 1917, construction was begun on a World War I Army training camp in New Jersey. This camp was named Camp Dix in his honor. In 1939 it became a permanent army post and was redesignated Fort Dix.

GEORGE HENRY WADLEIGH

Rear Admiral, U.S. Navy
American Civil War
Spanish-American War

Born: September 28, 1842, Dover, New Hampshire
Died: July 11, 1927, Dover
Education: U.S. Naval Academy, 1863

GEORGE H. WADLEIGH WAS BORN IN DOVER, NEW Hampshire, on September 28, 1842. He attended the U.S. Naval Academy at Annapolis, Maryland. He became midshipman in 1860 and was graduated in 1863, in the midst of the Civil War. He was immediately assigned to combat duty on the steam sloops *Lackawanna* and *Richmond* blockading New Orleans and other Gulf of Mexico ports.

When the Civil War ended, Lieutenant Wadleigh sailed in European and Mediterranean Waters. In July 1865, he was assigned to the USS *Ticonderoga* and was promoted to lieutenant commander in March 1868. For the next decade, Wadleigh had shore duty. He was an instructor at the Naval Academy, teaching communications and torpedo work.

Back on sea duty, he served as executive officer on the gunboat *Shawmut*, the monitor *Canonica*, the schoolship *St. Mary's* and the sloop *Pensacola*. In 1881, he was skipper of the USS *Alliance*, his first sea command during an arduous Arctic cruise searching for survivors of the ill-fated Jeanette expedition.

Commander Wadleigh served at the Portsmouth Navy Yard in 1878 and returned in December 1882 for a second tour. He also served at the Boston Navy Yard. His next sea duty was as commander of the *Michigan* into the 1890's. He was promoted to captain in July 1894 and then commanded the *Richmond* and the *Minneapolis*.

Captain Wadleigh served as president of the General Court Martial Board at Norfolk, Virginia, and captain of the yard at Boston Navy Yard until June 1898. These were very busy months, as the Navy prepared ships for the Spanish-American War operations. From July 1898 until December 1901, Captain Wadleigh was commanding officer of the cruiser *Philadelphia* in the Pacific and the *Wabash* at Boston Harbor.

George Wadleigh was promoted to rear admiral in February 1902. He served briefly as the commandant of the Philadelphia Navy Yard and president of the Board of Inspection and Survey before retiring from active duty in July 1902. He returned to his hometown of Dover, New Hampshire and lived there until his death, July 11, 1927.

On April 5, 1943, the keel of the destroyer DD-689 USS *Wadleigh* was laid at the Bath Iron Works in Maine. The ship was launched on August 7, 1943, sponsored by Miss Clara Wadleigh, daughter of the late Rear Admiral George Wadleigh.

The DD-689 *Wadleigh* saw extensive service during World War II in the Marshall Islands and the invasion of Saipan Island. Following escort runs to Eniwetok and Guadalcanal, the *Wadleigh* supported the invasion of Palau.

While on mine-sweeping duties the ship was badly damaged. The *Wadleigh* limped back to Pearl Harbor and then on to Mare Island, California, for repairs. She returned to Pacific duty and was stationed near the battleship *Missouri* when the Japanese signed the official surrender papers ending World War II.

In 1961, the *Wadleigh* was part of the naval group to recover New Hampshire astronaut Alan Shepard after his history-making ride into space.

JOHN L. THOMPSON

Brigadier General, New Hampshire Cavalry
American Civil War

Born: 1835, Plymouth, New Hampshire
Died: 1888, Chicago, Illinois
Buried: Groveland Cemetery, Chicago
Education: Dartmouth and Williams Colleges, 1852-1856
Harvard Law School, 1858
Battles: Fredericksburg
               Port Royal
               Cedar Mountain
               Second Bull Run
               Chancellorsville
               Middleburg
               Gettysburg

JOHN THOMPSON GREW UP IN PLYMOUTH, NEW Hampshire, and attended Kimball Union Academy. At seventeen, he entered Dartmouth College. He transferred to Williams College for his sophomore year and then to Worcester, Massachusetts, where he studied law. Thompson entered Harvard Law School in 1856 and graduated in 1858. That same year, he was admitted to the Massachusetts bar. He studied at universities in Munich, Paris, and Berlin, then returned to the United States and practiced law in Chicago.

Thompson enlisted as a private on April 19, 1861, in the First Illinois Light Artillery. He completed his ninety-day enlistment as a corporal, but poor health forced him to resign and he returned to Worcester. While recuperating there, he was commissioned by New Hampshire Governor Berry as a first lieutenant in A Company, part of an all New England cavalry regiment. This regiment became part of the First Rhode Island cavalry which rode to Washington, D.C. in the spring of 1862. The unit was then attached to General McDowell's forces at Fredericksburg, Virginia.

The regiment fought at Port Royal, Cedar Mountain, Virginia, the second battle at Bull Run (Manassas), Fredericksburg, and Chancellorsville. The unit moved west where they fought at Middleburg, Virginia, in June 1863. At this battle, the regiment with only 250 men was surrounded by Confederate General Jeb Stuart's Virginia Cavalry and 175 men were killed or captured. Good recruiting in New Hampshire soon brought the strength back up to two hundred men. The regiment fought at this strength July 2-4, 1863, at Gettysburg.

Thompson's promotions were rapid, e.g., only five days from first lieutenant to captain, nine months to major, ten days to lt. colonel and eleven months to full colonel. The Civil War battles were fought using old-fashioned tactics, such as frontal assaults against heavily fortified enemy. This resulted in massive casualties in a single unit, where commanding officers in the lead in front of their unit were wounded or killed outright. The next officer in the chain of command was suddenly the new Colonel.

In January 1864, the New Hampshire battalion separated from the First Rhode Island Cavalry and became the nucleus of the First New Hampshire Cavalry. Thompson resigned his commission for four months but returned to command the First New Hampshire Cavalry at Harper's Ferry. The regiment fought with General Philip Sheridan's forces at Winchester, Virginia, and at Cedar Creek. At Waynesboro, Thompson's men were the first to breach the enemy's breastworks and capture its artillery.

General Sheridan recognized the bravery of the First New Hampshire Cavalry by putting them in charge of escort/guarding fifteen hundred rebel prisoners and getting them one hundred miles to Sheridan's base. The mission was successful and Thompson was brevetted to brigadier general on March 13, 1865.

General Thompson was well respected by his men and others for his courtesy, soldierly bearing, and constant concern for the welfare of his men. After the war, he returned to his Chicago law firm. He was active in many Chicago social clubs, but chose never to enter the political arena. He is buried at Groveland Cemetery in Chicago.

GILMAN MARSTON

Brigadier General
American Civil War

Born:	August 20, 1811, Oxford, New Hampshire
Died:	July 3, 1890, Exeter, New Hampshire
Buried:	Exeter
Education:	Dartmouth College, 1837
	Harvard Law School, 1840
Battles:	First Manassas (Bull Run)
	Fredericksburg
	Williamsburg
	Gettysburg
	Fair Oaks
	Drury's Bluff
	Richmond
	Cold Harbor
	Malvern Hill
	Petersburg

GILMAN MARSTON SERVED IN THE NEW HAMPSHIRE House of Representatives, from 1845 to 1849. In 1859 he was elected to the U.S. Congress as a member of the newly formed Republican Party. He served from 1859 to 1863 and 1865-67. His congressional service was interrupted by the Civil War.

He was appointed colonel of the Second Volunteer Regiment which mustered on June 4, 1861. Rev. John Wesley Adams was his regiment's chaplain. Only weeks later, Colonel Marston's arm was shattered by a Confederate musket ball at the first battle at Bull Run. He wisely refused amputation and recovered in time to lead the Second New Hampshire as part of General Joe Hooker's Second Division at the Battles of Williamsburg, Fair Oaks, Richmond, Malvern Hill, and Fredericksburg.

When military operations were suspended for the winter of 1862-63, Marston returned to Washington, D.C. where he attended

to his congressional duties. In April 1863, he was appointed brigadier general of volunteers.

Marston led the Second New Hampshire at Gettysburg where
more than 60 percent of the regiment was killed, wounded, or
missing. The Second and Twelfth New Hampshire Regiments were
combined into a brigade. Marston commanded them as guards and
established a prisoner-of-war camp at Point Lookout, Maryland,
from July 1863 through April 1864.

In late April, he led the brigade in the assault on Drury's Bluff,
Virginia. They then moved on to Cold Harbor, where in less than
an hour his unit lost five hundred men. The survivors marched to
join the siege at Petersburg, Virginia, and then to James River. Marston became ill and took sick leave. He never fully recovered and
resigned his commission after the fall of Richmond. The Second
New Hampshire Regiment had marched over 6,000 miles and
fought in twenty battles, 1861-1865, under the command of Colonel
Marston. The regiment lost more than one thousand of its three
thousand men during those four years.

Back in New Hampshire, Marston was reelected to Congress
in 1865, after which he returned to Exeter to practice law. In 1870,
he was offered appointment as the first governor of the Idaho territory, but declined. He organized the Exeter Water Company, which
local citizens refused to support. Marston filled a short vacancy
in the U.S. Senate, from March 4 to June 18, 1889. He remained in
Exeter until his death in 1890.

KOREAN EXPEDITION

1871

FREDERICK H. FRANKLIN

Quartermaster, U.S. Navy
Korean Expedition, 1871

Born: 1840, Portsmouth, New Hampshire
Died: May 10, 1873,
Buried: Proprietors Cemetery, Portsmouth
Award: Medal of Honor

Citation
G.O.#169, 8 February 1872

"On board the USS Colorado *during the attack and capture of the Korean forts on Kangwha Island, 11 June 1871.
Assuming command of Company D, after Lt. McKee was
wounded, Franklin handled the company with great credit
until relieved."*

James F. Merton

Landsman, U.S. Navy
Korean Expedition, 1871

Born: 1845, Cheshire, England
Entered service: Portsmouth, New Hampshire
Died: Unknown
Buried: Unknown
Award: Medal of Honor

Citation:
G.O.#180, October 10, 1872

"Landsman, USS Colorado, *Merton was severely wounded in
the arm while trying to force his way into the fort."*

THE FIFTEEN MEDALS OF HONOR AWARDED FOR THE ACTION
in Korea, 1871, were the first presented for foreign service against
an enemy.

Two of those Medals of Honor went to New Hampshire men.
Both were Navy men who served aboard the USS *Colorado*. Their
citations are brief and poignant.

In 1866, the American merchant ship *General Sherman* was
destroyed and its crew massacred in the Taedong River below
Pyongyang, Korea. U.S. ships were sent to investigate but resolved
nothing. This incident led commanders of the Asiatic Squadron to
interest themselves in the possibility of a treaty to open Korea to
trade using "gunboat diplomacy." This took on the semblance of
Admiral Perry's expedition to Japan.

A force of five U.S. ships-of-war totaling eighty five guns,
dropped anchor at the mouth of the Han River. Unlike Perry's
expedition or Admiral Rodgers' force against the Bey of Tunis, who
quickly capitulated, the king of Korea was out of range of the big
naval guns. The Korean king ordered his troops to open fire on the
Americans. Admiral Rodgers ordered an attack on the Choji forts
on Kanghwa Island. Although Rodgers had sufficient strength to
capture the forts, he could not force Korea to sign a treaty.

On July 3 the American expedition withdrew. Seth Allen, U.S. Navy, and Denis Hanrahan, U.S. Marine Corps, were buried on Boisee (Jakyak) Island. Lt. Hugh Wilson McKee, USN, wounded in action, died aboard the USS *Monocacy*. He was buried in his hometown of Lexington, Kentucky. For this action, Medals of Honor were awarded to six U.S. Marines and nine sailors, including New Hampshire's Frederick Franklin and James Merton.

Indian Campaigns

1861–1894

THE TERM "INDIAN WARS" IS MISLEADING BECAUSE IT groups American Indians under a single heading. The Native Americans, referred to as Indians, are a diverse category of people and tribes, each with its own history.

The Indian Wars were, instead campaigns—a series of battles with various tribes from colonial times to the closing of the American frontier in the 1890s. To see the Indian Wars as a racial conflict between natives and European settlers, also misunderstands the complex historical facts. For example, during the American Revolutionary War, the Oneida tribe of the Iroquois Nation sided with the American colonists while four other tribes of their Iroquois Confederacy, sided with the British.

Many battles against Native Americans were fought in the South (the Creek and Seminole Wars, 1818-1835), also in the old northwestern territory of Ohio and Indiana (Blackhawk War, the Battle of Tippecanoe in1811).

Generally, the Indian campaigns era is regarded as those battles fought in the west from 1861 through 1890.

Apache and Navajo, 1861-1886
Sioux Uprising, 1862
Red Cloud's War, 1866-1868
The Colorado War, 1864-1865
The Modoc War, 1872-1873
Black Hills War, 1876-1877
Massacre of Wounded Knee, December 1890

Fear, fatigue, poor rations, and little appreciation from his countrymen—that was the lot of the U.S. soldier whose job it was to enforce the nation's arrogant and often confusing Indian policies. In 1845, the territory from the Mississippi to the Pacific was home to more than three hundred thousand proud and possessive Indians. Less than fifty years later, the army had established complete control over the West.

The common soldier probably did not approve of all that happened during those bloody years, but generally he got the job done, despite appalling odds. In 1867, at the Wagon Box fight, forty soldiers stood off one thousand native warriors. Once, when an officer was asked why his troop had not set up a stronger defensive position, he snapped, "I have no troop, only three men."

At times of rest or easy duty, the soldiers may have found they actually enjoyed the easy camaraderie of the western outposts. But more often they were out on the plains making, as the saying went, "forty miles a day on beans and hay," praying they would never see an Indian, yet half wishing they would so they could have it out for once and for all and return home.

The U.S. Army, in 1905, created a campaign medal for the "Indian Wars." It was awarded retroactively to any U.S. Army soldier who participated in military actions against Native American Indians—for the period of 1865-1891.

The medal (campaign ribbon) was issued as a one-time only decoration. No devices or service stars were to accompany it to denote participation in multiple actions. The only attachment to the medal was the Silver Citation Star for meritorious or heroic conduct. The Silver Citation Star was the predecessor of the Silver Star Medal.

LEONARD WOOD

Major General, U.S. Army
Indian Campaigns
Spanish-American War
World War I

Born: October 9, 1860, Winchester, New Hampshire
Died: August 7, 1927, Boston, Massachusetts
Buried: Arlington National Cemetery
Education: Harvard Medical School
Awards: Medal of Honor, Indian Campaigns, 1886
               Distinguished Service Medal, WWI, 1919
Commands: First Volunteer Cavalry "Rough Riders,"
                  Cuba, 1898
               Military Governor of Cuba, 1899-1902
               Governor General, Philippines, 1903-1908
               Chief of Staff, U.S. Army, 1910-1914

Medal of Honor Citation
LEONARD WOOD
Assistant Surgeon, U.S. Army

*In Apache Campaign, summer of 1886. Entered Service at
Massachusetts. Birth: Winchester, New Hampshire. Date of
Issue: 8 April 1898.*

   *Voluntarily carried dispatches through a region infested
with hostile Indians, making a journey of 70 miles in one night
and walking 30 miles the next day. Also for several weeks, while
in close pursuit of Geronimo's band and constantly expecting
an encounter, commanded a detachment of Infantry, which was
then without an officer, and to the command of which he was
assigned upon his own request.*

LEONARD WOOD WAS THE OLDEST OF THREE CHILDREN
born to Charles Jewett Wood and Caroline Hagar Wood. The
Woods were seventh generation Americans from Cape Cod. Charles
studied medicine in Boston and at Dartmouth College without
receiving a degree. The family lived in Winchester, New Hamp-

shire, for ten years, where Leonard was born. During the Civil War, Charles joined the Union Army, serving as a hospital steward.

After returning from the war, Charles moved his family back to Cape Cod. There, Leonard grew to strong manhood, developing his father's traits of reserve, quiet humor, and self-control and his mother's attention to details. Leonard didn't mind the hard work shoveling coal for the family enterprise. In his spare time, he enjoyed sailing and duck hunting.

Finished with his schooling at eighteen, Leonard wanted to go to the Naval Academy at Annapolis, but did not receive an appointment. His family was firmly opposed to his attending West Point. In the midst of this, his father died. Leonard decided to attend Harvard Medical School.

At Harvard, Leonard Wood did well in most of his classes. His favorite professor was Oliver Wendell Holmes, who taught anatomy. Wood enjoyed Boston's sights and museums and the sociability of his fellow students.

After graduating from Harvard, he interned for a year at Boston City Hospital. Upon completing his internship, Leonard took the examinations to become an Army physician. He did well and was commissioned a first lieutenant assigned to Fort Huachuca, Arizona. During the summer of 1886, Lieutenant Wood served in the campaign against Geronimo and the Apaches. He was awarded the Medal of Honor for his heroic actions.

After four years in Arizona, Wood was assigned to the Presidio, an Army post in San Francisco. While there, he organized the "army" football team that beat the University of California. The tedium of official duties at the Presidio was broken by a trip to Washington, D.C., where Leonard met Louise Adriana Condit-Smith. He returned to Washington five months later and the couple was married on November 18, 1890.

The newlyweds set up housekeeping at the Presidio briefly, then were reassigned to Fort McPherson in Atlanta, Georgia. While at Fort McPherson, Leonard enrolled in classes at the Georgia School of Technology (Georgia Tech). He became a coach and player on their first football team, leading them to their first victory, beating the University of Georgia 28 to 6.

Wood was called the "Iron Man" because he seemed so hard to hurt. He was cut over his eye, but finished playing the game. In the locker room, he sewed up the cut himself, looking in a mirror.

In 1895, the Woods were posted to Washington, Louise's hometown. Leonard became the personal physician to Presidents Grover Cleveland and William McKinley through 1898. During that period, he developed a friendship with Theodore Roosevelt, who was then Assistant Secretary of the Navy. They would go on extended walks together and Roosevelt remarked that, "Leonard is the only man that can outwalk me!"

When the war with Spain began, in 1898, Leonard Wood was given authority as colonel to raise the First Volunteer Cavalry Regiment, commonly known as "the Rough Riders." Lt. Col. Theodore Roosevelt, second in command, took charge when Wood was promoted to general. Colonel Wood commanded the First Regiment at Las Guasimas and two regular cavalry regiments at the famous charge and taking of San Juan Hill. On July 8, 1898, he was appointed brigadier general for these actions.

After the surrender of Santiago City, Wood was appointed governor of the captured city. Later he was made governor of all of eastern Cuba. In this capacity, he was responsible for improving the food and water supply and sanitation of the province by building public works and maintaining order. On December 7, 1898, he was appointed major general for his services to the people of the captured territory. One year later, General Wood was appointed military governor of Cuba. He continued in this position until the territory was transferred, as an organized republic to the duly elected Cuban government and Thomas Estrada Palma, the newly elected president on May 20, 1902.

During this period of reorganization, laws and sanitation regulations were enforced. It was under General Wood's supervision that Major Walter Reed and his assistants in the medical division, conducted experiments that led to the discovery that mosquitoes transmit yellow fever (malaria) and, consequently, its control. The death rate on the island was greatly reduced. In 1903, Wood was confirmed as major general in the Regular Army. In March of that year he was transferred to the Philippine Islands and became governor of Moro Province. In 1906, he was named to command the Philippine division of the Army after suppressing the Moro uprising.

General Wood returned to the United States in 1908 and served two years as commander of the Department of the East. President Taft appointed Wood to the post of Army Chief of Staff in 1910, a position he held for four years. Throughout this period, he labored to advance the nation's military preparedness. The establishment of reserve officers training camps at Plattsburg, New York was largely the result of his efforts and direction. During World War I, General Wood was not given an overseas post. He was passed over by a junior officer, John J. Pershing, who commanded the American Expeditionary Force. Wood's contribution to the Allied victory was considerable, as he organized and trained the 89th Division and the 10th Regular Division at Camp Funston, Kansas.

The government created a furor in June 1918 by relieving Wood of his command of the 89th Division just before its embarkation for Europe. This apparent hostility toward the general had the effect of making him a hero in the eyes of President Wilson's critics. In 1920, Wood solicited the presidential nomination of the Republican Party. He was one of the leading candidates, receiving 314 votes on one ballot before the decision to go with Warren G. Harding was made in the famous "smoke filled room."

In 1921, the University of Pennsylvania chose Wood to be its leader, a position he held only briefly. He was granted a leave of absence to become Governor General of the Philippines, a post he held until his death. He was disturbed by the economic instability of the islands and the weakened position of his office. He endeavored to correct both by firm and at times autocratic rule. Although successful, he was vilified by the independence-minded Filipinos and severely criticized in Washington. He returned to the United States seeking treatment of a tumor resulting from an earlier head injury. He died on the operating table of a Boston hospital.

General Wood is buried in Arlington National Cemetery with his wife, Louise Adrianna Wood (1869–1943) and their son, Captain Leonard Wood, Jr. (1892–1931). Fort Leonard Wood, Missouri, is named in his honor.

George Emerson Albee

Captain, U.S. Army
Indian Campaigns

Born: January 27 1845, Lisbon, New Hampshire
Died: March 24, 1918
Buried: Arlington National Cemetery

While serving with the 41st Infantry Regiment Albee received the Medal of Honor for action at Brazos River, Texas, on October 28, 1869.

Medal of Honor Issued 18 January 1894

CITATION

"For action at Brazos River, Texas, 28 Oct. 1869, Lt. Albee, with two men, attacked a force of eleven Indians, drove them from the hills and reconnoitered the country beyond."

LIEUTENANT ALBEE ENTERED THE SERVICE FROM Owatomma, Minnesota.

  His wife, Mary Hawes Albee, is buried with him in Arlington National Cemetery, Virginia.

Spanish-American War

1898

WHEN THE FIGHT FOR INDEPENDENCE BROKE OUT IN THE Spanish colony of Cuba in 1895, Spain took vigorous action to crush it. The U.S. government saw no grounds for intervention, but the American public, stirred by tales of Spanish brutality, developed a belligerent spirit.

The Spanish minister in Washington made derogatory remarks about President McKinley and six days later (February 15, 1898) the battleship *Maine* was blown up in Havana Harbor, killing 260 American sailors and Marines. Although Spain had agreed to end hostilities in Cuba, McKinley and Congress yielded to popular clamor and in April took the country to war.

Commodore George Dewey sailed the Asiatic squadron of six ships into Manila Bay, Philippines, on May 1st. This was a key Spanish outpost. America's small peacetime army of twenty-one hundred officers and twenty-eight thousand men was doubled. The call went out for volunteers—more than a million Americans volunteered.

General William Shafter landed the first American troops in Cuba on June 20. The principle campaign lasted from June 30 to July 13 resulting in the capture of Santiago on the southeast coast. The Spanish fleet had slipped unseen into Santiago Harbor. During this fighting, Colonel Theodore Roosevelt, under General Leonard Wood, led the First Volunteer Cavalry (the Rough Riders) in the dramatic capture of San Juan Hill.

The Spanish fleet in Santiago Harbor attempted to withdraw on July 3, but was demolished by American warships, thus ending Spain's ability to continue the war. General Nelson Miles overran Puerto Rico and on August 13 American troops in the Philippines captured Manila. Although the combat performance of the U.S. Army and Navy looked impressive, it actually revealed many serious shortcomings, which led to a major reorganization of the defense establishment.

On August 12 a truce was effected. In the treaty, signed in Paris on December 10, 1898, Spain relinquished Cuba, Puerto Rico, and Guam outright and ceded the Philippines for twenty million dollars in payment for public improvements. The treaty was denounced by many Americans as blatant imperialism. For better or worse, the American flag now flew over lands in far off places.

The Spanish-American War brought the U.S. government serious problems regarding the ultimate status of these conquered lands. In Cuba, where the U.S. professed no claim, General Leonard Wood was placed in charge of a provisional government as a virtual protectorate. However, Cuba was given self-governing status in 1902. The Philippines remained a territory until granted independence in 1946.

WALTER SCOTT WEST

Private, U.S .Marine Corps
Spanish-American War

Born: March 13, 1872, Bradford, New Hampshire
Died: September 14, 1943
Buried: Forest Hills Cemetery, Jamaica Plain, Massachusetts

MEDAL OF HONOR—CITATION—
7 JULY 1899—G.O. #521

"On board the U.S.S. Marblehead *during the operation of cutting the cable leading from Cienfuegos, Cuba, 11 May 1898. Facing the heavy fire of the enemy, West displayed extraordinary bravery and coolness throughout this action."*

A MONTH BEFORE THE BATTLES OF EL CHANEY AND SAN Juan Hill, the cruisers USS *Nashville* and USS *Marblehead* were dispatched to cut the underwater cables at Cienfuegos, Cuba. These cables were the main communication lines between Havana and Spain.

Two steam launches, one from each ship, sailed with fifty-two sailors and Marine sharpshooters to provide cover. Each launch was armed with a one-pound Hotchkiss gun. The launches had to drag the ocean floor with grappling hooks within range of intense small arms fire from shore.

One at a time, the six-inch armored cables were hoisted and laboriously cut with axes and handsaws. Spanish reinforcements arrived, increasing the deadly fire on the two launches, which were hit repeatedly and began to sink. Finally, the second cable was severed and the sailors and marines left the rain of enemy fire.

During this operation, three Americans were killed, and six were wounded. Walter Scott West was cited for his bravery and coolness while protecting his comrades.

Robert Henry Rolfe

Colonel, U.S. Army
Spanish-American War
World War I

Born: October 16, 1863, Concord, New Hampshire
Died: October 27, 1932, San Antonio, Texas
Buried: Arlington National Cemetery
Education: Dartmouth College, 1884

ROBERT H. ROLFE WAS THE SON OF HENRY PEARSON ROLFE, U.S. district attorney and Mary (Sherburne) Rolfe. He graduated from Concord High School. At Dartmouth College, Rolfe was a member of Kappa Kappa Kappa fraternity, a champion long distance runner, and a member of the first Dartmouth football team. He graduated with a bachelor of arts degree in 1884.

Rolfe married Grace Stearns, the daughter of New Hampshire Governor Onslow Stearns. They had three children, Mary Rebecca Rolfe, Grace Stearns Rolfe, and Onslow S. Rolfe (a West Point graduate awarded the Distinguished Service Cross for gallantry during World War I, and brigadier general commanding the 71st Division in World War II).

In 1884, Rolfe began his long military career as an enlisted man in the Third Regiment of the New Hampshire National Guard, rising to command that unit as its colonel in 1894. When war with Spain was declared in 1898, Rolfe was named Colonel of the first New Hampshire Volunteer Infantry. The unit was assigned to duty at Chickamauga, Tennessee. The fighting was over before they were sent to Cuba.

Following Rolfe's honorable discharge from volunteer service, he was appointed captain in the regular army in the Quartermaster Corps. He accompanied General Brooke to Cuba, serving under him and General Leonard Wood as Inspector General from 1899 to 1902. Rolfe's duties of inspecting civilian monetary accounts and transportation took him all over Cuba, giving him an intimate knowledge of the people and the geography of the island.

From 1902 through 1905, Major Rolfe had charge of the construction of Fort Rosecrans, near San Diego, California. He built the post from a "site of sage brush to a complete military post."

He was assigned to Nagasaki, Japan from 1905 to 1907 as the Army Depot Quartermaster, handling and repairing transport ships, purchasing and accepting of eighty thousand tons of coal and food supplies annually. During his off-duty time, he traveled through mainland China and Korea as well as Japan.

In 1912, Colonel Rolfe spent a month in Mexico visiting all the U.S.–Mexican border crossing points from Brownsville, Texas, to Yuma, Arizona. In 1913, while at Fort Sam Houston, Texas, Colonel Rolfe was issued the first auto truck purchased by the United States Army.

In 1917, while at the Philadelphia Depot, Colonel Rolfe purchased and organized (including a garage unit) a fleet of thirty three-ton Packard trucks for military use—the forerunner of the Army Transportation Corps.

During World War I, Rolfe served in Washington, D.C., and then was assigned to Gievres, France, in 1919 under General Pershing. He went on to London, for eighteen months to settle and close the U.S.-English accounts for the war. He handled 196 million dollars from the comptroller general. He returned to Washington in 1921 where he remained until 1924. Colonel Rolfe was assigned to Fort Sam Houston, Texas, for two years. "Fort Sam," at the time, was one of the largest posts in the U.S. Army. Rolfe was responsible for the disbursement of more than one million dollars annually. He supplied food, fuel, pay, clothing, quarters and transportation for twenty-five hundred soldiers and eighteen hundred animals.

In 1926, Colonel Rolfe was assigned to Fort Huachuca, Arizona, where he stayed until October 16, 1927, at which time he reached the age of sixty-four and passed from active duty to the retired list of Army officers. He and his wife moved to San Antonio, where they lived until his death in 1932. He was buried with full military honors at Arlington National Cemetery.

During Colonel Rolfe's forty-three years of military service, he served in two wars and never fought a battle in combat. Colonel Rolfe is considered a "man of granite" for his continuous, sustained excellent service that kept the combat soldiers fed, clothed, and supplied with weapons and ammunition; provided horseshoes and hay for the horses, tires and gas for the trucks.

THE BOXER REBELLION

1900

"BOXERS" WAS THE NAME GIVEN TO MEMBERS OF A CHINESE secret society that spearheaded a violent anti-foreign movement in northern China in 1900. China had been defeated and humiliated in wars with Great Britain, Japan, and France. Western communities were established on Chinese soil, yet were not subject to Chinese law. Missionaries freely taught their doctrines, which contradicted the teachings of Chinese sages.

Some Manchu princes gave their encouragement and protection to the Boxer movement and persuaded the embittered dowager empress that the Boxers could be used to drive the hated foreigners and their works from their country. When anti-foreign troops and Boxers moved into Peking (now Beijing), the foreign community in the capital was seriously threatened.

The crisis came in June 1900 in Peking. The senior foreign minister, Great Britain's Sir Claude MacDonald, requested a sizable relief force be sent, just before the telegraph lines were cut. More than 430 sailors and Marines from eight countries (including fifty-six Americans from the USS *Oregon* and USS *Newark*) arrived at legations in Peking on June 4. On June 9, the Boxers began their attack.

One allied force departed the city of Tientsin on June 10 under the command of British Admiral Sir Edward Seymour. However, strong opposition by the Boxers and Imperial Chinese Army forced Seymour's column to return to Tientsin on June 22. After regrouping, Seymour assembled a larger force of twenty thousand men (two thousand Americans, five hundred of which were sailors and Marines). After fighting two major battles against huge Chinese forces, the relief column reached the foreign legations at Peking on August 14. China suffered a devastating blow to her prestige and power. The weakened Chinese state could not interfere in the 1904–05 Russo-Japanese War, which eventually secured Japanese domination in the Far East.

The United States was able to play a significant role in suppressing the Boxer Rebellion because large numbers of American ships and troops were stationed in the Philippines as a result of the conquest of the Philippine Islands during the Spanish-American War. The Boxer Rebellion, in military minds, reinforced the need to retain control of the Philippines and to maintain a strong presence in the Far East.

William E. Holyoke

Boatswains Mate First Class, U.S. Navy
China Relief Expedition: Boxer Rebellion

Born: March 13, 1868, Groveton, New Hampshire
Died: April 3, 1934
Buried: Charles Evans Cemetery, Reading,
              Pennsylvania

MEDAL OF HONOR CITATION

"In action with the relief expedition of the allied forces in China 13, 20, 21 & 22 June 1900. During this period and in the presence of the enemy, Holyoke distinguished himself by meritorious conduct."

WORLD WAR I

1917–1918

PRESIDENT WOODROW WILSON'S HOPE TO PROMOTE world peace was rudely dashed with the drift of Europe toward war. Nationalism, militarism, and imperialism were under rapid, rabid development. The triple alliance of Germany, Austria, and Italy stood face-to-face against the triple entente of Great Britain, France, and Russia—each waiting for the other to blink first. American diplomacy to prevent an explosion proved futile.

A month after the assassination of Austrian Archduke Francis Ferdinand in Sarajevo, Austria declared war on Serbia (July 28, 1914). Within days, Germany and Austria were at war with Russia, France, Belgium, and Great Britain. President Wilson exhorted the American public to "be impartial in thought as well as in action."

Under international law, neutrality is a precise relationship between belligerent and neutral nations. Both Great Britain and Germany's navies broke the rules of neutrality. The significant difference in the violations was that British ships stopped vessels to confiscate contraband; the German submarines sank the merchant ships taking lives. The torpedoing of the British ship *Lusitania* on May 7, 1915, which drowned two thousand people, including more than one hundred Americans, sent a wave of warlike emotion through the United States.

President Wilson protested the incident, but learned that diplomacy, not backed by military force, was ineffectual. America was unprepared for war until Congress moved to build up the Army,

135

Navy and Merchant Marine by creating the Council of National Defense to mobilize the country's resources.

Originally a European war, this conflict had mushroomed into a World War involving Italy, Turkey, Greece, and Portugal as well as large military contingents from Australia, New Zealand, and India. Fierce fighting continued on the eastern front in Russia and on the southern front in Turkey, Palestine, Syria, and Arabia.

While fighting dragged on in the western front in Europe, Germany resorted to unrestricted submarine warfare. More American vessels were sunk. Wilson finally admitted the failure of his pacifist methods on April 6, 1917, and asked Congress for a declaration of war between the United States and Germany. Germany seriously underestimated the amount and kind of American involvement in the war. The United States, since 1915, had been shipping to the Allies vast amounts of food, metals, and explosives on credit.

The U.S. Navy blockaded the North Sea. In June 1917, the first ground units—Army and Marines—of the American Expeditionary Force, landed in France. The AEF was commanded by Major General John J. "Black Jack" Pershing and was assigned a quiet sector at the right of the western front between Belfort and Verdun, France. The main force of American troops arrived in March 1918. The 250,000 Americans then in France increased to one million by July and two million by November. Two-thirds of the twenty-nine U.S. divisions saw combat.

In March 1918, Germany launched its massive campaign to end the war. The submarine campaign had failed, but the collapse of Russia allowed Germany to concentrate on France. The German strategy was to drive a wedge between the British and the French units. This thrust was blunted by the American divisions, now organized as a field army. The Battle of Argonne began on September 26, 1918, with forty-six days of continual fighting. The twenty-one American divisions contributed greatly to shattering the German forces along the entire front.

The British minister of munitions, Winston Churchill, later wrote, "The moral consequence of the United States joining the allies was indeed the deciding cause in the conflict."

During the course of World War I, many significant techno-
logical advances were made. The horse cavalry was replaced by
armored tanks. Horse-drawn wagons and artillery pieces were now
hauled by trucks. Machine guns decimated troops, making frontal
assaults obsolete, and mustard gas made its deadly way into the
muddy trenches.

Airplanes, originally used for observation and reconnaissance,
dropped bombs and dueled each other in the skies. Machine guns
mounted on aircraft straifed troops on the ground.

Even after entering the war, President Wilson continued his
efforts to seek a peace settlement. Wilson proclaimed his Fourteen
Points on January 8, 1918, as the basis for lasting peace. Germany
relied on those points when it requested an armistice. The armistice
that came on November 11 saw Germany acknowledge extreme
defeat. The United States, without determining if peace had really
come, rushed headlong into a demobilization of its armed forces,
leaving itself vulnerable to the Japanese attack which would come
in 1941.

Japan joined the Allies in World War I. Her military contribution was limited to the conquest of German-held Tsingtao and
the occupation of German Pacific islands. As a result of this minor
participation, the Japanese empire, at a cost of three hundred lives,
gained control of more than six hundred islands and a vast expansion in the Pacific.

George Dilboy

Private First Class, U.S. Army
World War I

Born: February 5, 1896, Alatsata, Greece
Died: July 18, 1918, Belleau Wood, France
Buried: Arlington National Cemetery
Entered the service in Keene, New Hampshire
Served in Company H, 103rd Infantry Regiment,
     26th Division
Battle: Belleau Wood, France

He was killed in action and posthumously awarded the Medal of Honor. President Wilson presented the medal to his father, Antonios Dilboy.

MEDAL OF HONOR CITATION
General Order No. 13, War Department 1919

After his platoon had gained its objective along a railroad embankment, PFC. Dilboy, accompanying his platoon leader to reconnoiter the ground beyond, was suddenly fired upon by an enemy machinegun from 100 yards. From a standing position on the railroad track, fully exposed to view, he opened fire at once, but failing to silence the gun, rushed forward with his bayonet fixed, through a wheat field toward the gun emplacement, falling within 25 yards of the gun with his right leg nearly severed above the knee and with several bullet holes in his body. With undaunted courage he continued to fire into the emplacement from a prone position, killing two of the enemy and dispersing the rest of the crew.

GEORGE DILBOY GREW UP IN ALATSATA, NEAR SMYRNA, Greece. His family emigrated to America in 1908, settling in Keene, New Hampshire. In 1909, when George was only thirteen, he returned to his homeland to join the Greek army, fighting the Turks. He fought in Thessaly during the first Balkan War of 1912, and stayed on to fight in the second Balkan War of 1913 in Macedonia.

George returned to America attending school in Somerville, Massachusetts. In 1916, he enlisted in the U.S. Army and saw action during the Mexican Border War, 1916–1917. He was honorably discharged, but only a few months later in Keene, he enlisted in the New Hampshire National Guard's Company H, 103 Infantry Regiment. His unit was assigned to the 26th "Yankee" Division on its way to France and World War I. At twenty-one, George had already fought in three wars.

In France, near Belleau Wood, George led an attack against an entrenched German machine gun crew. In his charge, he was mortally wounded, but continued the attack driving the enemy from their position. For is courage, he was posthumously awarded the Medal of Honor. General John Pershing listed George Dilboy as one of the ten greatest heroes of World War I.

PFC Dilboy was buried in France, but at his father's request, the body was shipped to Greece and buried in Alatsata, where it rested peacefully until 1922. That year, during an invasion by the Turks, Dilboy's coffin was dug up.

President Warren G. Harding was enraged by these actions. He ordered the *Litchfield* to retrieve Private Dilboy's remains and demanded an apology from the Turkish government. He got both.

An article in the *New York Times*, Nov. 1, 1923, described the incident. "The Turkish government has made full official amends for the desecration at Alatsata near Smyrna, Greece, at the time of the Turkish advance, Sept. 1922.

On Sept. 7 at Chesmeh, southwest of Smyrna to which PFC. Dilboy's body was brought, an American Honor Guard landed and was saluted by a Turkish Guard of Honor drawn up beside the coffin, which was covered with an American flag.

The coffin was then formally delivered to the American officials and carried aboard the *Litchfield*, full military honors being rendered by both detachments."

PFC Dilboy's body was returned to America, where it was reinterred at Arlington National Cemetery with full military honors. Calvin Coolidge presided at the ceremony.

Dilboy's father, Antonios, wore his son's medal at parades. When the 26th Division passed he would square his shoulders and remember his brave young son.

Antonios, reportedly sent the medal to his family on the island of Crete. During the Second World War, the Nazis raided the home and stole the medal as a souvenir. It was never returned. In April 1999, U.S. Ambassador to Greece Nicholas Burns presented a replacement medal to nephew of Dilboy, Georghios Rosakis of Athens.

Reference:

Georgie! My Georgie! Eddie Brady, Xlibris Books, 2005.

CHARLES A. DOYEN

Brigadier General, U.S. Marine Corps
Spanish-American War
Philippine Insurrection
World War I

Born:	September 3, 1859, Concord, New Hampshire
Died:	October 6, 1918, Quantico, Virginia
Buried:	Arlington National Cemetery
Educated:	U.S. Naval Academy, Annapolis, 1881
Awards:	Distinguished Service Medal, World War I
Battles:	Cuba—Spanish-American War
	Chateau Thierry, France—World War I
	Belleau Wood, France—World War I

CHARLES DOYEN WAS BORN IN CONCORD AND GRADUATED from the U.S. Naval Academy in 1881. He served as a midshipman in the U.S. Marine Corps from 1881 through 1893. He was promoted to second lieutenant in July 1883. Doyen received subsequent promotions until 1898, when he was appointed colonel. He was stationed shipboard off Cuba and Puerto Rico during the Spanish-American War.

During the Philippine Insurrection, 1904-1906, he commanded a Marine battalion and regiment. From 1913 to 1914 he commanded a Marine brigade. Colonel Doyen was reassigned to the United States and was in command of the U.S. Marine barracks in Washington, D.C., at the outbreak of World War I. He was promoted to brigadier general on March 22, 1917. General Doyen left Washington in command of the 5th Marine Regiment on June 5, 1917.

Upon reaching France, he was also put in command of the 6th Marine Regiment and the 4th Machine Gun Battalion comprising the 4th Marine Brigade. In October 1917, General Doyen commanded the 2nd Division until he was replaced by Army General Omar Bradley.

Doyen saw active combat duty in the front line trenches at Chateau-Thierry and Belleau Wood, France. Due to strenuous

141

activity, he was invalided (probably a heart attack) and shipped home in May 1918. He later assumed command of the Marine Training Center at Quantico, Virginia, and remained there until his death in 1919.

General Doyen was buried with full military honors at Arlington National Cemetery. His wife, Claude Fay Doyen, is buried with him.

Two U.S. Navy ships have been named USS *Doyen* for Charles A. Doyen. The first *Doyen*, destroyer DD-280, was commissioned in 1919 and decommissioned in 1930. The second *Doyen*, transport (AP-2/APA-1) was commissioned in 1943 and decommissioned in 1946. The *Doyen* received six battle stars for World War II Service.

INTERIM

1934–1939

JEAN DONAT GRENIER

Second Lieutenant U.S. Army Air Corps
Air Mail Pilot

Born:	November 24, 1909, Manchester, New Hampshire
Died:	February 16, 1934, Oakley, Utah
Buried:	Mount Calvary Cemetery, Manchester
Education:	University of New Hampshire, 1930

JEAN GRENIER WAS BORN IN 1909, THE SON OF MR. AND Mrs. Alphonse Grenier. His father was a well-known contractor in Manchester. Jean attended Hevey Elementary School, and graduated from Manchester West High School in 1926. At West High he distinguished himself academically and was a star athlete in boxing, football, and basketball.

Jean Grenier enrolled at the University of New Hampshire in the fall of 1926. While there, he excelled in athletics, lettering in boxing as co-captain. He was pitcher for the baseball team and quarterback on the football team and was a member of Theta Kappa Phi fraternity.

When former Army Mail Service pilot Charles Lindbergh made his epic solo flight across the Atlantic Ocean in 1927, Grenier and many other young men became aviation enthusiasts. Jean Grenier made his dream a reality.

After graduating from the University of New Hampshire in 1930, he was commissioned through ROTC. Lieutenant Grenier graduated from flight school at Kelly Field, San Antonio, Texas, in July 1933. He was assigned to the third air attack group at Fort Crockett, Galveston, Texas, and in February 1934 was assigned to Salt Lake

City to fly a government mail route. Lieutenant Grenier was selected to fly an advance route between Salt Lake City and Cheyenne, Wyoming, to determine flying time and distance. On February 16, 1934, Lieutenant Grenier and his crew-mate, Lieutenant Edwin D. White, were killed when their aircraft, a Curtis A-12 "Shrike," tail number 33-244, crashed in bad weather in Oakley, Utah.

The Army Air Corps Mail Operation (AACMO) was established by President Franklin D. Roosevelt in February 1934. Roosevelt directed Postmaster General James F. Farley to cancel air mail contracts with commercial airlines due to contract irregularities. Major General Benjamin Foulois directed the Army operation.

Army pilots selected for AACMO were young lieutenants, most with less than two years of experience, less than fifty hours flying time, and no instrument flying experience. The winter of 1934 was severe and the eager young pilots would clear themselves to fly in the most hazardous weather conditions. Their planes had open cockpits and no radios or flying instruments. This was seat-of-the-pants flying relying on compass needle, ball, and airspeed.

The deaths of Lieutenant Grenier and White were among a dozen pilots in sixty-six crashes. Despite all the hardships, these young pilots were out to prove that the Army Air Corps could do the job. With the coming of spring and better weather, the crashes and casualties declined. On June 1, 1934, new air mail contracts were signed with the airlines. The Army Air Corps was relieved of its responsibility for carrying mail.

For all the difficulties, the operation pointed to inadequacies of equipment, training, and operation. Investigations and the recommendations of the Drum and Baker Boards led to the establishment of the General Headquarter Air Force in March 1935—the first long stride in the establishment of an independent Air Force.

The young lieutenants like Grenier and White who suffered and died during that terrible winter of 1934 deserve a large share of the credit. Valor takes many forms, in peace as well as in war. Lieutenant Jean Grenier was buried with full military honors at the Mount Calvary Cemetery in Manchester. On January 23, 1942, the Army air base at Manchester, New Hampshire, was named Grenier Air Base in honor of Lieutenant Jean D. Grenier.

USS SQUALUS

U.S. Navy Submarine #192
World War II

Keel Laid: October 18, 1937, Portsmouth Navy Yard
Launched: September 14, 1938, Portsmouth Navy Yard
Sunk: May 23, 1939
Renamed: USS *Sailfish*
Decommissioned: October 1945
12 War Patrols, South Pacific
Presidential Unit Citation

THE USS *SQUALUS*, A 1450-TON SARGO-CLASS SUBMARINE, was built at the Portsmouth Navy Yard and entered service in 1939. On May 23, 1939, while conducting a test dive fifteen miles off Portsmouth, Skipper Lieutenant Oliver Naquin gave the order to dive. On board were the crew of fifty-eight officers and men.

In the control room, Machinist's Mate Alfred Prien was on duty watching the "Christmas tree," a control board so called because of its red and green lights. The lights indicated which valves were open and which were closed. As the dive progressed, Prien shut the valves to keep out the seawater. He watched as the lights changed to green, indicating valves closed. As the dive continued and reached a depth of fifty feet, seawater began flooding the engine room.

Lieutenant Naquin was informed and blew the ballast. Regardless of the indication of valves on the Christmas tree, the main induction valves were still open. As more water rushed in, the *Squalus* lost her trim and went twenty degrees bow up. While the forward bulkhead door closed automatically, the door between the engine room and control room remained open allowing four men to swim through to safety. Finally the men pushed the 200-pound door shut and secured it.

The *Squalus* slipped down and at 242 feet hit the bottom stern first, with the bow tilted up at twelve degrees. As the seawater reached the controls and batteries, the lights went out, leaving the

USS Squalus*—Disaster struck on May 23, 1939 when the Portsmouth submarine USS* Squalus, *while on sea trials, sank off the Isles of Shoals.* Squalus *was raised on September 13, put out of commission two months later, rebuilt and recommissioned as USS* Sailfish *just a year after she sank. The bridge and conning tower of* Sailfish *are located on the Shipyard mall as a memorial to the 26 officers and men lost on* Squalus. *Photo courtesy of Portsmouth Naval Shipyard.*

boat in darkness. With no moving machinery or galley stove to generate heat, the interior of the submarine grew cold, 34 degrees Fahrenheit. The *Squalus* did carry a supply of soda-lime compound that neutralized the carbon dioxide in the atmosphere. The men had enough oxygen for four days. While the depth was within limits for the ascent using the Momsen Lung escape gear, the cold water temperature voided its use.

Skipper Naquin ordered the release of the new rescue device, a phone buoy. The buoy went up and released a red dye marker on the surface and floated high enough to be visible to rescuers. As they settled down to wait, Lieutenant Naquin made a roll call.

There were thirty-three men and officers in the forward compartments. That left twenty-six people aft, fate unknown.

On the surface, their sister ship, the *Sculpin* was circling the area and spotted the dye marker and telephone buoy. The *Sculpin* brought the phone on board where Captain Wilkin could talk to Naquin. As they spoke, the rough seas snapped the telephone line. Captain Wilkin was able to send a message to Portsmouth giving the exact position, depth, and heading of the sunken submarine. He also radioed that he was anchored over the *Squalus* and could remain there.

A tug spent the rest of the afternoon dragging the bottom in an attempt to get a line on the sunken boat. This was accomplished, although no one was sure until the following day when divers could be sent down.

On the morning of May 24, the rescue vessel USS *Falcon* moored above the *Squalus*. The *Falcon* carried a team of divers and a McCann rescue chamber. The divers were commanded by Lt. Commander Charles "Swede" Momsen, who had invented both the Momsen Lung and the rescue chamber. After securing a cable to *Squalus*, the nine-ton rescue chamber—a large diving bell that could be secured to the escape hatch in the deck over the forward part of the sub, was used to bring up the survivors.

The rescue chamber went down with William Badders and John Michalowski guiding it. They opened the *Squalus'* hatch and took up six men and one officer. They lowered blankets, sandwiches, and hot soup to those below. Two more trips brought up nine men each time. At 8:30 that night, the last trip brought up the final eight survivors, including Lieutenant Naquin. On the way up a cable threatened to break and delayed the trip. After repairing the cable, other trips were made to the *Squalus* in an attempt to discover more survivors, but there were no more, only the thirty-three.

Four of the rescue team, William Badders, Orson Crandall, James McDonald, and John Michalowski, were awarded the Medal of Honor for their extraordinary heroism throughout the rescue and salvage operation. Lieutenant Naquin remained in the Navy, but was transferred to the surface fleet and never served in submarines again. He retired as a rear admiral in 1955.

The *Squalus* was raised in the summer of 1939 and towed back to Portsmouth for repairs. After extensive maintenance, the sub was recommissioned as the USS *Sailfish*, a name suggested by President Franklin Roosevelt. Sailors usually consider renaming a ship bad luck, but the *Sailfish* (sometimes referred to as "*Squalfish*" by her crew) survived a dozen World War II combat patrols in the South Pacific.

The *Sailfish* sank a total of seven Japanese ships, forty thousand tons, on those twelve patrols. Ironically, *Sailfish* sank the Japanese escort carrier *Chuyo*, which was carrying half the surviving crew members of the *Sculpin* the ship that had located the sunken *Squalus* in 1939. Only one of those American sailors being transported by the *Chuyo* survived to spend the remainder of the war as a slave laborer in Japan.

One result of the *Squalus'* sinking was the redesign of the diving controls, so the main induction and negative tank flood levers could be easily distinguished by touch—even in total darkness. One theory was that the vent operator had accidentally opened the induction when he attempted to close the negative flood valve, which was located next to it.

In January 1945, the *Sailfish* returned to the Atlantic, where she performed training duties for the remainder of World War II. She was decommissioned in October 1945 and assigned to be expended as a target. She was not used for that purpose, but instead was sold for scrap in June of 1948.

However, the conning tower of the *Squalus*, with the flag flying, remains to this very day at the place of her birth: the Portsmouth Navy Yard.

References:
Submarines at War, Edwin P. Hoyt, 1983
The Terrible Hours, Peter Maas

WORLD WAR II

1941–1945

WORLD WAR I WAS CALLED THE "WAR TO END ALL WARS," but of course, it wasn't! Leaders in Germany, Japan, and Italy were overcome by visions of extreme power by dominating people and countries other than their own.

Emperor Hirohito and former General, then Prime Minister, Tojo wanted the Pacific Ocean and all surrounding countries to become part of the Japanese Empire. Korea had been under their control since 1910. Japan systematically began its invasion and occupation of Manchuria, China, Indo-China, Burma, Siam, and in 1941, the Philippine Islands.

Italy's Benito Mussolini, deposed King Victor Emanuel and bullied his way into North Africa and Ethiopia in 1935. The Mediterranean Sea would once again be a Roman/Italian Lake. In 1940, Italy joined the axis—Japan and Germany.

Germany had fallen under the spell and control of madman, Adolph Hitler. Hitler's dream in his book, *Mein Kampf,* was world domination. Germans would become the master race by ethnic cleansing—exterminating Jews and homosexuals. Hitler promised the German people, still in disgrace from their defeat in WWI, that "a November 1918 will never be repeated in German history."

Germany spent over ninety billion dollars building up their "defenses." In September 1939, Germany invaded Poland beginning their Blitz Kreig—lightning war. Fighter bombers attacked from the air while troops followed tanks over-running ground defenses. In April 1940, Norway and Denmark fell. In May, Belgium and the Netherlands were overrun. In June, Germany went over and around France's vaunted impregnable Maginot Line. General Charles de Gaulle and other soldiers from the overrun countries fled to England in hopes of again fighting the Germans.

In July 1940, Germany began the systematic aerial bombing of England beginning the Battle of Britain. The first air assaults on British airfields in August were designed to destroy the RAF— Royal Air Force. The force of five hundred German bombers and fighters was met by spirited opposition from British Hurricanes and Spitfire fighters. Although seriously outnumbered, the RAF fighter pilots held off the attacks. September 16 was the decisive day in which the Germans lost one hundred eighty five planes. After that, the bombing raids dwindled. The RAF had downed 1,867 German aircraft while losing only 621. Although bombings continued, these were no longer a preparation for a German assault on the British mainland. This was Germany's first set-back of the war.

In January 1941, Germany invaded Greece and the Balkans. In June, Russia was invaded. Operation Barberrosa continued until the winter of 1941-42 when the Germans were halted at the siege of Stalingrad by Marshall Zhukov.

Meanwhile the Japanese were progressing in their conquests on the rim of the Pacific, which they hoped to become the Japanese Ocean. After the invasion of Indo-China in 1940, the U.S. stopped exporting steel and iron scrap to Japan. Until the Japanese attack on Pearl Harbor, Hawaii, on December 7, 1941, the United States provided aid to England, but remained neutral.

On December 10, the Japanese invaded the Philippine Islands, then a U.S. territory. The U.S. army units there were under the command of General Douglas MacArthur. The combined Army, Navy, and Filipino Scouts held off the Japanese until February 23, when MacArthur was ordered to proceed to Australia. General Wainwright, left in command, had to surrender all U.S. Forces on May 10. Prisoners were forced to march to Bataan, during which the sick and wounded were beaten or killed by beheading. Although resistance by regular U.S. forces ceased in 1942, guerilla warfare continued throughout the war.

With most of the U.S. Pacific fleet destroyed or damaged, the U.S. Navy mounted its offense with a small task force built around two aircraft carriers—the *Enterprise* and the *Yorktown*. The success of Admiral Halsey's task force in the Marshall and Gilbert Islands led to more aircraft carriers being built and sent out on such patrols.

On April 18, 1942, General James Doolittle led a group of 16 U.S. Army B-25 medium bombers on a raid against Tokyo. The aircraft were launched from the U.S. Navy carrier *Hornet*, bombed their Tokyo targets, and then proceeded to China. While not a significant military success, the raid against the Japanese capital boosted American's spirits.

The war in the Pacific continued to be mostly naval battles and island assaults by Marines and Army troops like stepping stones leading to Japan. Midway, Wake Island, Truk, the Solomons, New Guinea, Guadelcanal, Iwo Jima, Okinawa, were all hard-fought long, bloody battles against an entrenched fanatical enemy that was told to die rather than surrender. While U.S. submarines sank enemy ships in the Pacific, German U-boats were doing the same in the North Atlantic Ocean.

On the other side of the world, the American forces landed in North Africa to support British General Bernard Montgomery's troops. The British had lost desert tank-battles to General Erwin Rommel's Afrika Korps. The defeat at Tobruk put twenty-eight thousand British prisoners into the Germans' hands. Rommel raced his exhausted and over-taxed tanks to his next objective—Cairo. At El Alamein, the British defense held fast. The scales of war finally tipped against Rommel, the Desert Fox.

The newly arrived American II Corps was commanded by General George Patton who engaged some of Rommel's Afrika Korps and then proceeded to invade the German-defended Italian Island of Sicily. Combined British and U.S. troops captured Sicily and continued up the Italian peninsula toward Rome, fighting entrenched German forces. After the defeat of Sicily, Italy left the axis group. From captured airfields in Sicily and Italy, U.S. bombers attacked the Romanian oil fields at Ploesti in a daring daylight raid. The B-24's flew in at low-levels, some planes that made it back to their base, had corn stalks trapped in the bomb-bay doors.

The fighting continued on the Russian front through 1942-1943 with severe low temperature taking its toll on the German Soldiers.

In 1942, there came a distinct change in the strategic aspects of the air war over western Europe. Prime Minister Winston Churchill directed their air offensive against German production, transportation, and invasion fortifications. This bombing was conducted at night to prevent attacks by German fighter aircraft. In July 1942, General Carl Spaatz was appointed Commander of the U.S. Air Force by General Dwight Eisenhower, the Supreme Commander of all forces in Europe. Under General Spaatz, the U.S. Eighth Air force, now stationed at airfields in England, began daylight bombing of Germany with mass numbers of B-17 flying fortresses.

The war in China continued. Allied forces were stationed in India, then part of the British Empire. The C-B-I, China-Burma-India Theater of operation was vital in maintaining Chinese General Chiang Kai-Shek's army fighting the Japanese in mainland China. Supplies were trucked into China over the Burma Road. The Japanese cut this route. The alternative was for allied planes to fly from India to Chinese airfields. Pilots referred to this air route of five hundred miles over the Himalayan Mountains as flying "the Hump."

In 1942, American engineers with Chinese laborers began building a new ground route from Ledo, India, to the old Burma Road. The American pilots in General Cheunault's Flying Tiger squadron were still flying out of airfields in southern China. The Japanese captured these airfields believing that they were the source of General Doolittle's raiders. The Japanese also resorted to a scorched-earth strategy, burning rice fields and graineries, literally starving the Chinese people. In 1943, General Frank Merrill's specially trained combat team trekked through three hundred miles of jungle to join with two Chinese divisions, to re-open the Burma Road. Japanese assaults on rail-heads in India were repulsed by British troops.

The war in the Pacific continued with U.S. submarines, based in Hawaii, operating along the Formosa Strait, sinking Japanese cargo ships. B-17 bombers based in Australia and New Zealand supported ground assaults on islands in New Guinea, New Britain, and the Japanese naval base at Truk.

The Russian campaign also continued. In 1943, after two years of fierce fighting, the Russians took the offensive, retaking their own land. The Germans had systematically destroyed everything they left behind in Russia and had forced ten million Russian civilians into slave labor. By April 1944, the Russian strength totaled three hundred divisions outnumbering the Germans two to one. During the previous two years, the U.S. and Great Britain shipped the Russians 15,500 planes, 10,200 tanks and 190,000 trucks and jeeps. Russian tanks under General Konev, defeated six German Panzer divisions, cutting the key rail line between Odessa and Lwow, thereby cutting off German supplies.

Although the allied efforts in Europe were focused on the invasion of France, the drive in Italy had to be continued in order to tie up the greatest number of German Divisions. Initial assaults on coastal Anzio and inland Cassino in January were repulsed by heavy German resistance. The bitter cold weather halted most activity until May when the fifth and eighth U.S. armies launched coordinated thrusts. Better weather also enabled allied bombing to neutralize the salient on Monte Cassino.

Meanwhile in England, Supreme Commander Eisenhower and his staff had been planning the invasion of France—Operation Overlord. The plan called for an assault by sea-borne troops crossing the English Channel, landing on beach-heads on the Normandy coast. Two airborne divisions, the 82nd and 101st would parachute at night behind the coastline to capture bridges and disrupt enemy communications. The troops assaulting the beachhead would be covered by naval gunfire.

D-Day was June 6, 1944. After days of bloody fighting, allied troops began pouring onto French soil. The total allied strength amounted to 61 U.S., 13 British, 5 Canadian, 10 French and 1 Polish division (the average division consisted of 17,000 men). Ground units fought their way toward Paris and air raids on German industrial targets continued. Some underground factories continued undisturbed by the bombings. Allied air raids on German aircraft production facilities did slow the production of Luftwaffe fighter planes. Approximately 18,000 tons of allied bombs were dropped. The Luftwaffe lost 641 fighters against losses of 148 British and 232 U.S. bombers (each U.S. B-17 bomber had a crew of 10 airmen).

The invasion of Normandy was a success. Cherbourg was taken on June 26. The allies had also tricked the Germans into believing the main invasion would be at Pas-de-Calais, thus holding the 15th German army away from Normandy. On August 25, French General LeClerc accepted the surrender of the Germans and allied troops entered Paris.

The allies continued toward Germany crossing into Germany on November 18th. The retreating Germans launched a surprise counter-offensive in December 1944 in Belgium at Bastogne—the Battle of the Bulge. As the weather cleared, aerial resupplies reached the ground troops and allied fighters maintained safety from above. Patton's Third Army captured Weimar giving Americans possession of the concentration camp at Buchenwald. As the allies were driving into Germany from the West, the Russian army was pushing in from the East. On April 25, 1945, patrols of the U.S. 69th Division met elements of the Russian 58th Guards Division in the Torgav area on the Elbe River.

On April 30, General Mark Clark announced that "troops of the Fifteenth Army have so smashed the German armies in Italy that they have been virtually eliminated as a fighting force." A German communiqué of May 1, 1945, stated that Hitler had died in action—actually he had committed suicide. On May 7, leaders of the German military signed their unconditional surrender. The war in Europe was over—VE Day (Victory in Europe).

Continued victories in the Pacific were steadily advancing U.S. forces nearer to mainland Japan. The island of Iwo Jima was taken by U.S. Marines in March after twenty six days of continual combat at a cost of 4,305 dead and 20,196 wounded. The capture of Iwo Jima and its key airfield put Japan only fourteen hundred miles away.

On March 24, the battle for Okinawa began. This was a joint operation consisting of U.S. Army and Marines supported by naval gunfire and air support. After eighty-two days of fighting, Okinawa was taken. Battle casualties were 21,342 U.S. Army, 16,313

U.S. Marines, 9,721 U.S. Navy. Enemy casualties were estimated to be one hundred twenty thousand. Okinawa was not only the last major ground battle of the war, but the costliest single engagement in the Pacific.

America victories in the battles for Leyte and Luzon broke the Japanese domination of the Philippines. While these did not completely liberate the islands, a large number of isolated actions eliminated the Japanese occupation. Now mainland Japan was subjected to air bombardment. Airfields in the Mariana Islands were built up to accommodate greater numbers of B-29 super-fortress bombers. After Iwo Jima became available for emergency landings, greater bomb loads were carried and constant fighter support was provided.

The tide of the war in China and Burma also changed in favor of the allies. Chinese divisions joined by General Joseph Stilwell's forces were pushing the Japanese back toward Canton. Lord Mountbatten's joint forces of U.S., British, and Chinese, opened the way to Siam and Malaya. The Battle of Burma was declared ended on July 28, 1945. General Douglas MacArthur assumed command of all U.S. Army forces in the Pacific on April 6, 1945. He and Admiral Nimitz began preparing for the invasion of Japan. They realized that the Japanese had planned an inland defense which would inflict disastrous casualties upon them.

On August 6, 1945, President Truman announced that an American B-29 had dropped an atomic bomb on Hiroshima. On August 9, a second bomb was dropped on Nagasaki. A demand for unconditional surrender was eventually agreed to by the Japanese emperor and his staff. The formal surrender document was signed on the deck of the battleship *Missouri* in Tokyo Bay on September 2, 1945. Five days later, General MacArthur entered Tokyo and raised the American flag over the American Embassy. It was the same flag which had flow over Washington, D.C. on December 7, 1941. Thus ended the military phase of the most far-reaching and destructive war the world has known thus far. Three years, eight months, and twenty-six days after the Japanese attacked the United States at Pearl Harbor.

FRANK DOW MERRILL

Major General, U.S. Army
World War II, Far East

Born:	December 4, 1903, Hopkinton, Massachusetts
Died:	December 11, 1955, Fernadina Beach, Florida
Buried:	West Point
Education:	U.S. Military Academy, West Point, 1929
	MIT, Cambridge, Massachusetts

Commanded the 5307th Composite Unit known as Merrill's Marauders and led them in combat in Burma.

Awards:	Distinguished Service Medal
	Legion of Merit, 2 OLC
	Bronze Star
	Purple Heart
	Combat Infantryman's Badge
	Ranger Tab
	Presidential Unit Citation

FRANK MERRILL WAS RAISED IN AMESBURY, MASSACHUSETTS, just across the New Hampshire border. As a boy, he frequently hunted and fished in New Hampshire. At age sixteen, he enlisted in the U.S. Army saying that he was over 18, which was technically true, as he had written the number "18" on the bottom of both shoes.

Merrill was promoted to sergeant before being accepted to the U.S. Military Academy at West Point, an extremely rare occurrence in pre-war times. He graduated in the class of 1929 and was commissioned as a second lieutenant of cavalry. He later received a bachelor of science degree in military engineering from the Massachusetts Institute of Technology.

In 1938, Captain Merrill was assigned to the U.S. Embassy in Tokyo as a military attaché. His wife, Lucy, and two sons, Frank, age six and Thomas, three months old, accompanied him to Tokyo. While there, Merrill studied Japanese weapons, and the Chinese and Japanese languages.

In 1941, when he was assigned to the Philippines, his family moved to North Woodstock, New Hampshire. Frank Merrill was promoted to major and assigned to Manila as General Douglas MacArthur's intelligence officer. On December 7, 1941, when the Japanese attacked Pearl Harbor, Merrill was in Rangoon, Burma, on a mission for MacArthur. He remained there and became an aide to General Joseph W. Stillwell, commanding the China-India-Burma theater.

Merrill was promoted to lieutenant colonel in the spring of 1942 and was decorated for actions in Burma, including the Purple Heart for wounds received in combat during March through May.

In August 1943, at the Quebec Conference, President Franklin Roosevelt and Winston Churchill agreed to form a U.S. military unit in Burma based on Colonel Orde Wingate's "Chindits." The new unit would specialize in guerrilla tactics, jungle warfare, and long-range penetrations. Frank Merrill was selected to plan, train, and lead the unit, whose code name was Galahad.

In October 1943, Merrill was General Stillwell's operations officer. As such, he organized the 5307th Composite Unit. The call for volunteers for hazardous duty went out and three thousand men responded. Most were veterans of combat in New Guinea. Colonel Charles Hunter was the unit's second in command. Soldiers were selected based on jungle experience as well as pack troops and mule-handlers. Three dozen Nisei (American-born of Japanese parents) soldiers volunteered. Their expertise was valuable as they cut into Japanese army communications lines or crept close enough to overhear conversations concerning enemy supplies, ammo dumps, or troop movements.

Frank Merrill was promoted to brigadier general and led the first campaign attacking and defeating the 18th Japanese Division after a hundred mile march. The 18th Division had been victorious at Singapore and in Malaya. This victory gave General Stillwell control of the Hakawing Valley.

During the second campaign, in March 1944, Merrill led the assault at Hsamshingyang. He suffered a heart attack and was evacuated to Ledo. He returned to duty on May 17, and led the attack on Myitkyina, capturing the airfield there. During that long trek, the 5307th, now known as Merrill's Marauders had lost seven hundred men and had to be reinforced with Chinese troops.

To reach Myitkyina, the marauders had marched 750 miles through jungles and fought five major engagements and thirty-two skirmishes with the Japanese army. Casualties were high. Only thirteen hundred of the three thousand marauders reached the objective. Of these, 679 had to be hospitalized including General Merrill who was suffering with malaria and then a second heart attack. On August 3, 1944, Myitkyina was taken.

Merrill's Marauders were the first American infantry unit to fight on the mainland of Asia. In July 1944, the 5307th was awarded the Distinguished Unit Citation, which was later up-graded to the Presidential Unit Citation.

Merrill was promoted to major general on September 9, 1944, in command of the Allied Liaison Group. He later became the deputy U.S. commander in Burma. In 1945, he was chief of staff of the Tenth Army at Okinawa. In 1947, General Merrill was transferred to the military advisory group in the Philippines. He later served as Sixth Army commander in San Francisco. He retired from the Army in 1948 and joined his family back in North Woodstock, New Hampshire.

Merrill was appointed New Hampshire Highway Commissioner by Governor Sherman Adams, who became President Eisenhower's chief of staff. General Merrill was elected to head the American Association of State Highway officials. As a personal friend, Adams gave Merrill access to the Oval Office. This may have had some influence on why the Interstate Highway Act was passed.

Camp Frank D. Merrill in Dahlonega, Georgia, is named in his honor. Camp Merrill is the home of the U.S. Army's 5th Ranger Battalion of the 75th Ranger Regiment's mountain training center. The 75th Ranger Regiment traces its lineage back to the 5307th— Merrill's Marauders.

References:
The Marauders, Charlton Ogburn, 1959
Personal Correspondence from Thomas Merrill
USMA Records provided by Dr. Grove, USMA Historian
U.S. Special Forces, A. & F. Landau, 1992

Richard H. O'Kane

Rear Admiral, U.S. Navy
World War II—South Pacific

Born: February 2, 1911, Dover, New Hampshire
Died: February 16, 1994, Petaluma, California
Buried: Arlington National Cemetery
Education: U.S. Naval Academy, 1934
Submarine Commander, South Pacific
Awards: Medal of Honor
              3 Navy Crosses
              3 Silver Stars
              Legion of Merit
              Purple Heart

Medal of Honor Citation:

For conspicuous gallantry and intrepidity at the risk of his life above and beyond the call of duty as commanding officer of the USS Tang *operating against two enemy Japanese convoys on 23 and 24 October 1944, during her fifth and last war patrol. Boldly maneuvering on the surface into the midst of heavily escorted convoy, Comdr. O'Kane stood in the fusillade of bullets and shells from all directions to launch smashing hits on three tankers, coolly swung his ship to fire at a freighter and, in a split-second decision, shot out of the path of an onrushing transport, missing it by inches. Boxed in by blazing tankers, a freighter, transport, and several destroyers, he blasted two of the targets with his remaining torpedoes and, with pyrotechnics bursting on all sides, cleared the area. Twenty-four hours later, he again made contact with a heavily escorted convoy steaming to support the Leyte campaign with reinforcements and supplies and with crated planes piled high on each unit. In defiance of the enemy's relentless fire, he closed the concentration of ship and in quick succession sent two torpedoes each into the first and second transports and an adjacent tanker, finding his mark with each torpedo in a series of violent explosions at less than 1,000-yard range. With ships bearing down from all sides, he charged the enemy at high speed, exploding the tanker in a burst of flame, smashing the transport dead in the water, and blasting the destroyer with a mighty roar which rocked the Tang from stem to stern. Expending his last two torpedoes into the remnants of a once powerful convoy before his own ship went down, Comdr. O'Kane, aided by his gallant command, achieved an illustrious record of heroism in combat, enhancing the finest traditions of the U.S. Naval Service.*

RICHARD O'KANE WAS RAISED IN DURHAM, NEW Hampshire, where his father, Walter, was a professor at the University of New Hampshire. He studied at Phillips Andover Academy and the University of New Hampshire before entering the U.S. Naval Academy, from which he graduated 1934. In 1936, he married Ernestine, the girl who lived next door to him in Durham.

Upon completion of submariner training at New London, Connecticut, the young couple moved to Hawaii. When the war broke out on the morning of December 7, 1941, Mrs. O'Kane was living at Pearl Harbor. Lieutenant O'Kane was aboard the USS *Argonaut*, the first of three submarines he would serve on during World War II in the South Pacific.

The *Argonaut* was one of the two submarines to deliver Carlson's Raiders to Mankin Island on August 8, 1942. The second group of subs made a feint, or mock landing, at another island to draw the Japanese attention away from Mankin. The *Argonaut* skipper's overly cautious actions eventually led to his dismissal from active duty.

O'Kane was transferred to the submarine USS *Wahoo* four months prior to its sinking off New Britain Island in July 1943. Aboard the *Wahoo*, O'Kane was executive officer to Commander Dudley "Mush" Morton, whose more aggressive leadership, tactics, and success in battle earned the *Wahoo* its enviable nickname "one man wolf pack."

O'Kane assumed command of the USS *Tang* in 1943. He engaged in five war patrols sinking a record thirty-one ships and damaging two others—more than 227,000 tons. The *Tang* sank a Japanese ship every eleven days on those five patrols. It also rescued scores of American fliers whose planes were shot down on raids on Japanese ships or bases.

During one patrol in Formosa Strait, Oct. 23-24, 1944, the *Tang* sank 110,000 tons of Japanese shipping including one destroyer. The sub then fell victim to her last torpedo when it malfunctioned, circled back, and hit the *Tang* killing all but nine of the eighty-seven-man crew.

O'Kane and the other survivors swam for eight hours before being taken prisoner. They spent the last ten months of the war in a Formosa prison camp and were then transferred to a secret prison near Tokyo where they were subjected to beatings and a starvation diet. When he was released from that prison camp, Richard O'Kane weighed only eighty-eight pounds. He, like most of the other prisoners, suffered from rickets and beriberi.

After the war, he was promoted to captain and commanded the Submarine School in New London, Connecticut. For his wartime service, Richard O'Kane was awarded America's highest military award, the Medal of Honor.

He retired from active duty in 1957 as a rear admiral. He wrote two books about his wartime experiences—*Clear the Bridge* in 1977 and *Wahoo* in 1987. Admiral O'Kane died at age eighty three of pneumonia on February 16, 1994, at a nursing home in Petaluma, California. He is buried in Arlington National Cemetery.

In 1998, an aegis-class destroyer, the USS *O'Kane*, DDG-77, was commissioned at the Bath Iron Works Shipyard, Bath, Maine, honoring a true hero.

References:

Submarines at War, Edwin P. Hoyt, 1983
Wahoo, Adm. Richard H. O'Kane, 1987
Clear the Bridge, Adm. Richard H. O'Kane, 1977

HARL PEASE JR.

Captain, U.S. Army Air Corps
World War II, Pacific Theater

Born: April 10, 1917, Plymouth, New Hampshire
Died: October 8, 1942, New Britain
Buried: American Military Cemetery, Manila, Philippines
Education: University of New Hampshire, 1939
Awards: Medal of Honor
                Distinguished Flying Cross
                Purple Heart
                Air Medal
                Army Aviator Badge

HARL PEASE JR. WAS BORN AND RAISED IN PLYMOUTH, New Hampshire, the son of Harl and Bessie (Fox) Pease. He attended Tilton Academy and graduated from the University of New Hampshire in 1939 with a degree in business administration.

He enlisted in the Army Air Corps after graduation to enter flight training. In 1940, he was commissioned a second lieutenant. and awarded his pilot rating at Kelly Field, Texas. He was immediately called to active duty to participate in a mass flight of Boeing B-17 bombers from March Field, California, to Honolulu, Hawaii. His next assignment was another mass flight of B-17s this one from Albuquerque, New Mexico, to the Philippines. Lieutenant. Pease remained at Clarke Field, near Manila.

In 1942, as General Douglas MacArthur was about to leave the Philippines, he and his entourage were waiting at the muddy airfield at DelMonte for three B-17s to evacuate them to Australia. These aircraft were the remnants of those at Clarke Field that had escaped a destructive Japanese air attack. Two of the B-17s did arrive but one had hydraulic problems—no brakes—and was intentionally "ground looped" to keep from going off the end of the airfield.

This did not impress General MacArthur, and he was even less impressed when he saw the young pilot, First Lieutenant Harl

Pease, as he got out. MacArthur is reported to have said, "He's only a boy!" General MacArthur angrily rejected both aircraft as unsafe for his evacuation to Australia. The general and his party and Lieutenant Pease and his flight crew rode to Australia in U.S. Navy submarines.

Upon reaching Australia, Pease and his crew were assigned to the Nineteenth Bomb Group. They participated in bombing missions and Pease was promoted to captain. It was during one of these missions, on August 5, 1942, that one engine of Captain Pease's B-17 (#41-2439) failed and he was forced to return to his base in Australia. His unit was scheduled to deploy to Papua, New Guinea, to support a maximum-effort bombing mission on August 7. It would require all available aircraft. Captain Pease and his crew, with their aircraft out of commission, were not scheduled to fly. Determined not to miss this big mission, the crew voluntarily found a good engine from among some unserviceable B-17s at the base. They rejoined the Nineteenth at Port Moresby, Papua New Guinea, at one in the morning after having flown almost continuously since early the preceding day.

With only three hours of rest, Captain Pease took off with the group to bomb targets at Rabaul, New Britain. About fifty miles from the Vunakanua airfield target, the bomb group was attacked by more than thirty Japanese fighter aircraft. Pease's crew shot down several of the enemy, fought their way to the target, and bombed successfully.

After leaving the target area, Pease's aircraft was hit by several bursts from the Japanese fighters. Their crippled B-17 fell behind the rest of the formation. Pease elected to turn his aircraft back toward the target in order to draw the attacking fighters away from the bomb group. He was seen to have dropped a flaming bomb-bay fuel tank. It was originally believed that he and his crew were shot down in flames and that there were no survivors of B-17 #41-2439.

In September 1942, Father George Lepping, a Roman Catholic priest, was taken prisoner to a Japanese camp near Rabaul. He reported that he found Captain Pease and one of his crewmen at that prison camp. Pease was well respected by his fellow prisoners and even by some of the Japanese guards, who called him a captain of a Boeing (as they referred to the B-17). The younger guards would ask if he was "Captain Boeing." Father Lepping reported that on October 8, 1942, Captain Pease, two Australians, and three American prisoners were given picks and shovels and taken into the jungle. It is believed they were forced to dig their own graves and were executed by the sword.

On December 2, 1942, President Franklin D. Roosevelt awarded posthumously the Medal of Honor, the Distinguished Flying Cross, and the Air Medal to Captain Harl Pease Jr. for his heroism in combat. The awards were presented to his parents.

In 1946, the bodies of slain prisoners at the camp near Rabaul were recovered for burial with full military honors at the military cemetery in Manila.

On September 7, 1957, Portsmouth Air Force Base, in Newington, New Hampshire, was rededicated as Pease Air Force Base in honor of Captain Harl Pease. The ceremonies included a fly-by by the Air Force's precision flying team, the Thunderbirds. On September 19, 1997, the air base was formally rededicated as Pease Air National Guard Base.

Rene Arthur Gagnon

Corporal, U.S. Marine Corps
World War II

Born: March 7, 1925, Manchester, New Hampshire
Died: October 12, 1979, Hooksett, New Hampshire
Buried: Arlington National Cemetery
Raised the American Flag, Battle of Iwo Jima
Awards: Presidential Unit Citation
            American Campaign Medal
            Asia-Pacific Campaign Medal
            China Service Campaign Medal
Battle: Iwo Jima, 1945

RENE GAGNON WAS BORN IN MANCHESTER, NEW HAMPSHIRE, the son of Henry and Irene Yvonne Gagnon. He completed only two years of high school before taking a job in one of Manchester's many textile mills. At age 18, in May 1943, he joined the Marine Corps, training at Parris Island, South Carolina, recruit depot. Rene was promoted to private first class in July 1943 and transferred to the Marine Guard Company at the Charleston, South Carolina, Navy Yard. He remained there for eight months, then joined the Military Police Company of the 5th Marine Division at Camp Pendleton, California. On April 8, 1944 he was transferred to Company E, 2nd Battalion, 28th Marines.

After training at Pendleton and Hawaii, Gagnon's unit landed on the beaches of Iwo Jima on February 19, 1945. Rene and his buddies in "Easy" company and the 28th Marines fought and clawed their way from the beach-head inland past the entrenched Japanese to the base of Mount Suribachi. That 546-foot high mount was an extinct volcano full of pillboxes, gun emplacements, fortified caves, tunnels, and storage areas.

On the fifth day of fighting, the Marines finally reached the summit of Suribachi, on February 23. Someone had raised a small American flag to show the top had been reached. But an officer said that he had a larger flag that would be seen more easily. Six

Marines from Easy Company took the larger flag, tied it to a pole, and hoisted it upright. Rene Gagnon, from New Hampshire; Ira Hayes, a Pima Indian from Arizona; Harlon Block, a farm boy from Texas; Michael Strank, an immigrant from Czechoslovakia; Franklin Sousley, a countryboy from Kentucky; and Jack Bradley, from Wisconsin, were the six. Nearby, Joe Rosenthal, an Associated Press photographer snapped a photo that became one of the most powerful and recognizable images of World War II. That photograph dramatically changed the lives of those Marines forever.

A week later, still on Iwo Jima, their outfit joined another assault on heavily fortified terrain. Easy Company came under intense sniper fire. Mike Strank, now a sergeant and their squad leader, led Hayes, Block, and Sousley to cover under a rocky outcrop. A shell exploded nearby and killed Strank. Block took over command of the squad. A few hours later he was killed by a mortar round.

Jack Bradley, the corpsman (medic), was wounded by shrapnel and medically evacuated to Guam. Sousley was shot to death by a sniper. Gagnon and Hayes and the remnants of Easy Company hung on. The battle for Iwo Jima finally ended after a month of bitter fighting. More than twenty-five thousand American Marines were dead or wounded. The Japanese garrison of twenty-two thousand was annihilated. Very few Japanese surrendered to become prisoners.

By the time Iwo Jima was secured, the Rosenthal photograph of the six Marines' flag raising had become a rallying point for American pride and patriotism. Rene Gagnon and the two other survivors, Hayes and Bradley, were assigned to temporary duty with the U.S. Treasury Department for appearances during a "war bond drive." They were wined and dined and greeted like heroes across the United States. They were glad to be alive, but, as with many survivors, suffered feelings of guilt over the loss of their Easy Company buddies who died on Iwo Jima.

The war bond tour ended on July 5 and Gagnon was ordered to San Diego for further duty, then transferred overseas. Before leaving, he married Pauline Georgette Harnois, of Hooksett, New Hampshire, in Baltimore, Maryland on July 7, 1945. He was assigned to a replacement unit and in November joined the Second Battalion, Twenty-Ninth Marines, Sixth Marine Division, in Tsingtao, China. He later served with the Third Battalion of the Twenty-Ninth.

After five months duty with occupation forces in China, he was ordered back to the United States. Gagnon was promoted to corporal after three years in the Marine Corps, fourteen months of which was overseas duty. He was only twenty-one years old when discharged on April 27, 1946.

Rene Gagnon died on October 12, 1979, after having suffered from years of alcoholism and unemployment that his family attributed to his unwanted fame. He was buried at Mount Calvary Cemetery in Manchester. At his widow's request, Gagnon's remains were reinterred, with full military honors, in Arlington National Cemetery on July 7, 1981. Two other flag raisers are buried at Arlington—Sergeant Michael Strank and Corporal Ira Hayes. Gagnon is the flag raiser buried closest to the Marine Corps Memorial, the statue in Washington, D.C., which depicts the Iwo Jima flag raising.

On the back of Rene Gagnon's tombstone is written, "For God and his country, he raised our flag in battle and showed a measure of his pride at a place called Iwo Jima, where courage never died."

Reference:
Flags of our Fathers, James Bradley, 2000

HARRY ALFRED PARKER

Captain, U.S. Army Air Corps
World War II, Europe

Born: January 29, 1919, Pasadena, California
Missing in Action: April 2, 1945, Austria
Presumed Killed in Action, Klagenfurt, Austria
Education: University of New Hampshire—one year
Awards: Silver Star, one Oak-Leaf Cluster
               Distinguished Flying Cross, one Oak-Leaf Cluster
               Air Medal, sixteen Oak-Leaf Clusters
               Partisan Medal (Austria)
               Army Aviator Badge

HARRY ALFRED PARKER WAS BORN IN PASADENA, California, the second of four sons of Hannah (Craig) and Truman Parker. All four Parker boys served in World War II. The family moved to Merrimack, New Hampshire, and Harry graduated from McGaw Institute (high school) in Reeds Ferry, New Hampshire, in 1933. The family moved this time to Milford, New Hampshire.

Harry attended the University of New Hampshire for one year before moving to Florida. He enlisted in the U.S. Army Air Corps on October 29, 1940, and took his basic training in Tampa, Florida. He studied sheet-metal work at Chanute Field, Illinois. Parker qualified for flight duty and trained as a pilot at Maxwell Field, Alabama; at Ocala, Florida, and at Shaw Field, South Carolina. He received his wings and commission as a second lieutenant on April 29, 1943, at Spence Field, Georgia.

In May 1944, Harry Parker was assigned to Italy, where he joined the 15th Air Force in the mediterranean theater of operations as a fighter pilot flying the P-51 Mustang. Parker was assigned to the 325th fighter group, whose P-51s were identified by their cherry-red nose-spinners and the yellow and black checkerboard pattern on their vertical stabilizers (tails). The 325th was known as the checkertails.

The main mission of the checkertails was to serve as bomber escort, to fly protective cover for B-17 and B-24 bombers from North Africa over Italy and to the oil fields of Ploesti, Romania. Their base, at Foggia, Italy, was a dirt strip that turned into a field of mud when it rained.

During his service with the 325th, Harry Parker was promoted to captain and served as flight commander and later as unit operations officer. Parker still flew combat missions escorting the heavy bombers on raids such as that on Bucharest, Romania. On that raid, he dove his aircraft into a formation of forty-two German fighters, destroying four ME-10s and damaging six others. His action caused the attacking Germans to break off their attack.

Captain Harry Parker flew 273 aerial combat missions. He shot down thirteen enemy aircraft, becoming a double-ace and New Hampshire's leading World War II air ace. While flying a strafing mission on April 2, 1945, southwest of Vienna, Parker radioed that a plane was flying below the formation and that he would investigate. He was last seen in the vicinity of Klagenfurt, Austria. He was listed as missing in action, and a year later his mother was notified that he was presumed dead.

For his actions he was awarded the Silver Star Medal with oak-leaf cluster, the Distinguished Flying Cross with oak-leaf cluster, the Air Medal with sixteen oak-leaf clusters (one award for flying 25 combat missions) and the Partisan Medal, bestowed by the Austrian government.

Capt. Harry A. Parker was honored in his hometown of Milford, New Hampshire, when they dedicated a tree in his name at the World War II Memorial Park, along with the names of twelve other Milford servicemen who lost their lives in World War II. Parker's name was also included in the Concord, New Hampshire, monument honoring New Hampshire airmen of distinction.

References:
The Granite Town, Winifred A. Wright, 1979
Milford in World War II, Winifred A. Wright, 1949

NORMAN JOHN FORTIER

Lieutenant Colonel, U.S. Air Force
World War II
Berlin Airlift, 1948-1949

Born:	May 30, 1922, Pelham, New Hampshire
Died:	November 20, 2005
Education:	University of New Hampshire, 1947
Awards:	Distinguished Flying Cross, three Oak-Leaf Clusters
	Air Medal, fourteen Oak-Leaf Clusters
	AF Commendation Medal
	French Croix de Guerre
	Army Aviator Badge

NORMAN "BUD" FORTIER GREW UP IN PELHAM, NEW Hampshire. Like many families during the Depression, the Fortiers did whatever they could to make ends meet. Bud recalled walking the railroad tracks with his father picking up coal, that had fallen off steam engines' coal tenders, in order to heat their house.

After graduating from high school, Fortier enrolled at St. Anselm's College in Manchester, New Hampshire. During his second year at St. Anselm's, he turned eighteen. In June 1941, Bud Fortier enrolled in the Civil Pilot Training Program. He made his first solo flight in a J3 Piper Cub at the Nashua Municipal Airport and eventually qualified as a private pilot.

In January 1942, one month after the Japanese attack on Pearl Harbor, Fortier enlisted as a flying cadet, U.S. Army Air Corps. He did his basic training and primary flight training at various bases in the South. At Spence Field, Moultrie, Georgia, he completed advanced flight training. On January 14, 1943, one year after enlisting, Norman "Bud" Fortier received his silver pilot's wings and commission as a second lieutenant—an officer and a gentleman.

Shortly after graduation, he was assigned to the 354th Fighter Group at Orlando Air Force Base, Florida. This unit would be flying the new Republic P-47 Thunderbolts, affectionately called the "Jug" because of its shape. The P47's wide-spaced landing gear made for easily controlled take-offs and landings.

The 354th was shipped north to be billeted at Camp Kilmer, New Jersey. The unit flew training missions off Cape May and the Jersey coast. The unit finally received travel orders for Europe. They crossed the Atlantic aboard the *Queen Elizabeth*. This was no luxury cruise, as the liner normally carrying three thousand passengers, now carried sixteen thousand U.S. troops to war. The 354th reached England and was assigned to the airfield at Steeple Morden, formerly an RAF bomber training base. The men and pilots were billeted in a series of Nissen huts, each barely large enough for fourteen cots and a stove.

Training missions were flown daily until all sixty aircraft were received. Fortier's P-47 (and his P-51 later) was designated WR-N. Some pilots had nose-art painted on their individual aircraft. Fortier thought, "If the Krauts see a fancy painting on a P-47's nose, the pilot must be a big wheel. But a guy with no artwork must be a peon—not worth shooting at." Fortier's WR-N kept a clean nose.

His P-51 Mustang wore the unit's distinctive and recognizable red tail and proudly sported six small swastikas indicating his six air-to-air victories. In addition to escorting and protecting bombers enroute to German targets, the 354th also strafed airfields, trains, and aircraft on the ground. This low-level flying had its hazards too, as 50-caliber and 20mm machine guns protected the airfields.

After nearly two years of combat flying, Bud Fortier had logged 113 combat missions, became a fighter "Ace," was promoted to major and at twenty-three years old he became the "Old Man"—the commanding officer of the 354th Fighter Squadron. With the end of World War II, young men like Bud Fortier could go back to civilian jobs, eat civilian food, and marry the American girls they had been missing for the long "duration" of the war. Most enlisted men became instant civilians. Some officers and NCOs remained on active duty. Some pilots, like Fortier, chose to retain their commissions as reserve officers, but enjoying civilian life.

Bud Fortier enrolled at the University of New Hampshire, graduating in 1947 as a premed major. Due to the huge number of ex-GIs applying for medical school, he was not selected. His only marketable skill was flying airplanes and Fortier became an airline pilot.

Before the ink was dry on the unconditional surrender documents, Russia began flexing her muscles, dividing Germany and Berlin, and precipitating the Cold War. Europe was a bombed-out heap of rubble. Rail lines, highways, power stations, factories, and cities had been damaged or completely destroyed. The European people were starving.

General George Marshall was far-sighted enough to realize that America, in winning the war, now had to win the peace. He instituted the European Recovery Program. His "Marshall Plan" of humanitarian aid for the Europeans called for $5.3 billion during its first year. Federal aid was supplemented by C.A.R.E. packages sent by individuals and groups of U.S. citizens. But Russia had blocked all ground routes to Berlin.

The first major challenge for the newly formed U.S. Air Force was to begin round-the-clock flights of military cargo planes to airlift food and supplies to the starving Germans. U.S. pilots were recalled to active duty including Major Bud Fortier. Fortier traded his dream job flying for Northwest Orient Airlines to pilot C-47s in and out of Berlin. He flew thirty-eight of these humanitarian missions during the Berlin Airlift, from June 1948 through May 1949.

The Berlin Airlift was unofficially called "Operation Vittles" with the 102 C47s flying into Tempelhof Airport. The smaller C47s were replaced by Douglas C54s, which carried four times the load of C47s. The aircraft took off at three-minute intervals around the clock. During a ten-month period more than 2.3 million tons of food and supplies (including coal) were flown into Berlin.

As the aircraft made their landing approaches to Tempelhof, German children would wave from the airport fences. Aircrews began dropping candy in handkerchief-parachutes. Pilots would wiggle their wings to signal a candy drop to the kids below. The project became known as "Operation Little Vittles." Air Force personnel world-wide donated their candy rations for the German kids. This amounted to twenty-three tons of treats to the kids of West Berlin.

On May 12, 1949, after more than 277,685 flights, the Soviets relented and opened the ground routes. Seventy-eight U.S. and British airmen died during the airlift.

Bud Fortier decided that he would remain on active duty. His first assignment was in Morocco as an instructor in American-made jet fighters for French pilots. Fortier who was bilingual, was an excellent choice. After Morocco, he was assigned to the Pentagon for several years. From the Pentagon, he became a military attaché at the American Embassy in the Hague, Netherlands. This diplomatic assignment was for two years.

Fortier's longest and last assignment was as commander of an organizational maintenance squadron at Pease Air Force Base in Portsmouth, New Hampshire. While at Pease, he remained on flying status as command pilot of a B-47 bomber. His Air Force career spanned twenty years and one day.

He retired in 1964 as a lieutenant colonel and began his new career as a schoolteacher, "the best job I ever had," he told his son. Fortier was a teaching principal at the Epsom Center School from 1965 through 1972. He also taught the fifth and sixth grade at Dover's Horne Street School from 1972 to 1991.

He encouraged his students to keep a daily journal, urging them to write. Bud Fortier wrote his WWII memoirs, *An Ace of the Eighth* in 2003 published by Ballantine Book/Presido Press. When he died, in 2005, he was writing a book about his teaching years.

Norman "Bud" Fortier lived eighty-three good years to the fullest. He is survived by his wife, Jane; sons John and Robert; daughter Diana; and six stepchildren.

References:

An Ace of the Eighth, Norman Fortier, Presido Press, 2003.
"A Memoriam," Anne Downey, *University of New Hampshire Magazine*, Winter 2006.
Personal correspondence with John Fortier.

KOREAN WAR

1950–1953

ALTHOUGH THE INVASION OF SOUTH KOREA BY THE North Korean Army took place in June 1950, the seeds of the Korean War were planted in 1904. The Japanese, fearing Russian expansion into Korea, fought and won the Russo-Japanese War. In 1907, Japan forced the Korean emperor to abdicate. In 1910, Korea became a colony of the Japanese Empire. This control continued thirty-five years until the end of WWII.

In 1945, Korea was divided at the 38th parallel with Russia occupying the northern zone and the U.S. occupying the south. The demarcation line became the equivalent of a frontier. When Russo-American negotiations broke down, the problem was referred to the United Nations, in September 1947.

Elections were held in South Korea in May 1948. By July, an assembly was convened and a constitution was adopted. Dr. Syngman Rhee was elected first president of the Republic of Korea. In the north, the People's Republic was formed and claimed jurisdiction over the entire country.

On December 12, 1948, the United Nations General Assembly formally recognized the southern Republic of Korea as the only lawful government of Korea. Unrest and rebellion in the south negated President Harry Truman's request for $150 million in aid for the new republic.

In the north, the military build-up continued. The Soviet-trained northern army numbered over 100,000 troops.

The U.S. congress reversed its earlier stance and voted to send sixty million dollars in aid in May 1950. Ambassador John Foster Dulles, on June 19, 1950, told the South Koreans, "…You are not alone, you will never be alone." Six days later on June 25, 1950, the Korean War began as tanks of the North Korean Army rolled southward expecting to join forces with the insurgents south of 38th parallel. In four days the capital of Seoul was in the hands of the communists. The well-prepared and well-equipped northern army would have swept to Pusan had it not been for the U.S. ground forces stationed in Japan, sent by President Truman to fight a delaying action until the United Nations could make its decision to send troops. The invasion tide was stayed at Taejon by the U.S. regular army troops, including a large proportion of young soldiers with no prior combat experience.

General Douglas MacArthur, the U.S. supreme commander in the Far East, was named Commander-in-Chief of the United Nations forces in an unprecedented decision to enforce its decrees by arms. Australia, Belgium, Canada, Columbia, Ethiopia, France, Greece, Luxembourg, Netherlands, New Zealand, the Philippines, Thailand, Turkey, Union of South Africa, and the United Kingdom contributed ground, air, and naval forces to augment the U.S. and ROK forces already in battle. India, Norway, Panama and Sweden sent non-combatant aid. The seventeen United Nations armed forces were represented in the ribbon of the United Nations service medal—seventeen stripes, nine blue and eight white.

Fierce hand-to-hand fighting lasted from July 5 through September 15 when the United Nations troops, supported by air and naval forces, gained a preliminary victory following the amphibious landing at Inchon. Led by General MacArthur, these forces cut the communist perimeter at Pusan. On September 29, Republic of South Korea (ROK) troops re-entered Seoul in triumph.

On October 1, 1950, ROK troops crossed the 38th parallel invading North Korea. The Northern capital of Pyongyang capitulated to the United Nations forces. Within another week UN and ROK troops had marched to the Yalu River the Manchurian border and the historic action of the United Nations seemed on the verge of conclusion.

However, on November 5, 1950, thousands of Chinese troops crossed the Yalu from Manchuria joining the North Koreans. This event was unforeseen by the U.S. and UN. The Chinese Army was large in numbers, comprised of seasoned, well-equipped troops. The U.S. Seventh Infantry Division launched a counter-offensive and the war continued with renewed hardship and misery through the icy winter of Northern Korea.

On February 1, 1951, the United Nations General Assembly resolution named the communist Chinese as the aggressors in Korea. The Chinese launched an offensive in March taking Seoul. Six days later, UN retook Seoul, which by now had been reduced to rubble.

The supply line of the communist army stretched two hundred fifty miles north to the Yalu and was under continuous air attack by the U.S. Air Force and Marine fighter squadrons. To protect their supply route, the Chinese communist sent Soviet built MiG-15 jet fighters to counter the U.S. Air Force's F-86's. Although the MiG-15 was superior in speed and maximum ceiling, the skill and tenacity of the U.S. pilots resulted in the overwhelming percentage of air victories, two hundred MiGs destroyed, only fifty-six F-86's lost in air combat.

For many years, U.S. pilots insisted that the Chinese communist MiGs were being flown by Soviet pilots. Finally in 2002, the Russian pilots who had actually flown the MiGs in air combat in Korea, broke their enforced silence and admitted their presence in the Korean sky.

By the summer of 1951, the 38th parallel, midway across the Korean peninsula, became a military deadlock. Russian UN delegate, Jacob Malik proposed a truce to take place along the 38th parallel. Preliminary truce talks occurred at Kaesong, but were eventually moved to Panmunjom, a more neutral location. On November 27, a provisional cease-fire line was drawn-up. It was generally assumed that the truce would be signed in 1952, but that would not happen.

General Matthew Ridgeway who had succeeded General MacArthur in April 1951, was in turn, succeeded by General Mark Clark in May 1952. During the summer and fall of 1952, heavy fighting resumed while the truce talks at Panmunjom continued. Field commanders were directed to either take or hold a piece of ground (while taking heavy casualties) only to be told days later to abandon that same area. "Pork Chop Hill" and "Heartbreak Ridge" were two such battle areas. Intense fighting which flared up in May and June, now ceased and both parties moved back two kilometers from the battle lines, leaving a demilitarized zone between them. On July 27, 1953, the armistice agreement was signed more than two years after the truce had been proposed.

Return of United Nations prisoners confirmed reports of communist atrocities, including torture to obtain false confessions of germ warfare. The U.S. forces suffered over one hundred forty-two thousand casualties (23,345 dead); South Korea over 1,312,000 casualties including 415,004 dead.

The demilitarized zone near the 38th parallel exists today with armies of both opposing sides nervously watching each other.

HARRISON REED THYNG

Brigadier General, U.S. Air Force
World War II
Korean War

Born: April 12, 1918, Laconia, New Hampshire
Died: September 24, 1983, Concord, New Hampshire
Buried: Barnstead, New Hampshire
Education: University of New Hampshire, 1939
Awards: Silver Star, two Oak-Leaf Clusters
              Distinguished Flying Cross, four Oak-Leaf Clusters
              Air Medal, thirty-three Oak-Leaf Clusters
              Legion of Merit
              Purple Heart
Battles: WWII—European Campaign
              WWII—African Campaign
              WWII—Pacific Campaign
              Korea

GENERAL THYNG WAS THE EPITOME OF A FIGHTER PILOT.
He was one of six men who are aces (five victories) flying both conventional aircraft and jet aircraft. He was also one of only seven pilots who were aces in two wars—WWII and Korea. General Thyng had air victories over German, French, Italian, Japanese, and Russian aircraft.

Harrison R. Thyng was born in Laconia, New Hampshire on April 12, 1918. He was raised in Barnstead, and graduated from Pittsfield High School in 1935. He received a bachelor of arts degree in pre-law from the University of New Hampshire in 1939 and was commissioned as a second lieutenant Infantry in the U.S. Army.

After graduation, he enlisted as a cadet in the Army Air Corps flight program. Lieutenant Thyng was awarded his wings in March 1940, and was assigned to the 94th Squadron, First Pursuit Group at Selfridge, Michigan. When the United States finally entered WWII, First Lieutenant Thyng was designated commanding officer of the 309th Fighter Squadron, 31st Fighter Group, which was ordered to

General Harrison Thyng and F-86. US Air Force photo, courtesy of James Thyng.

England. The British equipped this unit with Spitfire fighters, the aircraft that won the Battle for Britain. Lieutenant Thyng led the first fighter raids out of England, and was credited with the USAAF's first encounter with a German Foke Wulf 190, on November 8, 1942, near Shoreham, England.

The unit was secretly shipped to Gibraltar. Lieutenant Thyng led his squadron into Oran and shot down a Vichy French 520 fighter on that first mission, paving the way for the North Africa invasion.

Thyng's unit took over Oran airfield after chasing away the Vichy French air unit. Oran was in the desert, subject to frequent sandstorms. The unit's standard procedure after a sandstorm was to thoroughly clean their aircraft engines. One day, the unit took off immediately after a sandstorm, reasoning that the German fighter planes would be on the ground having their engines cleaned. The mission was a success. Many German ME-109s were destroyed by strafing.

On the way back to Oran, Lieutenant Thyng's engine froze. He glided two miles and crash-landed inside enemy lines. He avoided capture and was rescued by a U.S. Army patrol alerted by his wingman.

A week later, while in pursuit of a German ME-109, Thyng's Spitfire was shot down by British antiaircraft groundfire. The Brits were aiming at the ME-109 he was chasing. Lieutenant Thyng parachuted to safety, but broke his ankle. Back at Oran, the squadron doctor wanted to ground him. In Harrison Thyng's words, "at dawn the next day, my crew chief lifted me into an airplane, strapped my leg to the rudder (pedal), and I flew four missions that day." After North Africa had been secured by the joint British and U.S. ground troops, Thyng had logged 162 combat missions. Battle weary and wounded, he was sent home, an ace with eight confirmed air kills.

Harrison Thyng was promoted to full colonel at age twenty-six and was made commander of the 413th Fighter Group, flying P-47s, which he activated and trained. He led this group making the first single-engine fighter plane crossing of the Pacific Ocean, from Hawaii to Ie Shima, in June 1945. Colonel Thyng flew twenty-two missions and shot down a Japanese fighter while escorting B-29s on bombing raids over China and Japan. One of those missions was to escort the B-29 during the atomic attack on Nagasaki. At war's end, he was transferred back to the United States.

Thyng was commissioned as a regular officer in the U.S. Air Force in 1946. From September 1947 to May 1950, he was an Air National Guard instructor. During this time, he organized the Maine, Vermont, and New Hampshire Air National Guard. Colonel Thyng began flying jet aircraft in 1948 and commanded the jet-equipped 33rd Fighter Wing. In 1951, he was assigned to be commanding officer of the 4th Fighter Wing at Kimpo Airfield, near Seoul, Korea.

In Korea he inherited a unit that was outnumbered by 750 MiG-15s flying from five bases north of the Yalu River. Without enough equipment and parts to keep his aircraft flying, Thyng risked his career by going directly to Air Force Chief of Staff Hoyt Vandenberg, saying he could not be held responsible for air superiority unless he had the parts to keep his unit's F-86s flying. The parts arrived within ninety-six hours, but Colonel Thyng's career took a hit for bucking the chain of command.

Thyng scored more air victories than the five he is credited with by official sources. It is well known that he gave credit for several of his air kills to the wingmen who flew with him and kept him safe. During this tour of duty at Kimpo, he flew a total of 113 combat missions in his F-86 saber jet.

This was an exhilarating and heady time for fighter pilots. As Tom Wolfe wrote in his novel *The Right Stuff*, this was "*...fighter jock heaven! Using F-86's mainly, the Air Force was producing aces, pilots who had shot down five planes or more, as fast as the Koreans and Chinese could get their Soviet MiG-15's up to fight them.*" "*Col. Harrison R. Thyng...glowed like Excalibur when he described his 4th fighter-interceptor wing: 'like olden knights the F-86 pilots ride up over North Korea to the Yalu River, the sun glinting off silver aircraft, contrails streaming behind, as they challenge the numerically superior enemy to come up and fight.' Lances and plumes! I'm a knight, come on up and fight! Why hold back! Knights of the right stuff!*"

Colonel Thyng described one of his maneuvers, "Suddenly you go into a steep turn. Your Mach drops off. The MiG turns with you, and you let him gradually creep up and out-turn you. At the critical moment you reverse your turn. The hydraulic controls (of the F-86) work beautifully. The MiG-15 cannot turn as readily as you and is slung out to the side. When you pop your speed brakes, the MiG flashes by you. Quickly closing the brakes, you slide onto his tail and hammer him with your 50's."

When Colonel Thyng went home from Korea, he was given a farewell dinner. On September 29, 1952, General Glenn Barcus, commanding officer of the 57th Air Force, named him one of the greatest fighters of all time. He was an ace in two wars and, more important, a leader willing to take risks for the benefit of his men.

Before retiring, Brigadier General Thyng served as Western Air Defense Force deputy of operations, air division commander, sector commander, and NORAD vice commander. He logged over seven thousand hours flying time, of which three thousand hours were in jet fighters.

In 1966, Harrison Thyng made an unsuccessful bid for U.S. senator from New Hampshire. He was the founder and first President of New England Aeronautical Institute, which merged with Daniel Webster Junior College to become Daniel Webster College in Nashua, New Hampshire. He died September 24, 1983, at a hospital in Concord.

In 2004, General Harrison R. Thyng was honored by the people of Pittsfield, New Hampshire, when they dedicated a memorial to him. Its four sections represent the four theaters of war, in which he fought and flew—Europe, North Africa, the Pacific, and Korea.

References:
Knights of the Air, Volume I, Jerry Valencia, 1980.
The Right Stuff, Tom Wolfe, 1979
Korean War Aces, Robert Dorr, 1955

JOSEPH C. MCCONNELL JR.

Captain, U.S. Air Force
Korean War

Born: January 30, 1922, Dover, New Hampshire
Died: August 25, 1954, Edwards AFB, California
Buried: Victorville Cemetery, California

Joseph McConnell remains the leading American Jet Triple
Ace with sixteen air victories over MiGs in the Korean War.

Awards: Distinguished Service Cross
             Silver Star
             Distinguished Flying Cross
             One Air Medal—WW II
             Three Air Medals—Korea

JOSEPH C. MCCONNELL JR. BEGAN HIS MILITARY CAREER
in 1940, joining the Army at age eighteen. At the time of his enlistment he applied for pilot training, but was assigned to the Medical
Corps instead.

During World War II, Joe McConnell was a medical corpsman
assigned to Fort Devens, Massachusetts. He met Pearl Brown,
whom he affectionately called Butch, in nearby Fitchburg. McConnell wanted to be a pilot and paid for civilian flight instruction in
light airplanes at the Fitchburg airport. After two years of duty,he
was successful in being transferred to the Army Air Corps.

Joe and Pearl married and moved to Texas, where Joe completed training to become a navigator. During World War II, McConnell flew sixty combat missions as navigator on B-24 bombers
assigned to the 448th Bombardment Group, 8th Air Force.

After the war, he remained in the Air Force and in 1948 became
a pilot, qualified in the new F-86 Saber jet. At the outbreak of the
Korean War, he volunteered but it was not until late 1952 that he
was assigned to the 39th Fighter Interceptor Squadron of the 51st
Fighter Interceptor Wing. Assigned to Korea, he named his F-86 the
"Beauteous Butch," his wife's nickname.

McConnell scored his first victory on January 14, 1953, and the fifth—making him an ace—on February 16th. By the end of April, he had downed ten MiG-15s, making him a double ace. On April 12, 1953, while shooting down his eighth MiG, his own aircraft was shot down. He bailed out into the ocean and was rescued by an H-19 helicopter from Base K-16 in Korea.

Lt. Dean Abbott was flying as Joe McConnell's wingman on his final mission, on May 18. They were in hot pursuit of MiGs crossing the Yalu River in China, when suddenly three flights of MiGs appeared. Abbott yelled, "There must be thirty of them." McConnell responded, "Yeh, and we've got em all to ourselves!" The conversation is well documented, as the pilots' transmissions were being monitored by wing command.

In May, Joe McConnell shot down six MiGs, including three in one day on May 18. Those victories made him a triple ace and brought his final score to sixteen confirmed kills. Upon scoring these last victories, McConnell was ordered back to the United States by General Glenn Barcus, who didn't want his senior ace in any further combat. At that time, many USAF pilots insisted that the Russian-built MiG-15 fighters were being flown by Russian pilots, not North Korean or Chinese communist pilots. In 2002, the Russian pilots broke their enforced silence and admitted that they were, in fact, flying most of the MiG-15s in Korea.

Returning to the United States, McConnell continued flying F-86 Saber jets at George Air Force Base. He and his family lived in nearby Apple Valley, California, in a house built for them by the "appreciative community." He was attached to Edwards Air Force Base, California, as a test pilot.

On August 24, 1954, while on a test flight in an F-86-H model, serial #52-1981, the fifth production model, at Edwards, an elevator control malfunctioned caused by a missing bolt. Captain McConnell continued to fly the aircraft using only manual elevator trim, throttle, and rudder. Rather than bailing out immediately, he attempted to fly the crippled aircraft back to Edwards. Several miles short of the dry lakebed landing area, the attempt failed. McConnell ejected, but was too low for the parachute to open. The F-86-H crashed and Captain McConnell was killed.

Captain Joseph McConnell Jr. to this day remains the leading American triple jet ace.

References:
Time magazine: September 6, 1954
Time magazine: October 17, 1955
Documents supplied by the USAF History Support Office, Bolling Air Force Base, Washington, D.C.

LEON JOSEPH JACQUES JR.

First Lieutenant, U.S. Army
Korean War

Born: May 2, 1924, Milford, New Hampshire
Died: July 12, 1950, South Korea
Buried: St. Patrick's Cemetery, Amherst, New Hampshire
Education: U.S. Military Academy, West Point, 1947
Awards: Bronze Star for Valor
             Purple Heart
             Combat Infantryman Badge

LEON J. JACQUES JR. WAS ONE OF THE FIRST CASUALTIES of the Korean War. Leon was born and raised in Milford, New Hampshire, the oldest son of Leon, Sr. and Vera (Stoddard) Jacques. Leon senior repaired shoes in his shop on the oval in the center of Milford. The Jacques were a devout Catholic family. Leon's younger brother, Donald, was ordained a diocesan priest and his sister Jeanne became a nurse.

In high school, Leon was class president and lettered in baseball, basketball, and track. After graduation, in 1942, he studied at St. Anselm's College for a year. In 1943, he entered New York Military Academy at Cornwall-on-the-Hudson. In the summer of 1944, he entered the U.S. Military Academy at West Point in its advanced class and graduated in three years. He was commissioned a second lieutenant of infantry.

Jacques returned to Milford and married his high school sweetheart, Marion Woods. It was a double wedding ceremony when her sister, Evelyn, married Richard O'Neil.

The young couple went to Fort Benning, Georgia, where Jacques attended the Infantry Officers basic course. His first duty station was Fort Riley, Kansas. In 1949, Lieutenant Jacques was assigned to the 21st Infantry Regiment of the 24th Division at Camp Wood in Kumamoto, Kyushu, Japan. In December of that year, Marion gave birth to their son, Steven, at the U.S. Army's

118th Station Hospital in Fukuoka, about a three-hour jeep ride from Camp Wood.

Lieutenant Jacques served as the 21st Regiment, Third Battalion's S-2 (Intelligence) staff officer. At that time, the U.S. Army had been reduced in strength from ninety divisions to only ten divisions, most of them doing occupation duty in Germany and Japan after the end of World War II. The 21st Regiment was at 70 percent strength with only two, instead of three battalions.

Little or no anticipation or preparations for a war had been made when suddenly the North Korean Army invaded South Korea in Soviet-made tanks on June 25, 1950. On June 30, President Harry Truman approved the commitment of U.S. ground troops to aid and protect South Korea. The 21st Regiment, in Japan, was the nearest to Korea and was alerted. A 440-man force from the First Battalion, commanded by Lieutenant Colonel Brad Smith, was airlifted to Korea on July 1.

"Task Force Smith" arrived at Taejon on July 2. On July 5 they advanced to just north of Osan to engage the enemy. The infantry unit was not equipped to fight against the Russian-built T-34 tanks, but the First Battalion made a gallant stand. They delayed the enemy until their ammunition ran out and they withdrew from their defensive position. The North Korean Army swept past Colonel Smith's task force and pushed south.

On July 10, the Third Battalion of the 21st Regiment, commanded by Lieutenant Colonel Carl Jensen plus the survivors of the First Battalion made their stand at Chochiwon. In the command post with Colonel Jensen was Lieutenant Jacques. Their command post was on the high ground above the Kum River. The 21st delayed the enemy for three days before being forced to withdraw.

Colonel Jensen was killed in the command post bunker and Lieutenant Jacques was killed on July 12 as he was leading a group of men to safety. Most of this group were killed, but some were taken prisoner.

The Twenty-First Regiment lost 1,433 men, about 60 percent of its strength. The battle continued through July and August until Army reinforcements from Okinawa and the United States arrived, along with Marines and a British brigade from Hong Kong. The new units established the Pusan perimeter, which held until General MacArthur's landing at Inchon.

Lieutenant Jacques was posthumously awarded the Bronze Star for Valor, the Purple Heart, the Combat Infantryman Badge, and appropriate service medals. A service was held at St. Patrick's Church in Milford in January 1951. Burial with full military honors was held on May 20, 1951.

In 1954, the town of Milford voted to build a twelve-room school near the high school. It was completed in 1955 and named the First Lieutenant Leon Jacques School.

References:
From the Hudson to the Yalu, Harry Maihafer
The Granite Town, Winifred A. Wright, 1979
Correspondence from: Mrs. Marion Jacques Dube, Lt. Col. Ralph E. Culbertson, and Col. Edwin F. Merrill Jr.

SPACE PROGRAM

1957–

ALAN B. SHEPARD JR.

Rear Admiral, U.S. Navy
Naval Aviator, Astronaut

Born: November 18, 1923, East Derry, New Hampshire
Died: July 21, 1998, near his home, Pebble Beach, CA
Education: U.S. Naval Academy, 1944
First American in Space; Freedom 7, May 5, 1961
Third Lunar Landing; Apollo XIV, 1971
Fifth Man to Walk on the Moon
Awards: Congressional Medal of Honor—Space, 1978
               Distinguished Service Medal—NASA
               Distinguished Service Medal—Navy
               Distinguished Flying Cross—Navy
WWII Service: USS destroyer *Cogswell*; Pacific Theater,
               1944-1946

ALAN B. SHEPARD JR. WAS BORN AND RAISED IN EAST Derry, New Hampshire. His father was a retired Army colonel. Alan grew up on the family farm and went to local public schools. His elementary education was in a one-room schoolhouse where one teacher taught all grades 1-6. Young Alan completed the six grades in only five years, joking that his teacher just wanted to get rid of him quickly. He graduated from Pinkerton Academy, a public school in Derry. He prepped for the Naval Academy for a year at Admiral Farragut Academy in New Jersey.

As a youngster in East Derry, Alan was fascinated with flying. He would ride his bicycle ten miles to the Manchester airport (later named Grenier Field) to do odd jobs around the hangar in hopes of getting an airplane ride. He realized then that aviation would be his life's work.

After graduating from the Naval Academy in 1944, Ensign Shepard was assigned to sea duty for the remaining days of World War II. He served aboard the destroyer USS *Cogswell* in the Pacific from 1944 to1946. He married Louise Brewer, a young lady from Philadelphia whom he met while at Annapolis.

In 1947, Shepard took flight training at Corpus Christi and Pensacola. He won his naval aviator wings in 1947 and was assigned to Fighter Squadron 42 at Norfolk, Virginia, and Jacksonville, Florida. He made two Mediterranean cruises during 1948 and 1949.

Shepard graduated Navy Test Pilot School at Patuxent River, Maryland, in 1950. For the next two years at Patuxent, he helped perfect naval aircraft such as the F2H-3 Banshee, the F3H Demon, the F8U Crusader, the F11F Tiger, and the F5D Skylancer. He also did some high-altitude flying and helped to develop the Navy's in-flight refueling system. From 1953 to1956 Shepard served as operations officer in a night-fighter squadron on board a carrier off the West Coast.

After reassignment back to Patuxent, he was selected to attend the Naval War College at Newport, Rhode Island. After that, he was a staff officer for the Commander-in-Chief at the Atlantic Fleet Headquarters in Norfolk, Virginia, in charge of aircraft readiness for the fleet. Shepard was well-positioned to become commander of a carrier squadron, the plum for any career Navy aviator.

In 1959, the newly created National Aeronautics and Space Administration (NASA) invited 110 top-rated test pilots to volunteer for the manned space flight program. Alan Shepard was one of the seven chosen for Project Mercury. On April 8, 1959, he and the others—Scott Carpenter, Leroy Cooper, John Glenn, Virgil (Gus)

Grissom, Walter (Wally) Schirra, and Donald (Deke) Slayton, were presented to the public.

The seven Mercury astronauts were subjected to two years of intensive training and grueling physical and psychological testing. They studied and planned for every conceivable situation they might encounter in space. Alan Shepard, early in training, announced, "I know it can be done and I want to do it." His sense of humor helped the Mercury seven get through their tough training. His parody of José Jimenez's parody of the astronauts kept all in stitches. Each of the Mercury astronauts wanted to be the first in space, but Shepard was chosen for the first American manned mission into space. On April 15, 1961, only a few weeks before Shepard's flight, Soviet cosmonaut, Yuri Gagarin became the first human to reach outer space in a single orbit around the Earth.

Shepard's flight, on May 5, was still a historic event because he was able to maneuver his Freedom 7 space capsule himself. While the Soviet mission remained secret until its completion, Shepard's flight was seen on live television by millions, from blast off to recovery at sea by helicopters to a nearby aircraft carrier—a near perfect splash down.

Subsequent flights by Mercury astronauts Glenn and Grissom would soon surpass the achievements of Gagarin's flight. Shepard moved on to the next phase of the space program, Project Gemini.

Alan Shepard was scheduled to command the first Gemini mission when he was diagnosed with Meniere's disease, an inner-ear problem affecting his equilibrium. This problem kept him out of space travel for six years, but he remained with NASA as chief of the astronaut office. He waited patiently and watched the younger astronauts of Project Apollo prepare for travel to the moon. A launch-pad fire destroyed Apollo V claiming the lives of three astronauts, including Gus Grissom, a comrade from Project Mercury.

In 1968, Shepard underwent an operation, that restored his equilibrium and he immediately volunteered for a lunar mission. While Apollo XI and XII landed men on the moon, Alan had to bide his time and wait. Apollo XIII experienced technical problems and returned safely to Earth without making its scheduled lunar landing.

Finally, in 1971, Alan Shepard, now forty-seven, the oldest astronaut in the program, was chosen to lead the Apollo XIV mission to the moon. The lunar landing and the excursion were broadcast on live TV. Alan Shepard and his wonderful sense of humor will be forever remembered bouncing about in the low-gravity of the moon, then driving his golf balls a mile or so. Some future lunar explorer may be startled to find those white balls in a huge sand (dust) trap.

In 1978, Alan Shepard was awarded the Medal of Honor, Space. He was promoted to admiral and retired from the Navy and NASA in 1974, and moved to a home in Pebble Beach, California. There he took advantage of the nearby golf courses and drove some balls in one-gravity environment.

Alan Shepard died in 1998 after a two-year bout with leukemia. His wife of fifty-three years, Louise, died shortly afterward. In 2006 the U.S. Navy named a supply ship, T-AKE-3, the *Alan Shepard*, in his honor.

References:
We Seven, the Astronauts, 1962
The Right Stuff, Tom Wolfe, 1979
"The Mercury Astronauts," *Life* Magazine, Sept. 14, 1959

VIETNAM

1961–1975

VIETNAM WAS ONE OF THE THREE STATES OF THE FRENCH
Union (with Laos and Cambodia) comprising French Indochina, in
Southeast Asia. Vietnam is located on the eastern edge of Indochina
bordering the South China Sea with a 1,400 mile coastline. From
north to south, it consisted of three distinct areas—Tonkin, capitol
city—Hanoi; Annan, capital city—Hue; and the southernmost,
Cochinchina, capital city—Saigon.

Over 80 percent of the Vietnamese people are ethnically
Annamese, a mixed breed representing varied physical Asian
types. They were already a mature culture of the Bronze Age when
conquered by the Chinese in the third century B.C.

In the mountains of Tonkin are some uncivilized tribes,
notably the fierce Muongs. In southern Annam are a few isolated
groups of Chams—descendents of a great people influenced by
Hindu and Islamic culture, yet with a strong Malay strain. In the
Annam Central Highlands, are the primitive hill people known as
Moi—believed to be remnants of Indonesian tribes, which at one
time occupied the entire country. These tribes were known by the
French term, Montagnards, mountain-people.

The Chinese play the predominant role in trade and commerce.
Over one-half million are centered in the Saigon-Cholon region.

In 1940, during World War II, French Indochina was occupied
by the Japanese, who left control in the hands of the Vichy regime
of France. During WWII, Japan fostered separatism from France
and a feeling of Asian nationalism. In March 1945, Japan interned

the French Vichy administration and troops. Japan then proclaimed the autonomous state of Vietnam with Bao Dai, emperor of Annam, as the ruler. This puppet state collapsed with the defeat of the Japanese by the WWII allied forces.

Since France was not in a position to reoccupy Indochina, it was agreed at the Potsdam Conference that Vietnam north of the 16th parallel would be occupied by Chinese forces, while British troops would occupy the southern half. In August 1945, the Viet Minh League led by Ho Chi Minh, a communist, proclaimed the Democratic Republic of Vietnam. When the British forces landed in Saigon in September, they found the country in the hands of lawless bands and high anti-French feelings.

When the French took control of Cochinchina (South Vietnam) the local Viet Minh officials fled north of the 16th parallel. The Viet Minh were able to consolidate their position there and secure control of a provisional government at Hanoi. Sporadic fighting ensued between the French and Viet Minh forces until a convention was signed in Hanoi on March 6, 1946. By terms of this convention, France recognized the Democratic Republic of Vietnam as a free state within French Indochina and the French Union.

Marked differences between the interpretation of the convention by each of the parties soon became apparent, mainly concerning the future of south Vietnam—Cochinchina. The south held the fertile Mekong Delta, the "rice bowl of Asia." In December 1946, Viet Minh forces made an unprovoked surprise attack on Hanoi killing 140 French including women and children. Two hundred others were taken away as hostages, precipitating what might be called the "First Vietnam War."

Various political and religious groups who wanted a Vietnamese state, refused to follow the Viet Minh's twin paths of communism and terrorist revolution and gave their support to Bao Dai, as emperor. An agreement with France in March 1949, defined the status of Vietnam and its place within the French Union. On February 2, 1950, the President of France signed the ratification.

Meanwhile, fighting against the Viet Minh continued. By January 1951, 63,000 French troops were engaged against an estimated 150,000 communist forces. From 1950 onward supplies of American arms and weapons were provided to the French under the U.S. mutual defense assistance program.

The communists first invaded Laos in 1953. French General Henri Navarre attempted to break the organized communist resistance but was unsuccessful. The Viet Minh then began a fifty-five-day siege of Dien Bien Phu, a point in North Vietnam near the Laotian border. Dien Bien Phu fell on May 7. On July 21, 1954, armistice agreements were signed in Geneva, which set a demarcation line along the 17th parallel. The area to the north under Ho Chi Minh and the remainder to the south going to the so-called Saigon government under Bao Dai. People from each area could move north or south, but were deterred by terrorist Viet Minh tactics.

The Geneva agreement also called for holding elections in 1956 for a unified government in Vietnam. However, in 1955, South Vietnamese Premier Ngo Dinh Diem rejected a request for election talks. Premier Diem sponsored a referendum in South Vietnam in October 1955, in which Bao Dai was ousted as chief of state. Premier Diem proclaimed South Vietnam to be republic with himself as first president. Democracy in the Republic of Vietnam (RVN) had a shaky start. In November 1955 the U.S. formed the Military Assistance Advisory Group—(MAAG). Select officers and NCO's brought their families with them and advised their Vietnamese military counterparts on staff levels and field levels. This support had the complete backing of the U.S. Congress, President Eisenhower, and in 1959, the over-whelming support of the American people. For example: the NY Times in July 1959 editorialized, "with American's help (Vietnam) has been made less vulnerable from a military point of view . . . a five-year miracle has been carried out. Vietnam . . . is becoming stronger . . . there is reason to salute President Ngo Dinh Diem."

By 1959, the setting for American involvement in the second Vietnam War was complete. By the end of the year there were 760 U.S. military personnel in South Vietnam and the North Vietnamese were beginning to move men and supplies to the south.

Shortly after John F. Kennedy's election victory in November 1960, the National Liberation Front was formed in Hanoi. In January 1961, President Kennedy approved a Vietnam counter-insurgency plan that called for government reform and military restructuring as the basis for expanding U.S. assistance. Kennedy visited Fort Bragg, NC, and became an ardent supporter of the elite U.S. Army's Special Forces—the Green Berets. Viet Cong insurgents continued making small, swift, deadly attacks throughout the country. In June, President Diem requested U.S. troops to train the Army of South Vietnam (ARVN). In December, the first U.S. combat units arrived in country—the U.S. Army's 8th and the 57th Transportation Companies, both helicopter units flying the antiquated H-21's. Bill Mauldin's cartoon gave impetus to eventually replacing the old H-21s with the new turbo-jet HU-1s (HUEYS). Within two weeks of the U.S. helicopter unit's arrival, ARVN troops were airlifted into battle. U.S. military strength now totaled 3,205.

In 1962, the U.S. Military Assistance Command—Vietnam (MACV) was formed and the U.S. Air Force deployed the Second Air Division. The U.S. Special Forces deployed teams from Okinawa on temporary duty (TDY) status. On the other side of the world, the Cuban missile crisis occurred. By year's end there were 11,000 U.S. personnel in Vietnam.

In January 1963, the Viet Cong defeated the ARVN at the battle of Ap Bac. Throughout the summer, Buddhist monks staged demonstrations and one monk set himself on fire. President Diem ordered government forces to attack Buddhist pagodas. Ambassador Henry Cabot Lodge received a State Department cable stating that the U.S. can no longer tolerate Ngo Dinh Nhu's influence on President Diem's regime. On November 1, the South Vietnamese combined military staged a coup overthrowing President Diem. Diem and Nhu were both killed. Three weeks later in Dallas, Texas, President John F. Kennedy was assassinated and Vice President Lyndon Johnson assumed the presidency.

At the beginning of 1964, there were 16,000 U.S. military in South Vietnam. Communist North Vietnam began the infiltration of regular army units into the south. In April, in an attempt to sever the country, the North Vietnamese Army (NVA) was defeated at the battle of Do Xa.

In August, the U.S. destroyers *Maddox* and *Turner Joy* were attacked by North Vietnamese patrol boats in the Tonkin Gulf.

The U.S. Congress passed the Tonkin Gulf resolution escalating the U.S. military's advisory/ assistance role to armed conflict. In October, the Viet Cong attacked Bien Hoa Air Base destroying six B-57 bombers and killing five U.S. personnel. Soon after, the U.S. 5th Special Forces Group deployed from Fort Bragg, NC, to oversee its operations in Vietnam. U.S. forces reached 23,300, in-country personnel.

1965 saw increased Viet Cong (VC) attacks on U.S. military installations. The U.S. Air Force began its "Rolling Thunder" bombing of North Vietnamese targets to stop the flow of supplies to Viet Cong and North Vietnamese Army units in South Vietnam. The U.S. Marines landed at Da Nang and deployed an air wing to support marine actions in I Corps (northern part of South Vietnam).

Meanwhile, in the United States, the Students for a Democratic Society (SDS) staged an anti-war rally in Washington, DC, in April. In October, more anti-war protests were held in forty cities.

U.S. Navy units were deployed to interdict traffic on coastal waters and to seize or destroy enemy craft. Australia deployed the first battalion of the Royal Australian Regiment for combat operations in III corps area (Saigon, Bien Hoa). The Republic of South Korea (ROK) sent an infantry division and a marine brigade to help the Vietnamese.

The U.S. Army deployed the First Cavalry Division—Airmobile (Air-Cav) to the II Corps area (QuiNhon, An Khe, Plei Ku). The 173rd Airborne Brigade the First Infantry Division, and Third Brigade of the 25th Infantry Division were also deployed. November 14-16 was the first major battle of the war between regular U.S. troops and NVA forces. The Third Brigade of the First Cavalry Division defeated the NVA 32nd, 33rd, and 66th Regiments in the Ia Drang Valley southwest of Plei Ku. By the end of 1965, there were 184,300 U.S. personnel in South Vietnam, 636 Americans had been killed.

1966 saw the deployment of still more combat units—U.S. Air Force tactical and air commando wings, the 4th Infantry, the 9th Infantry, and 25th Infantry Divisions, the Army's First Signal Brigade and 44th Medical Brigade, the 196th and 199th Light Infantry Brigades, the 18th Military Police Brigade. By year's end there were

385,300 U.S. and 52,500 troops from Philippines, Korea and Australia in Vietnam.

As the war escalated in South Vietnam, the flow of war materials and reinforcements continued to flow down the "Ho Chi Minh Trail" in Laos unhampered due to restrictions ordered by politicos in Washington listening to the chants of anti-war protesters. Targets in Hanoi were restricted, tying the hands of Naval and Air Force bomber pilots. By the end of 1967, there were nearly a half-million U.S. troops in South Vietnam, over 16,000 U.S. killed in action. South Vietnam's troop strength was 798,000, over 60,000 killed in action.

1968 saw the siege of Marines at Khe Sanh and in February the Tet offensive by the NVA. During the Tet actions, the VC and NVA massacred over 2,800 civilians in Hue City.

In March, President Johnson announced a de-escalation of the war and stated that he would not run for re-election. Vice President Humphrey announced his candidacy. In November, Humphrey was defeated by Republican Richard M. Nixon.

In May, President Johnson stated that the U.S. and North Vietnam agreed to begin formal peace talks in Paris. The petty quarrels and protracted delays in starting the peace talks resulted in the needless deaths of thousands of men on both sides as the war continued. Parties in Paris argued as to the shape of the table they would sit at.

In September 1968, New Hampshire National Guardsmen were called to active duty. Guardsmen from Manchester, Nashua, Portsmouth, Franklin, Laconia, and Somersworth were assigned to Vietnam artillery fire bases. Twenty-eight Purple Hearts were awarded to New Hampshire soldiers from the 197th Field Artillery during their year in combat. In October, President Johnson ordered a complete halt to bombing of North Vietnam. By the end of the year, there were 536,100 U.S. military in Vietnam, 30,610 Americans had been killed in action.

1969 saw the swearing in of Richard Nixon as President. Nixon appointed Henry Kissinger to be National Security Advisor. In May, Nixon proposed and eight-point peace plan providing for mutual troop withdrawal. The U.S. military began withdrawing division-sized units. By the year's end, there were 475,200 U.S. military in Vietnam, 40,024 Americans had been killed in action.

In 1970, Henry Kissinger began secret peace talks in Paris with American POW's (Prisoners of War) used as bargaining chips. The war continued and the casualties on both sides mounted. More division-sized units were withdrawn. At the end of 1969, over 44,000 U.S. troops had been killed.

During 1971, the combat operations continued, more U.S. units were ordered home leaving those in-country more vulnerable. In November, Nixon announced that the U.S. ground forces were in a defensive role and offensive actions would be taken entirely by the South Vietnamese. By the end of December, the U.S. Air Force was told to resume bombing North Vietnam. By this time 45,626 U.S. servicemen and women had been killed.

The peace talks in Paris continued until Kissinger and LeDuc Tho deadlock on December 13, 1972. Finally, on January 27, 1973, a peace pact is signed by the U.S., the South Vietnamese, the Viet Cong, and the North Vietnamese. By March, the withdrawal of all American troops and the release of 590 U.S. war prisoners held by the communists in Hanoi, are completed. In September, Kissinger replaced William Rogers as Secretary of State. By year's end, only 50 U.S. military personnel remain, limited to U.S. Embassy guards.

In August 1974, Richard Nixon resigned as President, Vice President Gerald Ford assumed the presidency.

Although the peace accord had been signed and agreed to by all parties, the communist North Vietnamese began a series of attacks in December 1974 against Phouc Long Province and in March 1975, against Ban Me Thout, Quang Tri, the cities of Hue and Da Nang. In April, the cities of Qui Nhon, Tuy Hoa and Nha Trang were abandoned by South Vietnamese. In mid-April, the U.S. airlift of homeless Vietnamese children ended. Over 14,000 children were evacuated. April 30, 1975, the NVA captured Saigon. The Vietnam War ended.

MELVIN ZAIS

General, U.S. Army
World War II
Vietnam

Born: May 8, 1916, Fall River, Massachusetts
Died: May 6, 1981, Beaufort, South Carolina
Buried: Arlington National Cemetery
Education: University of New Hampshire, 1937
Awards: Distinguished Service Medal, three Oak-Leaf
             Clusters
             Silver Star, one Oak-Leaf Cluster
             Legion of Merit, three Oak-Leaf Clusters
             Distinguished Flying Cross, one Oak-Leaf
             Cluster
             Bronze Star
             Purple Heart
             Air Medal, twenty-six Oak-Leaf Clusters
             Army Aviator Badge
             Master Parachutist Badge
             Combat Infantryman Badge
             Numerous Foreign Awards
Major Commands:
CG I Field Force, U.S. Army, Vietnam, February 66-May 66
GG 101st Airborne Division, Vietnam, 1968-1969
CG XXIV Corps, U.S. Army, Vietnam, 1969-1970
CG 3rd U.S. Army, Fort McPherson, Georgia, 1972-1973
Cmdr. Allied Land Forces, Southeast Europe, 1973-1976

MELVIN ZAIS GRADUATED FROM THE UNIVERSITY OF NEW
Hampshire in 1937 with a bachelors degree in political science. He
was commissioned in the U.S. Army Reserve as a Second Lieutenant of Infantry. His initial tour of duty was for one year under
the provisions of the Thomason Act. After returning to civilian life,
he served as a Professor of Military Tactics at Tennessee Military
Institute, Sweetwater.

In 1940, Lieutenant Zais was recalled to active duty and assigned to the staff and faculty of the U.S. Army Infantry School, Fort Benning, Georgia. While there, he volunteered for assignment to the 501st Parachute Infantry Battalion, the original paratroop battalion in the Army. He served with the 501st at Fort Benning and later in Panama.

In 1943, following graduation from the shortened, wartime course at the Command and General Staff College at Fort Leavenworth, Kansas, Zais was selected as a major to command the Third Battalion 517th Parachute Infantry Regiment. He led the 517th from cadre training at Camp MacKall, North Carolina, to combat in Italy and France, including a night parachute assault into southern France. Major Zais then served as regimental executive officer during combat in Belgium and Germany until the end of World War II. He assumed command of the regiment at Fort Bragg, North Carolina, and commanded the 517th until its inactivation in January 1946.

His postwar service emphasized command, troop duty, and high-level staff positions. He served as G-1 and G-3 of the 82nd Airborne Division. General Zais attended the regular course at the Command and Staff College and was selected to remain at Fort Leavenworth for three years as an instructor.

In 1952 he was sent to Turkey, where he trained with the Turkish Brigade, and served as an advisor to that brigade when it was deployed to Korea.

Zais later commanded the 505th Parachute Infantry Regiment. He was selected as chief of staff of the 101st Airborne Division and subsequently to command the 187th Airborne Infantry Battle Group at Fort Campbell, Kentucky, during the initial tests of the "pentomic" concept.

General Zais' staff experience ranged from combat units to the joint staff, joint chiefs of staff in the Pentagon. He served in the G-3 section, headquarters, Department of the Army 1955-1956, and as deputy G-1 of the U.S. Army Europe 1958-1959. For the next three years he served as the G-3 of the Seventh Army in Germany.

Upon his return to the United States, he served with both the J-3 and J-5 staff elements of the U.S. Strike Command at MacDill Air

Force Base, Florida. General Zais completed the Advanced Management Program at Harvard University in 1963. He was promoted to brigadier general on June 1, 1964, and became the director of enlisted personnel, Department of the Army, until February 1966.

General Zais was transferred to Vietnam, where he was the deputy commanding general, First Field Force, and then assistant commanding general of the First Infantry Division. After returning from Vietnam in July 1966, General Zais served as the director for individual training, Headquarters, Department of the Army. On May 1, 1967, he was promoted to major general.

He and his wife Marjorie Aileen Emert, had two sons, Barrie E. and Mitchell M. Zais, both of whom became army officers. After Marjorie's death, General Zais married Patricia V. Light on August 6, 1967, at Fort Myers, Virginia. He became stepfather of David R. and John P. Light.

In July 1968, General Zais was reassigned to Vietnam, where he assumed command of the 101st Airborne Division. Being a rated Army aviator, he flew many combat missions in the UH-1 "Huey" helicopter. He was awarded the Air Medal for Valor and two Distinguished Flying Cross medals.

Ap Bia Mountain, dubbed "Hamburger Hill," was the commanding feature in the Ashau Valley near the border with Laos. The valley offered an easy route to the cities of Hue and Da Nang. The North Vietnamese had controlled the Ashau since 1966. In early May 1969, during a sweep through the valley, a battalion of the 101st Airborne Division found the enemy in strength on Ap Bia Mountain. The battle for Hamburger Hill ensued.

The attacking American unit, the Third Battalion of the 187th, was led by Lt. Colonel Weldon Honeycutt, who directed artillery and air strikes on the hill and led three infantry assaults up the steep slopes. Eleven days later, the North Vietnamese Army finally fled. The NVA lost 597 men killed, more than a battalion. The Americans lost fifty killed. Honeycutt's aggressive tactics, authorized by General Zais on the battlefield, produced heavy initial losses but saved American lives by avoiding a long, protracted battle. The hill was honeycombed with caves storing ammunition, hundreds of bags of rice, a hospital, and what had been the North Vietnamese Army's regimental headquarters.

General William Westmoreland said, in his book, *A Soldier Reports*, "To have left the North Vietnamese undisturbed on the mountain would have been to jeopardize our control of the valley and accept a renewed threat to the coastal cities. A prolonged siege would have been costly and tied up troops indefinitely. The commander of the 101st, Major General Melvin Zais, quite properly ordered an attack."

In June 1969, Zais was promoted to lieutenant general and assigned as the commanding general of the XXIV Corps in Military Region I of Vietnam. Following this two-year combat tour, General Zais returned to the Pentagon in August 1970 to the joint staff of the Joint Chiefs of Staff as the director of operations J-3.

General Zais assumed command of the Third U.S. Army at Fort McPherson, Georgia, in June 1972. He remained at Fort McPherson until June 1973. He was promoted to General (four stars) on July 13, 1973, and was named Commander, Allied Land Forces Southeastern Europe, Izmir, Turkey, that same month. He commanded NATO's southeastern flank during a volatile and trying period, witnessing the Cyprus crisis, Greece's withdrawal from NATO, and the U.S. arms embargo against Turkey, and the closure of American bases on Turkish soil.

General Zais was a graduate of the Command and General Staff College, the Armed Forces Staff College, the National War College, and Harvard Business School's Advanced Management Program. In 1971, he received an honorary Doctor of Science degree from the University of New Hampshire.

In 1974, General Zais was named the Twenty-Seventh Kermit Roosevelt lecturer by the Department of the Army. The exchange lecture series between the U.S. Army and the British Army is named for the late Kermit Roosevelt, second son of President Theodore Roosevelt, who served in the armies of both the United States and the United Kingdom in both World Wars.

General Zais retired from active duty in 1976 after thirty-nine years of service. He had commanded at every level available to an officer—platoon, company, battalion, regiment, division, corps,

Army and Army Group. In October 1978, the ROTC military science building at the University of New Hampshire was dedicated as General Melvin Zais Hall.

General Zais died of cancer on May 6, 1981, in Beaufort, South Carolina. He was buried with full military honors at Arlington National Cemetery.

References:

Dept. of the Army Biographical Data provided by Mrs. Melvin Zais.

Army ROTC, University of New Hampshire, Durham NH

U.S. Army Military History Institute, Carlisle, PA

A Soldier Reports, Gen. William Westmoreland, 1976

WILLIAM C. HAZEN

Lt. Colonel, U.S. Army
Special Forces "Green Beret"
Vietnam War

Born: February 3, 1936, Concord, New Hampshire
Education: University of New Hampshire, 1958
Awards: Bronze Star
                   Air Medal
                   Combat Infantryman's Badge
                   Senior Parachutist Badge
                   Ranger / Pathfinder

WILLIAM HAZEN WAS BORN IN CONCORD AND RAISED IN Henniker, New Hampshire. He graduated from Henniker High School, where he played baseball and basketball and represented his school at Boy's State. He graduated from the University of New Hampshire in 1958 with a bachelor's degree in business administration. He was commissioned as a lieutenant of infantry and completed the Infantry Officers course at Fort Benning, Georgia. Lieutenant Hazen became qualified as an Army parachutist, a Ranger and as a Pathfinder. He served as a platoon leader in the Second Infantry Division at Fort Benning from 1959 through 1961.

In 1960, Bill Hazen married his college sweetheart, Judith Manning. They had three sons and one daughter. The family adjusted well to army life with eventual tours of duty in Korea and Okinawa. In March 1962, Hazen completed the rigorous Special Forces training at Fort Bragg, North Carolina.

Bill Hazen was a Green Beret years before the first U.S. Army infantry units went to Vietnam. His first six-month tour of duty in Vietnam was in 1963-1964, before Robin Moore wrote his book *The Green Berets*, before Sgt. Barry Sadler wrote "The Ballad of the Green Berets," and before that war's first Medal of Honor was awarded to Army Captain Roger Donolan.

Bill Hazen won his green beret the hard way, back when, as the ballad goes . . . "one hundred men, we'll test today, but only

Captain William Hazen (right) (UNH-'58) and Captain William McGee (left) at Ya Lop (code name of operation Beau Geste) about 5 miles from Cambodian border, north of Ban Me Thout. December 1963.

three win the green beret." He was in Vietnam for the right reason, to free the oppressed—"de opresso liber"—the motto of the U.S. Army Special Forces.

Bill was assigned to the First Special Forces group in 1962 and the Hazen family moved to Okinawa. First Lieutenant Hazen's first assignment was for five months in Laos. His A-team's mission was training at the Laos NCO (Non-Commissioned Officers) Academy.

In 1963, Captain Hazen was assigned to the Republic of Vietnam for five months on TDY (Temporary Duty) from Okinawa where his family waited. The plus side of a TDY assignment was the sixteen dollars per diem. The minus side was that you didn't get credit for an overseas tour of duty for less than six months. Hazen's five month's TDY in Vietnam was commanding A-team #217 in the central highlands. The team's mission was to live with, recruit, and train men of the Rhade' montagnard tribe to fight the Viet Cong. The Rhade' was one of several primitive tribes of "mountain people," montagnards. They were hunter-gatherers whose weapons were blow-guns and cross-bows. The men wore loincloths, the women wore a sarong like cloth around their waist with breasts exposed. In the tropical climate, the children wore nothing.

The typical village consisted of bare ground with a series of thatched long-houses on three-foot legs. Six to eight families inhabited a single long-house. As the numbers in the family increased, the house was extended. Two sets of steps were in front of each long-house, one for men, one for women. In front of the long-house was a simple shrine dangling feathers and bones to their animistic deities. These were simple, honest, hardworking people you could trust and depend upon.

Hazen dubbed his mission "Operation Beau Geste" as their first operation point was set up near and old French Foreign Legion fort. When his A-team arrived in Vietnam, they inherited 350 Rhade' living in three different villages north of Ban Me Thuot. "Once the village defenders were established, the special forces team supervised programs to improve the quality of life for villagers. They established infirmaries and provided minor medical treatment, constructed shelters, improved sanitation and generally helped in any way they could. As soon as a mutually supporting cluster of villages had been established, the process was begun again to include other villages," said General Carl Stiner, in Tom Clancy's *Shadow Warriors*. Hazen very soon had a trained force of six hundred montagnard "strikers."

The A-team's area of operation was twelve kilometers wide and twenty kilometers north and south on the Ya Lop River. Although their western boundary was the Cambodian border, watch points and ambush points were deliberately set up on the Ho Chi Minh Trail inside Cambodia. This was mountainous and heavily wooded terrain. The team and its "strikers" walked everywhere. Everyone wore the same uniform—camouflage fatigues and a soft, wide-brimmed "boonie hat." While the American wore jungle boots, most of the montagnards preferred to go barefoot, as they had all their lives. The Green Berets carried AR-15 and M-1 rifles and shotguns. The strikers carried carbines and one B.A.R. (Browning Automatic Rifle) per squad.

When Captain Hazen's A-team initially set up its out-post, it was supplied by U.S. Army UH-1 helicopters flown by this author (see photo, page 206). The final third of their trek was on foot using elephants as pack animals to carry the heavy gear.

Bill Hazen had to dig deep into his memory to supply some of these facts. In his own words, "That was 43 years ago. I guess that . . . we were very young men then, half-way around the world, in a very different place trying to do something for our country and at the same time something for the local [Vietnamese] people. I think that I was lucky. I had the opportunity to work and live with the montagnards of the Rhade' tribe. That was a rare experience, which I really enjoyed."

Hazen completed the Infantry Officer's advanced course at Fort Benning, Georgia, 1964-1965. He returned to Vietnam in October 1966, serving as the S-4 of a Special Forces B-team in the Mekong Delta. After his promotion to major, he became the executive officer. He controlled three A-teams and was the adviser to the province chief of Kien Phong. The Special Forces compound was in Cao Lanh, the provincial capital.

At midnight on July 3, 1967, on the eve of the Fourth of July, the Viet Cong attacked the American compound with mortar rounds.

The Viet Cong simultaneously attacked a battalion of ARVN (Army of Vietnam) only three hundred yards from the U.S. compound. Many of the ARVN soldiers had their families with them. The ARVN took many casualties—dead and wounded—including Vietnamese women and children.

Major Hazen returned to the United States to complete the command and staff course at Fort Leavenworth, Kansas, in 1970. He was promoted to lieutenant colonel just prior to his assignment to the Republic of Korea. His family accompanied him, and lived on the Yong Son base near Seoul, Korea. He was assigned to the J-3 (Joint Staff) as a ground planner in the Eighth U.S. Army headquarters.

Colonel Hazen said, "I had very good results working with the ROKs [Koreans]. I had the opportunity to work with them at the ROK army headquarters and Joint Staff levels. I liked the Koreans, they were always honest with me and very professional."

Bill Hazen returned with his family to Durham, New Hampshire, where he became professor of military science in charge of the army Reserve Officers Training Corps (ROTC) detachment. He served in that capacity from 1976 through 1980. Colonel Hazen had the privilege to commission all three of his sons, two of whom served in Iraq.

In the course of his twenty-three-year army career, Bill Hazen made forty-five parachute jumps. He retired from active duty in 1981 and now lives in Kittery Point, Maine.

References:
Personal correspondence
The Shadow Warriors, Tom Clancy, 2002
The Two Vietnams, Bernard Fall, 1963

HOWARD WALKER KAISER

First Lieutenant, U.S. Air Force
Vietnam War

Born: March 25, 1941, Batavia, New York
Died: September 13, 1966, Vietnam
Buried: West Chesterfield, New Hampshire
Education: University of New Hampshire, 1963
Awards: Silver Star
               Purple Heart
               Air Medal, eighteen Oak-Leaf Clusters
               Aviator Wings—USAF
               RVN, Medal for Valor

HOWARD WALKER KAISER, THE SON OF BEVERLY AND
J. Howard Kaiser, was born in Batavia, New York, and raised in
West Chesterfield, New Hampshire. He graduated from Keene
High School in 1959. He was an all-state football player and a
member of the 1959 state championship football team.

Kaiser graduated from the University of New Hampshire in
1963 with a bachelor of arts degree in economics. While at the University of New Hampshire he was a member of Alpha Tau Omega
fraternity.

He was commissioned as a second lieutenant in the U.S. Air
Force. In 1964 he entered active duty at Laughlin Air Force Base,
Texas, and began pilot training, becoming qualified in T-33 and T-
37 jet aircraft. Lieutenant Kaiser was transferred to Travis Air Force
Base, California, for qualification in C-130 cargo/transport aircraft.
The flight training, from April through September 1965, included
Survival School in Nevada and further training at Edwards Air
Force Base, California.

In January 1966, Lieutenant. Kaiser was assigned to Vietnam.
At Song Be, he became qualified in the O-1 Cessna, a single-engine,
fixed-wing airplane he would fly in forward air control (FAC) missions. Top speed of the 0-1 was 110 miles per hour, far slower than
the T-28s and A-1 Skyraider fighter aircraft being flown by U.S. and

Vietnamese pilots. The mission of the FAC was to find targets on the ground, mark them with a smoke grenade, and communicate with fighter/bombers in the air guiding them to the ground targets, then observing and redirecting attacks. All of this was done at low level, well within range of rifles fired from the ground.

After two months of training, Lieutenant Kaiser began flying combat missions, which he continued to do on a daily basis. He flew more than six hundred flights with as many as five flights each day. From the end of May until his death on September 13, he flew every day. Although the missions were hazardous, Lieutenant Kaiser exhibited outstanding airmanship and courage while directing air-to-ground attack missions.

He received the Silver Star for a mission he flew on July 26, 1966. While flying his 0-1 aircraft on aerial reconnaissance, Lieutenant Kaiser spotted a well-camouflaged, hostile battalion near Phuoc Long, called for air strikes, and repeatedly flew through intense ground fire while directing attacks. Half the enemy battalion was destroyed and a major Viet Cong infiltration route was interdicted. The Republic of Vietnam awarded him the Medal for Valor for that same action.

On September 13, 1966, First Lieutenant Howard W. Kaiser was killed while piloting his reconnaissance aircraft in search of a downed U.S. helicopter. In addition to the Silver Star and Purple Heart, he was awarded the Air Medal with eighteen oak-leaf clusters (each award representing twenty-five flight missions), and the Vietnam Service Medal. All of these medals are on display at the American Legion Hall in West Chesterfield, New Hampshire.

On November 10, 2005, Lt. Howard W. Kaiser was inducted into the ROTC Hall of Fame at the University of New Hampshire in Durham.

IRAQ: DESERT STORM

1991

THE 1990 CRISIS IN THE MIDDLE EAST BEGAN ON JULY 17 when Saddam Hussein publicly threatened Kuwait and the United Arab Emirates with war. He accused them of shoving a "poisoned dagger" into Iraq's back by exceeding their oil production quotas set by OPEC. He said that their greed prompted them to conspire with the American and Israeli imperialists. They had stopped acting like Arab brothers. That same day U.S. intelligence received reports of unusual Iraqi troop movements just north of Kuwait.

King Fahd of Saudi Arabia saw Saddam as a thug and was not worried about him. Saddam had run Iraq as a military state for eleven years without turning on his Arab neighbors (Iranians are Aryans, not Arabs). But Saddam's blunt threats were unheard of in the Arab world. The United Arab Emirates were the first to ask for American help. They requested aerial tankers so they could keep their air force in the air to defend against an Iraqi attack. Colin Powell, Chairman of the Joint Chiefs of Staff, and Secretary of Defense, Richard Cheney, authorized the KC-135s be sent along with three U.S. ships into the Gulf of Arabia, whose radars would provide an early warning of an Iraqi attack.

Iraq had used the desert near Basra for military training before, but by the end of July the Iraqis were no longer in that area. Now they were pointed to the Kuwait border. Iraqi tanks had moved forward with helicopters and special-forces units. There was no doubt that there would be an attack. The Iraqis intent was to take the entire country, not merely Kuwait's Rumaila oil field. The Iraqis had planted agents in Kuwait to act as ground controllers for the forces entering Kuwait City.

Colin Powell directed General Norman Schwarzkopf to coordinate a plan to help Kuwait. The Joint Chiefs made it clear that although the U.S. might not go to war to aid Kuwait, they would go to war to aid and protect Saudi Arabia.

The invasion of Kuwait was still in its first hours when President George Bush determined that Saddam's aggression must be checked. The U.S. would fight if Iraq took the American embassy staff hostage. President Bush stated that an attack on Saudi Arabia would be a cause for America to go to war.

The conquest of Kuwait took less than three days. The same three divisions of Iraq's Republican Guard that led the attack into Kuwait, began massing tanks and artillery along the border of Saudi Arabia and bringing supplies forward. There was no doubt that the Iraqis planned to attack Saudi Arabia.

On August 4, generals Schwarzkopf, Powell, and Secretary Cheney met with President Bush and his inner staff at Camp David. Powell and Schwarzkopf were both veterans of Vietnam and had seen the disastrous results of sugarcoating the truth to please the President. They agreed that every piece of information they gave would be accurate. General Schwarzkopf explained to the group that Iraq's army, in size, ranked only behind China, Russia, and Vietnam (the U.S. ranked seventh). The Iraqi military consisted of 900,000 men organized into sixty-three divisions. Saddam's arsenal included some of the best weapons including Soviet T-72 tanks, South African 155mm artillery, French Exocet anti-ship missiles, Soviet MiG-29 fighters, and French M-1 Mirage fighters.

Schwarzkopf warned that although the U.S. could put the 82nd Airborne Division in that area right away, that unit could not withstand a full Iraqi attack. He cautioned that three months would be needed to mass enough combat power to halt the Iraqi forces. This was merely a contingency plan for the defense of Saudi Arabia. He then outlined his plan to drive the Iraqis out of Kuwait.

General Schwarzkopf was selected to go to Saudi Arabia and brief King Fahd. He was authorized to tell the king that America would commit forces if we had his permission. President Bush's message to King Fahd was delivered by Secretary Cheney "If you ask us, we will come. We will seek no permanent bases. And when you ask us to go home, we will leave." The king agreed and plans for the deployment began right away. Enroute home, the American entourage met with President Murbarak of Egypt and King Hassan of Morocco seeking support and help. Both men agreed to help, publicly condemning the Iraqi aggression.

General Schwarzkopf was selected as Commander-in-Chief of the operation that was designated Desert Shield. Tuesday, August 7, 1990, was the commencement day deploying the 82nd Airborne troops to Dhahrn, Saudi Arabia. The logistics of moving so many units with their organic equipment was an enormous task, but Yankee ingenuity made it work.

U.S. Air Force planners began working on a strategic bombing campaign, which ultimately became the first phase of Desert Storm. Meanwhile, an Iraqi defector arrived in Egypt with a map outlining the Iraqi invasion of Saudi Arabia showing three invasion routes. Although not sure of the genuiness of the map, General Schwarz-kopf ordered his ground commanders to emplace their units along the three proposed invasion routes.

President Bush addressed the nation calling for "the imme-diate, complete and unconditional withdrawal of all Iraqi forces from Kuwait." He continued that the United States' response was "not simply to protect resources or real estate, but to protect the freedom of nations."

The pentagon planners told Schwarzkopf that, "we don't want to destroy Iraq as a nation," the U.S. would continue to need Iraq as a regional counterbalance to Iran. The military mission was to silence Saddam and not to kill him. The plans for the retaliatory air campaign proposed to knock out Saddam's anti-aircraft instal-lations, airfields, missile sites, munitions plants, weapons labs, oil refineries, bridges, and railroads—hundreds of targets. It was plain to see how Saddam had transformed his country into an armed camp. The air force planners estimated they could neutralize all these targets within six days.

This original plan was expanded for an additional 2-4 days to bomb the Iraqi army, now occupying Kuwait. The White House proceeded with a naval blockade despite the fact that the United Nations Security Council had not yet granted permission to reinforce an embargo by military means. President Bush's next move was to call up the reserves using his authority to activate up to 200,000 reservists for up to one hundred eighty days without asking Congress. This action sent a powerful signal to the American people that we had a responsibility as a nation.

A steady flow of supplies, fighting equipment, and materials by sea and by air, was reaching the Saudi airfields and ports. On August 23, the U.S. command headquarters was moved to Riyadh. While General Schwarzkopf set up in Saudi Arabia, General Colin Powell took care of the military needs back in Washington.

To aid the coalition forces, King Fahd's nephew General Prince Khalid had been selected to head the Saudi forces. He had been educated at Sandhurst, the British military school. Khalid had attended the U.S. Air Force War College and held a master's degree in political science from Auburn University.

Throughout September, Washington was working hard to find a diplomatic solution to the crisis. However, the Gulf Arabs felt that a negotiated settlement would be a disaster. Saddam would still be sitting there with his huge arsenal waiting for an opportunity to make his neighbors pay for having cooperated with the West. The Arabs knew that anything short of an Iraqi defeat in Kuwait was a losing proposition.

Military planning and preparations continued through October and November. Finally on November 29, the United Nations Security Council authorized the use of force if Iraq did not leave Kuwait by January 15. The fuse of war had been lit.

In the meantime, the Egyptian military joined the coalition. Their presence was key as the entire Arab world was watching to see if Cairo would join the offensive. The Egyptians were experienced desert fighters. Their two armored divisions would spearhead the second prong of the attack and pin the Iraqis in Western Kuwait.

In that same time frame, the Iraqis were methodically building formidable barriers—mine fields, tank traps, high sandbanks, razor wire, trenches, and forts. These defenses had been built on the assumption that the coalition forces would attack head on. Saddam and his generals seemed oblivious of their exposed flank. Iraq's best chance for a successful defense was slipping away.

The air war commenced at 2:40 AM January 17, 1991. Warplanes from six nations with hundreds of tons of missiles, rockets, and bombs streaked toward Baghdad. A dozen U.S. Army special-operations UH-60 Blackhawk helicopters would start the attack. Flying in almost total darkness only thirty feet above the sand, they took out two early-warning radar installations on the Saudi-Iraqi border and returned safely to base. CW-2 Michael Durant's Blackhawk was credited with destroying the first Iraqi SCUD missile launcher.

As the fighters returned to re-fuel and re-arm, they reported targets hit—the telephone exchange was destroyed, Iraqi airfields and missile sites were destroyed, and the power plants were inoperable. The lights were out in Baghdad. The air attacks were staggered, as the fighter aircraft left their targets, the Tomahawk missiles would arrive. For the first forty-eight hours, the Iraqis had no rest from the relentless bombardment.

On the second day, seven Scud missiles were fired from Western Iraq toward Israel. People in Tel Aviv donned gas masks, but it was quickly ascertained that the Scuds carried conventional warheads, not poison gas. Dozens of Israeli jets were scrambled and took off but were recalled before reaching Saudi Arabian airspace, which would have created an incident detrimental to the coalition with Arab states.

The U.S. Army fired four Patriot missiles from Dhahran and destroyed a lone Scud fired from a mobile missile launcher in Southern Iraq. For as inaccurate as the Scuds were against pinpoint targets, they were effective as a terror weapon against civilian populations. Three more hit Israel, but the Israeli's did not launch reprisal attacks.

The Scuds were launched from mobile units about the size of an oil tanker truck and could drive away six minutes after firing. This made them elusive targets. Intercepts of incoming Scuds by the Patriot missiles were successful, but not one hundred percent. The inaccurate Scud launches tapered off. During the first week of Desert Storm, thirty-five Scuds were fired, eighteen during the second week, and thereafter only about one each day. Tragically, on February 25, a Scud fired at Dhahran struck a U.S. barracks. The explosion killed twenty-eight soldiers and wounded many more.

As the air war was systematically eliminating their targets, the ground troops were ready to attack. Morale was high. The troops knew that the order to attack would come soon. They were glad the long hours of sitting in the desert were about to end.

For the first ten days of the war, things had been quiet except for an occasional artillery duel or the random Scud launches. However, on January 29, Iraq's Fifth Mechanized Division launched a tank attack across the Saudi-Kuwaiti border to the Saudi town of Al Khafji. The town was not defended because it was within range of Iraqi artillery. The Iraqis Fifth Division (over 400 tanks) traveled down the coast highway, a prime target for Air Force and Marine fighters and helicopters.

The Fifth Division was cut off from retreat and was entirely destroyed by the air attack by General Khalid's Saudi armored brigade. The conclusion drawn from this early battle was that the Iraqi army was not as skilled or as well trained as it had been portrayed. The coalition's main concern now was Iraq's possible use of unconventional weapons—chemicals or biologicals.

After two weeks of war, most of Iraq's strategic targets had been eliminated. Now the bombing was shifted to the Iraqi forces in the Kuwaiti desert. The Republican Guard had gone underground, building bunkers for both men and tanks. The Iraqi air force was not effective—planes that took off from damaged airfields were either shot down or their pilots fled to Iran.

By early February, the coalition forces were ready to begin the ground war. Cheney and Colin Powell arrived to assess whether the U.S. was ready. General Schwarzkopf stated that the optimum time would be mid-February because of the good weather. Cheney returned to Washington for presidential approval. President Bush approved the military plan of attack for anytime after February 21. Through radio broadcasts and aerial leaflet drops, the Iraqis were encouraged to surrender and march "toward Mecca."

By February 15, coalition planes were flying missions night and day, bombing and strafing Iraqi positions. Intelligence estimated that the air missions had destroyed 35 percent of Iraqi tanks, 31 percent of its other armored vehicles and 44 percent of its artillery. Indications were that units had been bombed to fifty percent strength or less.

Schwarzkopf reminded his staff, "you can take the most beat-up army in the world, and if they choose to stand and fight, you're going to take casualties; if they choose to dump chemicals on you, they might even win." In the past, Saddam had used nerve gas, mustard gas, and blood-poisoning agents in battle. The possibility of mass casualties from chemical weapons was the main reason the U.S. had sixty-three hospitals, two hospital ships and 18,000 beds ready in the war zone.

By February 23, thousand of tanks and armored vehicles—U.S., Arab, British, and French—were poised along the Kuwaiti border in battle formation. Artillery had moved forward. To the west, the 101st air assault division was flying helicopter patrols deep into Iraq, reconning landing zones for the assault. To the east, the battleship *Missouri* was off the Kuwaiti coast with its huge sixteen-inch guns trained on Iraqi positions. Air strikes reached their maximum fury. The weather in the battle zone was clear except in eastern Kuwait, where the Iraqi troops were pillaging the city and setting fire to the oil fields. Thick, black clouds of smoke darkened the sky.

At 4:00 AM on the morning of February 24, the attack began in light rain. The first Marines crossed into Kuwait with M-60 tanks and Cobra helicopter gun-ships in the lead. The troops wore clumsy charcoal-lined suits to protect them from chemical weapons and carried gas masks on their belts. The Marines encountered no impassable mine fields, no walls of flame, no gas barrages, and very little resistance. Minor firefights resulted in few U.S. casualties and hundreds of Iraqis were taken prisoner.

The Saudis also made remarkably easy progress, driving past miles of bunkers and trenches before meeting only token resistance. They reported hundreds of Iraqi troops waving white flags. Meanwhile, far to the west, the French and U.S. forces were advancing almost unopposed. Around noon, reports came in that the Iraqis had destroyed Kuwait City's desalinization plant. Since there was no other source of drinking water, this indicated that the Iraqis intended to leave Kuwait permanently. This fulfilled the first of the coalition's three strategic objectives: to liberate Kuwait City, to kick the Iraqis out of Kuwait, and to destroy the invading forces so Saddam could never use them again.

During the few remaining hours of daylight, the troops were still accomplishing their objectives. The French and the 82nd Airborne were closing in on Al Salman, the 101st had established its fire base and Apache helicopters were blowing up trucks on Highway 8, the main route up the Euphrates Valley. The 24th Mechanized Infantry Division had already penetrated thirty-five miles into Iraq.

Report of units' progress filtered into the command post indicating remarkably few casualties (eight dead and twenty-seven wounded). While there was no way to calculate Iraqi casualties, over thirteen thousand prisoners had been taken.

On the evening of February 25th, President Bush called General Schwarzkopf for his evaluation of the situation, asking questions about the handling of Iraqi POWs and how the allies were getting along. When Schwarzkopf hung up the phone, he said, "I was struck by what the President had chosen "not" to say: he'd given me no order and hadn't second-guessed the decisions I'd made. His confidence in the military's ability to do its job was so unlike what we'd seen in Vietnam, that the conversation meant the world to me."

In the early hours of February 26, Baghdad radio made a public broadcast ordering the Iraqi troops out of Kuwait. This was only forty-six hours into the Desert Storm campaign and this was not a formal acceptance of the UN resolutions. General Powell confirmed that the attack was to continue. The standing orders to all coalition commanders were to inflict maximum destruction on the Iraqi military machine—their fighting equipment.

To the west, the coalition's VII Corps was ready for the largest tank battle in military history. The First and Third Armored Divisions, the First Infantry and First Cavalry Divisions along with the British First Armored Division would confront the elite Iraqi armored units that had spearheaded the invasion of Kuwait. The hour of reckoning had come for the Republican Guard.

On the eastern portion of the battlefield, the Iraqi retreat had disintegrated into chaos. Convoys and large units were bunching up near Basra where bridges had been destroyed. They made easy targets for the bombers. Of the forty-two Iraqi divisions at the start of the war, twenty-seven were destroyed and six more had been rendered "combat ineffective." Of the 400,000 Iraqi troops sent across the border, 38,000 were prisoners. Coalition casualties were twenty-eight dead, eighty-nine wounded and five were missing.

By the afternoon on February 27th, General Powell called General Schwarzkopf to confirm the cesession of offensive operations. President Bush made his announcement at nine o'clock, referring to Desert Storm as a "hundred hour war." Under terms of the cessation, the Iraqis had to abandon their equipment and walk north. Coalition forces remained at their positions in Iraq and destroyed the abandoned weapons.

On March 3, 1991, delegates from Iraq and the coalition forces met at Safwan to sign the terms of cease fire. This was done as the sky was shrouded in total darkness. The black smoke from hundreds of oil well fires, set by the Iraqis, covered the sky. General Schwarzkopf represented the coalition forces and General Ahmad signed for Iraq. When General Ahmad discussed prisoners, he stated that Iraq held forty-one. When told that the coalition held over 60,000 Iraqis, Ahmad's "face went completely pale: he had no concept of the magnitude of their defeat."

MICHAEL J. DURANT

Chief Warrant Officer, U.S. Army
Delta Force, Blackhawk Pilot
Desert Storm, Iraq

Born:	July 23, 1961, Berlin, New Hampshire
Education:	MBA-AVN, Embry-Riddle Aero University
Awards:	Distinguished Service Medal
	Distinguished Flying Cross
	Bronze Star, Valor
	Purple Heart
	Air Medal
	Master Army Aviator
Operations:	Prime Chance, Persian Gulf, 1988
	Just Cause, Panama, 1989
	Desert Storm, Iraq, 1991
	Gothic Serpent, Somalia, 1993

CW-4 MICHAEL DURANT WAS THE FIRST HELICOPTER pilot to engage an Iraq SCUD missile launcher during Operation Desert Storm.

Michael Durant was born and raised in Berlin, New Hampshire. He played football and hockey and loved to fish and hunt in the White Mountains of the Androscoggin River Valley. He is the son of a full-time First Sergeant in the New Hampshire Army National Guard.

His interest in flying began when he was fourteen years old. A friend of his father, Joe Brigham, a retired Army CW-4, owned an air transport business and took Michael on a ferry flight in his helicopter. Two years later Mike visited a National Guard base where he saw his first UH-60 Blackhawk. At that point, he knew he wanted to be an Army Aviator and fly the Blackhawk.

Michael enlisted in the Army in August 1979 at age eighteen. After basic training, he attended the Defense Language Institute in Monterey, California. He became proficient in Spanish and was assigned to the 470th military intelligence group at Fort Clayton, Panama, for two years.

In 1983, he enrolled as a warrant officer candidate and trained in TH-55 and the UH1 Huey helicopters at Fort Rucker, Alabama. In November 1983, Warrant Officer Durant trained as a pilot of the UH-60 Blackhawk.

His first flying assignment was with the 377th Medical Evacuation Company, Seoul, Korea. By the time he was twenty-four, he had flown more than 150 medical evacuation missions in Hueys and Blackhawks, some under extremely hazardous weather conditions.

After eighteen months in Korea, he was promoted to chief warrant officer-2 (CW-2). Durant was assigned to the 101st Aviation Battalion, Fort Campbell, Kentucky, supporting the famed 101st Airborne Division "Screaming Eagles." There he qualified as an Army instructor pilot. He volunteered and was accepted by the elite 160th Special Operations group in June 1988.

Durant flew combat missions in the Persian Gulf in Operation Prime Chance during 1988. In February 1989, he flew missions in operation Just Cause in Panama to unseat Manuel Noriega, the corrupt dictator ruling his country through fear and hatred.

In February 1991, during operation Desert Storm in Kuwait, Mike led a flight of the 160th Special Op's UH-60 Blackhawks on an armed reconnaissance mission to find and destroy SCUD missiles in the western desert of Iraq. He was the first helicopter pilot during Desert Storm to locate and engage an enemy SCUD missile launcher.

When the United Nations' 1993 humanitarian relief effort to distribute food to the starving people of Somalia was stymied by guerrillas, the United States sent Army rangers and the elite, clandestine Delta Force. Their mission was to find and capture the Somali guerrilla leader, Mohammud Farah Aideed, in operation Gothic Serpent. During the battle of Mogadishu on October 3, 1993, the assault on Aideed's hideout met with heavy resistance. Mike Durant's UH-60 Blackhawk, Super Six Four, was shot down by a rocket-propelled grenade. In the crash, his copilot, Ray Frank, died and Mike's back and leg were broken. He was pulled from the Blackhawk's wreckage by Sgt. Randy Shugart and Sgt. Gary Gordon while under intense enemy fire. Both were killed in the fire fight, and both would be posthumously awarded the Medal of Honor. Mike Durant was taken and held captive for eleven days. He was in constant pain from the crushed vertebrae and his broken leg.

During that October 3 assault in Mogadishu, six American soldiers were killed and nearly one hundred wounded by Somalis who didn't want United Nations food to be given to their starving countrymen.

Mike Durant's leg and back healed and he continued to fly Blackhawks for the 160 Special Operations Group. After twenty-one and a half years of active duty, Mike retired as a CW-4. He wore the wings of a master army aviator and had logged thirty-seven hundred hours of pilot flying time, more than fourteen hundred while wearing night-vision goggles.

Mike and his wife, Lisa, have four sons and two daughters. Now retired from the Army, Durant conducts seminars to military personnel about helicopter maneuvers and combat search and rescue operations. He is the author of the New York Times best seller, In the Company of Heroes. Mike's story was the inspiration for the book and movie, Blackhawk Down.

References:
Blackhawk Down, Mark Bowden, 2000
In the Company of Heroes, M.J. Durant, Steven Hartov, 2003
Shadow Warriors, Tom Clancy, 2002

EPILOGUE

THERE IS AN OLD SAYING, "IF YOU'VE BEEN TO A WAR, there's no need to talk about it with those who understand, and it's impossible to talk about it with those who don't."

Men of Granite is not a book about war, it is about men who have been to war and have made significant contributions to their country and countrymen. Wars or eras are summarized only to give a frame of reference to the men who served during those eras.

Who have been selected as a granite-stater? Of course, anyone born and raised in New Hampshire. But I have included men who have moved here and become New Hampshire residents. I have also included men who lived in Durham or Hanover while earning their degrees from the University of New Hampshire or Dartmouth.

Studying colonial American history at UNH, I concentrated on the Province of New Hampshire. Reading about the Revolutionary War led me to focus on the First New Hampshire Regiment of Volunteers and its first leader, Colonel John Stark. Stark became then and is still my hero of all time. Later reading about Robert Rogers' Rangers kindled my interest in other New Hampshiremen's military contributions to our history.

As a movie buff, I recall seeing Spencer Tracy as Major Robert Rogers in *Northwest Passage* and Jeff Chandler as General Frank Merrill in *Merrill's Marauders*. I nearly fell out of my theater seat when Alan Ladd, portraying Joe McConnell told his future wife that he was from New Hampshire, in *The McConnell Story*. The seeds that eventually blossomed to become this book were planted early.

As a young Army lieutenant, I took my fixed-wing flight training at Lowe Army Airfield, Fort Rucker, Alabama. Every day walking into our classrooms, I would pass by a picture of Professor Thaddeus Lowe in his Civil War observation balloon. Lowe, "the father of Army Aviation," was a New Hampshireman too!

I remembered that Pease Air Force Base in Portsmouth was named for native son, Captain Harl Pease a WWII B-17 pilot who received the Medal of Honor. Also I recalled that Rene Gagnon from Manchester helped raise the flag on Iwo Jima. I knew then that I would eventually write a book about all these men.

In 2004, I began research in earnest about these men and others from different eras and in 2005, I began writing *Men of Granite*. The more I read, the more names I found would need to be added. The last man, Sylvanus Thayer, was added after the final typing of the manuscript in late 2006.

Some stories are long and some are painfully short due to lack of information. Some men like Stark, Rogers or General Leonard Wood, have had volumes written about them. Some men are remembered only by the terse citations accompanying their Medal of Honor.

And so I ask the reader to remember that their gift of freedom was and is insured and protected by every man and woman who has ever worn the uniform of this country—those wounded, those whose lives were lost, those who endured captivity, and those still missing in action.

We should never forget any of our brave men.

Appendix I

MEDAL OF HONOR HOLDERS

Lieutenant George E. Albee
Lieutenant William Appleton
Private First Class George Dilboy
Boatswains Mate William Holyoke
Quartermaster Frederick Franklin
Landsman James Merton
Admiral Richard O'Kane
Captain Harl Pease
Private Walter Scott West
General Leonard Wood
Admiral Alan B. Shepard (space)

BURIED AT ARLINGTON NATIONAL CEMETERY

Lieutenant George E. Albee
Admiral George Belknap
Private First Class George Dilboy
General Charles Doyen
Corporal Rene Gagnon
Admiral Richard O'Kane
Colonel Robert Rolfe
General Leonard Wood
General Melvin Zais

NAMESAKES OF NAVAL SHIPS / MILITARY INSTALLATIONS

Fort Dearborn, Illinois
Fort Dix, New Jersey
Fort Leonard Wood, Missouri
Grenier Air Base, New Hampshire
Lowe Army Airfield, Alabama
Pease Air Force Base, New Hampshire
Destroyer DD-251, USS *Belknap*

Destroyer DDG-77, USS *O'Kane*
Destroyer DD-689, USS *Wadleigh*
Destroyer DD-280, USS *Doyen*
Supply Ship T-AKE-3, USS *Alan Shepard*

BECAME GOVERNORS

John Adams Dix, New York State, 1872-1872
James Miller, Arkansas Territory, 1819-1823
John Sullivan, New Hampshire, 1786, 1787, 1789
Leonard Wood, Military Governor Cuba, 1899-1902
Leonard Wood, Governor General, Philippines, 1902-1908

Appendix II

Civil War, 1861-1865
Edward Cross, colonel, volunteers
Thaddeus Lowe, civilian, chief aeronaut
William Appleton, lieutenant, U.S. Army
John Foster, general, volunteers
Jesse Gove, colonel, volunteers
George Belknap, lieutenant, U.S. Navy
George Wadleigh, lieutenant, U.S. Navy
John A. Dix, general, volunteers
John Thompson, lieutenant, volunteers
Gilman Marston, colonel, volunteers

Korean Expedition, 1871
Frederick Franklin, quartermaster, U.S. Navy
James Merton, landsman, U.S. Navy

Indian Campaigns, 1861-1890
Leonard Wood, lieutenant, U.S. Army
George Albee, lieutenant, U.S. Army

Spanish-American War, 1898
George Wadleigh, captain, U.S. Navy
Walter West, private, U.S. Marine Corps
Leondard Wood, general, U.S. Army
Robert Rolfe, colonel, volunteers
Charles Doyen, colonel, U.S. Marine Corps

Boxer Rebellion, China Expedition, 1900
William Holyoke, boatswain's mate, U.S. Navy

World War I, 1917-1919
George Dilboy, PFC, U.S. Army
Leonard Wood, general, U.S. Army
Robert Rolfe, colonel, U.S. Army
Charles Doyen, general, U.S. Marine Corps

Interim
Army Mail Plane Service, 1934
Jean Grenier, lieutenant, U.S. Army

World War II, 1941-1945
Frank Merrill, general, U.S. Army
Richard O'Kane, admiral, U.S. Navy
Harl Pease, captain, U.S. Army Air Corps
Rene Gagnon, corporal, U.S. Marine Corps
Harry Parker, captain, U.S. Army Air Corps
Norman Fortier, major, U.S. Army Air Corps
Harrison Thyng, colonel, U.S. Army Air Corps
Joseph McConnell, lieutenant, U.S. Army Air Corps
Alan Shepard, lieutenant, U.S. Navy
Melvin Zais, major, U.S. Army

Cold War—Berlin Airlift, 1948-1949
Norman Fortier, major, U.S. Air Force

Korean War, 1950-1953
Harrison Thyng, general, U.S. Air Force
Joseph McConnell, captain, U.S. Air Force
Leon Jacques, lieutenant, U.S. Army

Space Program, 1957
Alan Shepard, admiral, U.S. Navy

Vietnam, 1961-1975
Melvin Zais, general, U.S. Army
William Hazen, major, U.S. Army
Howard Kaiser, lieutenant, U.S. Air Force

Iraq-Desert Storm, 1991
Michael Durant, CW2, U.S. Army

Somalia, 1993
Michael Durant, CW4, U.S. Army

Bibliography

Ambrose, Stephen E. *Undaunted Courage*, Touchstone, Simon & Shuster, 1996
——. *Duty, Honor, Country*, Johns Hopkins University Press, 1999
The Astronauts; *We Seven*, Simon & Shuster, 1962
Bakeless, John. *Lewis & Clark—Partners in Discovery*, Dover, 1975
Barstow, G. *History of New Hampshire*, 1842
Bowden, Mark. *Blackhawk Down*, Penguin Books, 2000
Bradley, James. *Flags of our Fathers*, Bantam, 2000
Brady, Eddie. *Georgie! My Georgie!*, Xlibris Books, 2005
Clancy, Tom. *Shadow Warriors*, Putnam, 2002
Cross, Edward E. *Stand Firm and Fire Low*, University Press of New England, 2003
Cuneo, John. *Robert Rogers of the Rangers*, Oxford University Press, 1959
Dearborn, Henry. *The Revolutionary War Journals*, 1775-1783
Department of the Air Force, official documents on Harrison Thyng and Joseph McConnell
Department of the Army, official documents on Gen. Melvin Zais
Dorr, Robert F. *Korean War Aces*, 1955
Downey, Anne. "A Memoriam," *UNH Magazine*, Winter 2006
Durant, Michael J. *In the Company of Heroes*, Penguin, 2003
Fall, Bernard F. *The Two Vietnams*, Praeger, 1963
Forman, Sidney. *West Point, A History of the U.S. Military Academy*, 1950
Fortier, Norman J. *An Ace of the Eighth*, Presidio Press, 2003
Frisbee, John L. "The AACMO Fiasco," *Air Force Magazine*, March 1995
Hagedorn, Hermann. *Leonard Wood, a Biography*, 2 vols., 1931
Hawthorne, Nathaniel. *The Life of Franklin Pierce*, 1852
Hoyt, Edwin. *Submarines at War*, Stein and Day, 1983
Ketchum, Richard. *American Heritage History of the Revolutionary War*, 1958
Ketchum, Richard. *American Heritage History of the Civil War*, 1960

Kidder, Frederic. *History of the First New Hampshire Regiment*, 1868

Life magazine, "The Mercury Astronauts," September 14, 1959

Landau, Alan and Frieda. *U.S. Special Forces*, Lowe & Hould, 1992

Maas, Peter. *The Terrible Hours*, Harper-Collins, 2001

Maihafer, Harry. *From the Hudson to the Yalu*, 1993

New York Times, article on George Dilboy, November 1, 1923

Ogburn, Jr., Charlton. *The Marauders*, Harper, 1959

O'Kane, Richard. *Clear the Bridge*, Bantam Books, 1981

——. *Wahoo*, Bantam Books, 1987

Perrett, Bryan. *Impossible Victories*, Cassell & Co., 1996

Schwarzkopf, Norman. *It Doesn't Take a Hero*, Bantam Books, 1992

Stark, Caleb. *Memoirs and Official Correspondence of General John Stark*, 1877

Summers, Harry G. *Vietnam War Almanac*, Facts on File Publications, 1985

Time magazine, Article on J. McConnell, September 6, 1954

Time magazine, Article on J. McConnell, October 17, 1955

Tierney & Montgomery. *The Army Aviation Story*, Colonial Press, 1963

Valencia, Jerry. *Knights of the Sky*, volume I, 1980

Westmoreland, William. *A Soldier Reports*, Doubleday, 1976

Wolfe, Tom. *The Right Stuff*, Farrar, Straus, Giroux, 1979

Wright, Winifred. *The Granite Town*, Cabinet Press, 1979

Wright, Winifred. *Milford in World War II*, Cabinet Press, 1949

Index

ABOUT THE AUTHOR

WILLIAM "BILL" MCGEE WAS RAISED IN MILFORD, NEW Hampshire. He graduated Milford High School in 1955. That same year he enlisted in the New Hampshire National Guard as an Artilleryman. He graduated from the University of New Hampshire in 1959 and was commissioned a 2nd Lt., U.S. Army.

He took flight training at Fort Rucker, Alabama, at Lowe Army Airfield, which was named for another New Hampshireman. Bill was a rated Army Aviator in both helicopters and in fixed-wing aircraft. He served five years active duty. During his 12 months in Vietnam, he was promoted to Captain. He flew over 400 combat missions and rescued wounded American and Vietnamese soldiers while under intense enemy fire.

He left active duty and became the Associate Editor of Army Aviation Magazine. He spent 22 years with DuPont's Biotechnology Division in sales and marketing before founding his own business, Microtome Service Company.

Bill is an Eagle Scout and a Silver Beaver. During his forty-five years in Boy Scouting, he has been a Cub den leader, Scoutmaster, and Woodbadge trainer. He has served on the boards of the Lee Scouting Museum in Manchester, NH, and the Hillcourt Scout Museum near Syracuse, New York. He is still active in scouting.

Bill is a free-lance writer and has had his stories and articles published in England, Poland, and in the United States.

He considers Milford to be his home town.